Iris-Aya Laemmerhirt
Embracing Differences

*To my amazing mother Harumi Schneidewind*

**Iris-Aya Laemmerhirt** teaches American Studies and British Studies at TU Dortmund University where she is a post-doctoral candidate. Her research interests are the literature of the 1940s, Transnational Studies, and representations of Hawaii in the media. Currently, she is teaching as a Fulbright SIR at UVA Wise.

IRIS-AYA LAEMMERHIRT
# Embracing Differences
Transnational Cultural Flows between Japan and the United States

[transcript]

This thesis was accepted as a doctoral dissertation in fulfillment of the requirements for the degree »Doktor der Philosophie« by the Faculty of Humanities at Ruhr-Universität Bochum on the recommendation of Prof. Dr. Kornelia Freitag and Prof. Dr. Randi Gunzenhäuser (TU Dortmund) in 2008.

The dissertation was partly funded by the Wilhelm and Günther Esser Foundation grant from 2007-2008.

**Bibliographic Information published by the Deutsche Nationalbibliothek**
The Deutsche Nationalbibliothek lists this publication in the Deutsche Nationalbibliografie; detailed bibliographic data are available in the Internet at http://dnb.d-nb.de

© 2013 transcript Verlag, Bielefeld

All rights reserved. No part of this book may be reprinted or reproduced or utilized in any form or by any electronic, mechanical, or other means, now known or hereafter invented, including photocopying and recording, or in any information storage or retrieval system, without permission in writing from the publisher.

Cover layout: Kordula Röckenhaus, Bielefeld
Cover illustration: Replica of the Statue of Liberty, Iris-Aya Laemmerhirt, Tokyo 2007
Proofread by: Iris-Aya Laemmerhirt
Typeset by: Iris-Aya Laemmerhirt und Benjamin Lehmert.
Printed by: Majuskel Medienproduktion GmbH, Wetzlar
ISBN 978-3-8376-2600-1

# Contents

Acknowledgements | 7

Note on Japanese Terms | 9

**Exoticism, Imagination, and the Harajuku Girls** | 11
Cultural Imperialism and Globalization | 15
Gazing the Japanese | 18
Transnationalism | 23
Rethinking Japanese-American Cultural Relations | 26

**"Here Be Monsters": Early Japanese-American Cultural Exchanges** | 33
Japanese Monsters and American Barbarians | 35
Reciprocal Cultural Influences | 47

**Yōkoso Mickey Mouse! Disney in Japan** | 57
American Fantasyscapes | 59
The Disneyfication of America and the World? | 68
Tokyo Disney Resort | 72
Wonderland Re-Visited | 95

**A Taste of Difference: Sushi in the United States** | 101
Of Rice and Meat: A Short History of Japanese and American Food Relations | 104
Japanese Food in Culinary Texts | 112
Enter the Dragon Roll: Consuming Sushi in the United States | 132
Imagining Sushi Otherwise | 141

**Could We Have a Geisha in This Scene?
Transnational Depictions of Japan in Contemporary
Hollywood Movies** | 147
Flashback: Orientalizing Japan in Movies | 149
Subtitles and Subversion: Transnational Cinema | 160
*The Last Samurai*: A Masculine East | 166
Tokyo Irasshaimase! Two Americans Lost in Translation | 185
*Letters from Iwo Jima*: Japanese Writings – American Pictures | 196
Preview: A Transnational Turn in Hollywood | 207

**Conclusion** | 211

**Bibliography** | 219
Internet Sources | 247
Movies | 249
Miscellaneous | 255
TV Series | 255
Music | 256

**Index** | 257

# Acknowledgements

The printed pages of this dissertation do not only hold the outcome of years of research, but reflect the relationships with many inspiring and generous people I have met since beginning my doctoral thesis. First of all, I would like to gratefully and sincerely thank my advisor Prof. Kornelia Freitag who has guided me through this dissertation with thoughtful criticism and many valuable discussions. Her mentorship encouraged me to grow not only as a scholar but also as an independent thinker. I would like to thank Prof. Dr. Randi Gunzenhäuser, my second advisor, for her encouragement, input, as well as time and attention during busy semesters. I am further truly indebted to Prof. Walter Grünzweig for allowing me to teach courses in his department and for encouraging my future academic career. My research has benefited from a generous grant from the Wilhelm und Günther Esser Stiftung of the Ruhr-University Bochum.

Many of my colleagues at the Ruhr-University Bochum and TU Dortmund have read and provided helpful criticism on this thesis and have been essential to its thinking and rethinking. Katharina Vester, Sven Lutzka, Selma Bidlingmair, Eriko Ogihara-Schuck, Sina Nitsche, and Marcel Hartwig – thank you for your support and discussions which compelled and challenged me in many different ways. I am greatly indebted to Stefanie Hanneken, who helped to edit this book for her supportive comments and her keen eye for detail. I would like to thank Petra Schubert who was the first critical reader of the manuscript for this book and supported me in all my endeavors, Tammy Kirchner for her skillful readings, and Sandra Danneil who took time to give detailed feedback on my movie chapter. I further owe thanks to my friend and colleague Christian Lenz for his helpful and creative comments on the entire manuscript, for providing invaluable comments on my reading of *Lost in Translation*, and for cheering me up with his unfailing sense of humor.

I am very grateful for my invaluable network of supportive, forgiving, generous, and loving friends without whom I could not have survived the process of writing this thesis: Carla Kronenberger, Christine Arnold, Chantal Lenhardt, Janine Grabowski, Stefanie Simon, Carina Stella, Carina Laemmerhirt, Helge Laemmerhirt, Jan Hildenhagen, Jasmin Idek, Kai Flunkert, Ines Fries, Martin Fries, Lukas Wojarski, Ingor Baumann and Benjamin Krebs – thank you all for your support!

I would like to heartily thank Benjamin Lehmert, who never doubted that this book would be completed. Thank you for bearing my obsession with this project for the last three years and for constantly encouraging me to pursue my dreams.

I am deeply grateful to my family for their unfailing enthusiasm and support. I would like to thank my father, Prof. Dr. Dieter Schneidewind and his wife Khum-Hee Schneidewind-Choi. My father has been a consistent supporter and role model with his own work and fostered my love for literature and research, always encouraging my decision to work in the field of American Studies. He provided me with interesting articles, and constantly discussed ideas for my dissertation with me. I am further thankful to my brother Bert, his wife Anneke, my sister Birgit, and Renate Schneidewind for their constant encouragement.

My aunts Yoko Amari and Hisae Amari, made me look forward to every opportunity to visit them and supported my research, by willingly accompanying me again and again to Disney theme parks in Japan and by providing me with delicious food.

Finally, I dedicate this book to the memory of my amazing mother Harumi Schneidewind.

# Note on Japanese Terms

Standard romanization has been used for Japanese words. Macrons are used above vowels to indicate that the vowel is long. With the exception of place names, people's names, and company names, Japanese names and terms are given in italics. Japanese names are given in common Japanese order, surname first, except when referring to authors who have published in English. Translations of Japanese titles and from Japanese sources titles are, for the most part, my own.

# Exoticism, Imagination, and the Harajuku Girls

> Where mono – there's me, there's you (hoko-ten) / In a pedestrian paradise / Where the catwalk got its claws (meow) / A subculture in a kaleidoscope of fashion / Prowl the streets of Harajuku (irasshaimse)
> - GWEN STEFANI "HARAJUKU GIRLS"-

In her song "Harajuku Girls," which was released on her 2004 album *Love, Angel, Music, Baby*, American pop singer and fashion icon Gwen Stefani not only sings about her fascination with a particular Japanese fashion style, the Harajuku style, but she also blends Japanese words and phrases in her lyrics: "Where *mono* – there's me, there's you (*hoko-ten*)" [...] "Prowl the streets of Harajuku (*irrashaimase*)" or "n' cause it's (super *kawaii*), that means (super cute in Japanese)" ("Harajuku Girls"). The conflation of Japanese and English in this text mirrors the common practice of many Japanese entertainers of using English loan words in their songs and exemplifies how an American artist borrows from the Japanese culture and language.[1] In Stefani's song, the Japanese parts are sung by four Japanese background singers; "her" Harajuku Girls, who add an "exotic" and "authentic" flavor, while the translations explain and familiarize the foreign terms and phrases. Even though, or perhaps because, the song became very popular in the United States and Europe, Stefani was repeatedly criticized for employing the four background singers, who accompany her not only on tour but are also displayed on CD covers, posters, and in her music-videos. Since their

---

1 Jackie Hogan elaborated in "The Social Significance of English Usage in Japan" on the use of the English language in Japan.

main task is to pose behind the American singer, thereby adding a foreign flair to her appearance and performance, Stefani was accused by Korean-American actress Margaret Cho of reinforcing stereotypes of Japanese women as silent and submissive. Cho even went so far as calling the Harajuku Girl performance a "minstrel show" (Cho) and as the four women make Stefani's show more "exotic" it can be argued that the album indeed presents an "Orientalist" image of Japan for a Western audience.

The practice of exoticizing Japan and its people for Western consumers that helps to sell Stefani's music has been characterized as "Orientalism" and it is not at all new. Edward Said famously described this practice in his groundbreaking study under this title, explaining how in Orientalist discourses Europeans have been constructing an Orient according to their imagination for centuries, thereby defining, naming, and gaining power over foreign lands and people, while at the same time denying "The Orientalist Other" agency to represent him- or herself. This uneven power relation can be seen in the performance of Gwen Stefani as well. In her case, she is an American singer who defines the Harajuku-style for a Western audience; whereas the four Japanese women remain in the background and have to repeat Japanese phrases that fit Stefani's definition of Japan. The American singer creates a binary opposition between a mature Occidental self and an Oriental "Other" that is inferior and somehow childlike. Historically, this dichotomy of an enlightened West and uncivilized Orient became an "ultimately political vision of reality" (Said, *Orientalism* 43) which was used to justify colonialization.

Yet, at the same time, it has to be taken into consideration that Orientalism expresses a longing for the "Other." Henry Yu explains in *Thinking Orientals: Migration, Contact, and Exoticism in Modern America*, that when American merchants and missionaries sailed to Asia "the belief that the Orient was fundamentally different from America laid the foundation for Orientalism" (83) but the knowledge about the supposedly exotic "Other" was considered exciting and "something to be collected and objectified" (85). John MacKenzie has even argued that a relationship between the East and the West in the field of art was mainly grounded in admiration for the exotic (44). This notion is indicated as well in Stefani's song that admires the "Other" style and culture of the Harajuku Girls. In a similar vein, she sings in "Rich Girls" about what she would do "if [she] was a rich girl." One of her fantasies is that "I'd get me four Harajuku Girls / to inspire me and they'd come to rescue / I'd dress them wicked, I'd give them names / Love, Angel, Music, Baby / Hurry up and come and save me" ("Rich Girls"). Yet again while she is, on the one hand, very excited about the Harajuku Girls, on the other hand she objectifies them as she wants to "get" them, "dress [...] and give them names," thereby treating four grown-up women as if they were dolls. According to Yu, collecting and mastering the knowledge of the Orient has always functioned as "a fetish for elite white men and women" since the Orient represented "the adventure of the exotic" and "was the opposite of everything uninteresting in their own lives" (85). This attitude clearly motivates even Stefani when she hopes to be saved by the Japanese girls from her boring life by inspiration and in turn usurps them of their distinct identity, thus indicating a cross-cultural relationship with a very uneven distribution of power.

The concept of Orientalism can indeed be applied to Gwen Stefani's presentation of the four Harajuku Girls, who always appear in a group and wear the same outfit, which makes them hardly distinguishable for a Western audience. They create a stark visual contrast to the blonde, Caucasian Gwen Stefani, who further distinguishes herself from them by wearing a different costume than the Harajuku Girls. Visually she stands out from the exotic group and serves as a familiar reference point. Stefani, who promotes herself as a modern, independent, and unique woman of the twenty-first century, reinforces this self-perception by surrounding herself with the group of smaller, Japanese women who remain mute in interviews, follow Stefani silently, and affirm the Western stereotype that all Japanese women look the same.

While Stefani's performance borrows profusely from Orientalist stereotyping, interestingly enough, the lyrics of "Harajuku Girls" do not necessarily support the same attitude. Stefani voices her appreciation of the Harajuku style, which is named after a fashionable district of Tokyo where teenagers and young adults dress in various extravagant ways. This style has no rules or conventions except, maybe, the idea that the combinations of clothes worn have to be creative and individual. The song does not only acknowledge the distinctiveness of this Japanese fashion style, but emphasizes that despite all the differences to American fashion, it is a "Ping-Pong match between Eastern and Western [styles]" ("Harajuku Girls"). Indeed, the Harajuku style does not only include Japanese influences such as kimonos or anime-inspired fantasy costumes, but it is influenced by Western styles as well, i.e. by the 1950s retro-, punk, glam rock, gothic, and hip hop styles. Japanese and Western elements are mixed and matched in new, creative ways, thereby generating a unique fashion style that transcends national borders.[2] The lyrics of the song pinpoint exactly what Tiffany Godoy and Ivana Vartanian explain in the "Introduction" to *Style Deficit Disorder: Harajuku Street Fashion Tokyo*: "while the Harajuku district has long been a spot for a domestic audience to come into contact with foreign culture and style, today the influence has reversed: foreign fashion leaders are taking notice and being influenced by what's happening on Harajuku's streets" (10).[3] Thus, Western styles were first exported to Japan, and then adapted to the local culture and the result exported to the West, where Western consumers are free to use and recontextualize the stylistic mix again.

In her song, Stefani further confesses that she does not only admire the fashion of the Harajuku Girls but that she was inspired by them when designing fashion for her own label L.A.M.B. (an acronym of Love Angel Music Baby – the names given to the Harajuku Girls by Gwen Stefani). The lyrics of her song read, "Did you see your inspiration in my latest collection? / Just wait 'til you get your little hands on L.A.M.B." ("Harajuku Girls"). Her Harajuku-inspired fashion line, however, is very different from the Harajuku fashion worn by Japanese subcultures. Stefani's design no longer reflects the distinct and extravagant style worn in the Japanese suburb but appeals more to the American mainstream. The only markers of distinctiveness and Japaneseness are Japanese characters and images printed on T-shirts and sweaters. Gwen Stefani's Harajuku style may be inspired by the Tokyo street-fashion style but it remains *her* interpretation and it is streamlined for an American target group.[4]

---

2   As Takeji Hirakawa describes in "Harajuku's Start: The Roots of Tokyo's Street Fashion Scene," the style developed during the Occupation Era after World War II, when American officers and their families settled in a district called Washington Heights in Harajuku, and U.S. and Japanese fashion styles started to be mixed (22).

3   Since the 1980s the international fashion scene has been increasingly interested in Japanese designs and fabrics and Japanese fashion designers such as Issey Miyake and Kenzo continue to be internationally acknowledged (Kondo).

4   The commodification of different styles by the media is closely investigated by Dick Hebdige in *Subculture: The Meaning of Style*.

Binary oppositions of the East (Japan) and the West (America) can neither account for the complex, border-crossing nature of the Harajuku fashion style/s, nor the particular cross-cultural exchanges in the performance and the lyrics of the song. While Orientalist notions are still widespread, fashion and popular music display a much wider spectrum of cultural exchanges between Japan and the United States today. Despite its problematic features, Stefani's song reveals much about the growing influence of Japanese popular culture in the United States as it discloses how cultural influences cross national boundaries and how contemporary cultural interactions create not only new ties but perpetuate and recreate old tensions.

But how does one account for the changing interrelations? How should one conceptualize the new configurations of power and longing? Such a reading of Gwen Stefani's "Harajuku Girls" suggests that new and more complex approaches are needed when discussing Japanese-American cross-cultural relationships. Before inspecting the intricate interrelations between Japan and the US in the fields of amusement parks, cuisine, and movies in the three chapters of this study, some traditional as well as newer theoretical approaches to intercultural links and dynamics will be sketched. First it will be argued that formerly popular theories of cultural imperialism are no longer sufficient to explain contemporary Japanese-American relationships. Then attention will be drawn to a number of studies which have already endeavored to discuss Japanese-American cultural exchanges outside of the discourse of cultural imperialism. Finally an outline of the theory of transnationalism, which will serve as the theoretical basis for this study, will be given.

## CULTURAL IMPERIALISM AND GLOBALIZATION

The song "Harajuku Girls" reveals that cultural interactions between Japan and the United States are not unidirectional and consequently cannot be fully grasped in terms of simple binaries. Hence, the concept of cultural imperialism does not suffice when explaining Japanese-U.S. interrelations. Said, who wrote about the power of Western fiction as a tool to define and dominate other cultures, described cultural imperialism as practices, theories, and attitudes of a "dominating metropolitan center ruling a distant territory" (Culture and Imperialism 9) and John Tomlinson agrees with Said that theories of cultural imperialism "constrain the negatively marked notions of power, domination, or control" (20). This binary model of West-East cultural interaction has been challenged by various theorists. Richard Pells, for instance, criticizes the fact that the consumer is denied any agency in these theories, as dominant cultures supposedly "turn the masses all over the globe into robotic consumers of superfluous products and vacuous entertainment, unable to decide what was in their best economic interest or how to satisfy on their own, their personal or cultural needs" (265). The term "cultural imperialism" implies the one-way imposition of cultural practices and commodities by a stronger on a weaker nation. Although questions of economic power relations play an important role, the processes of cultural exchanges are more complex and less consistent than the center-periphery model suggests – and the changing character of cultural interaction over time has to be considered.

Through processes of migration and colonization, people and cultural practices have been traveling across borders for centuries. However, in the past they traveled for weeks, sometimes months before encountering different cultures. While many of those who traveled to unknown and distant places were, merchants, explorers, and missionaries, sometimes including refugees and economic migrants; unlike today, there were only few tourists. Their journeys mainly focused on trade, the claim of new territory, and the mission of converting supposedly uncivilized people (Ashcroft *Post-Colonial Studies* 112). Encounters with an unknown culture then and even now challenge the familiar, one's own culture. In order to cope with the unfamiliar, the unknown has always been evaluated in comparison to the known culture, which frequently resulted in the creation of binary oppositions that stress the differences and obliterate commonalities. In the past, the foreign "Other" was almost inevitably judged as exotic, backward, sometimes even dangerous and barbaric and the creation of such imaginary visions of the "Other" helped to justify Western interference in the East under the pretense of proselytizing campaigns. While intercultural processes of othering are still at work today, increased global and transnational interconnectivity, new technologies of transport, and new communication technologies such as the internet have made parts of apparently distant cultures a part of everyday life and it is becoming easier to get accustomed to them. Production and consumption of goods happens on a world-wide scale and instead of dangerous, inconvenient journeys on ships which took months to reach their destination, nowadays people can travel, both literally and metaphorically, within a few hours to almost all places around the globe. The internet allows users to inform themselves about other cultures or to order commodities online from all over the world, thereby further decimating boundaries of time and space and creating an "intense and immediate contact with each other – with each 'Other' (an 'Other' that is no longer simply 'out there', but also within)" (Morley and Robins 115).

Nevertheless, the current massive extension of cultural interactions, international trade, and the flow of goods and images between different nations is often accompanied by fears of globalization in the form of cultural imperialism. These terms became synonymous with the Americanization and homogenization of other cultures, which were believed to lead to the decline of national identities and the erasure of cultural uniqueness throughout the world. While the American cultural impact is still very strong, in the meantime Japanese anime, video games, and food, Indian Bollywood productions, and Chinese martial arts movies as well as other Asian popular cultural artifacts increasingly penetrate the global market and have become serious competitors in the fight for cultural dominance around the globe. Japanese scholar Iwabuchi Koichi argues in *Recentering Globalization* that the United States is no longer the only global player but has to share their central position with other nations. He criticizes the cultural imperialism thesis and acknowledges new sources of cultural influences and new marketplaces and further scrutinizes the successful export of Japanese culture and media to the West in order to shed light on Japan's decentralizing power in the globalization process (5).

Given this development of "recentering," the concepts of hegemonic globalization and cultural imperialism turn out to be hasty oversimplifications if applied to the contemporary cultural interactions that exist between the United States and Japan. The assumption that cultural transfer is one-sided, forced upon a weaker Japan by a stronger USA, can no longer be used to grasp the complex phenomena of the cultural interactions and exchanges between these two nations. Not only do the Japanese modify imported U.S. products according to their needs and thereby change the original meaning of these goods to create new, hybrid, and transnational products, but the export of Japanese cultural commodities to America yields vast profits for Japan and enhances its prestige within North America. From a Japanese perspective, the export of Japanese popular culture products "articulate[s] distinct 'Japaneseness'" and reinforces the pride of Japanese superiority and uniqueness that rests on Japan's own tradition of imperial supremacy in Asia (Iwabuchi, "Uses of Japanese Popular Culture" 202).

Manga and anime, for example, are among the most popular genres in contemporary U.S. popular culture (Goldberg 281) while domestic comic books are losing their appeal to the younger audience. Even in industrial sectors, Japan "threaten[s] to surpass the United States in the field of electronics and automobiles" (Pells 314).[5] With an increased interest and investment by large numbers of U.S. customers in Japanese (popular) culture, the image of Japan in the United States has shifted once again. While Japan was regarded by the first Americans to visit the island nation in the eighteenth century as an awkward, backward country, today it is primarily perceived as the bearer of technology and modernity. Hence, it is no longer possible for cultural theorists to deny Japan agency and apply concepts of simple center-periphery relations. It has to be acknowledged that within the worldwide flow of cultural practices, as well as commodities and images Japanese and U.S. cultural representations, experiences, and ways of life interact with and cross-pollinate each other in multiple ways.

## GAZING THE JAPANESE

A number of studies have been devoted to the images and stereotypes of Japan and the Japanese in the United States. While the common images of Japan and the Japanese mostly betray very one-sided notions of the other culture, they are far from being homogeneous. Sheila K. Johnson argues in her book *The Japanese Through American Eyes* that contradicting images of Japan as "cruel warriors," "harmony-loving worker bees," and "otherworldly aesthetes" have existed in the United States side by side or in succession since the first Americans set foot on Japanese soil (v). Similar observations are made by Ian Littlewood in *The Idea of Japan: Western Images, Western Myths*, who categorizes the images of the island-nation in

---

5   In the automobile industry, Japan produced eleven million vehicles in 1980 while the U.S. only produced eight million cars in the same year. This trend continues and Toyota even exceeded General Motors as the world's number one car producer in 2006 (W.Cohen and Kennedy 104).

terms of "Aliens, Aesthetes, Butterflies and Samurai" (xii). Both Johnson and Littlewood relate these conflicting stereotypes to Japanese-American history, which is marked by constant imaginings and re-imaginings of "the Japanese Other" either as enemy or as close ally.

In the nineteenth century, Japan was perceived as a backward but aesthetically appealing country with beautiful women whereas in the twentieth century Pearl Harbor and World War II atrocities resulted in a negative image of cruel, inhumane savages. This image was revised when Japanese people were elevated to the status of model minority in the late 1950s and 60s in the U.S. (Niiya 238-239). Yet, during the trade conflicts in the 1980s, when "Americans thought the Japanese economy more a threat than the Soviet military" (Wilkinson 140), negative war-time images reappeared and Japan once more became a nation of cruel, treacherous (business) warriors in the mindset of many Americans. Johnson explains that the radical changes in perception result from the very nature of popular stereotypes which are always greatly influenced by immediate historical events and cultural developments (ix-x). The constantly shifting image of Japan attests vividly to the fact that the idea of a nation or culture does not remain static through time, but is reconfigured and reshaped according to external influences. Nowadays, because of the multiple influences, especially in the realm of popular culture, Japan has a predominantly trendy, "cool," and yet still exotic allure in the United States. Yet, Japanese popular culture also constantly evolves in the face of external influences from other Asian countries and "the West".

Especially the American influence in Japan, visible in the omnipresence of American brands such as Starbucks, McDonald's, GAP, or Disney and U.S. film and TV, has been critically discussed by several scholars such as Joseph J. Tobin, Aviad Raz, and James Watson. They all agree that although there is a wide-ranging contemporary American cultural impact in Japan, American consumer items are not simply imposed, but fulfill a distinct Japanese need. As Japanese consumers actively adapt foreign cultural practices, these scholars reject the idea of an American cultural imperialism subduing Japan. Ian Condry explains, for instance, in "Japanese Hip-Hop and the Globalization of Popular Culture" how hip hop is not just taken over and/or copied by Japanese artists but actively and creatively reinterpreted. Here, as in other cases, what seems to be at first sight an invasion of American culture in Japan turns out to be a distinct, Japanese version of an

American original, as "Japanese rappers perform for local audiences in the Japanese language and use Japanese subjects to build their base of fans" (381).

Similarly, the collection *Re-Made in Japan: Everyday Life and Consumer Taste in a Changing Society*, edited by Joseph J. Tobin, analyzes a number of cultural adaptations in Japan such as the specific usage of the English language, the creation of Japanese versions of Disneyland, and the ways in which tango is popularized in Japan. However, most analyses in the book are still occupied with positioning Eastern and Western cultures as binaries, thereby completely ignoring the possibility of cultural hybridization or exchange. Mary Yoko Brannen's essay "'Bwana Mickey': Constructing Cultural Consumption at Tokyo Disneyland" that focuses on the adaptation of the American Disneyland theme park in Japan is a case in point. Her detailed analysis, in which she repeatedly explains how the dichotomy between "us" versus "them" is strictly preserved in the Japanese park, leads her to the conclusion that Tokyo Disneyland is a "Japanese form of cultural imperialism" (227). It will be argued in the second chapter of this study that although it is important to acknowledge the differentiation between Japan and the United States within the park in order to understand how Japanese consumers perceive Tokyo Disneyland, the adaption of Tokyo Disneyland to Japanese consumer demands resulted in a hybrid product that contains American *and* Japanese influences.

Aviad Raz also focuses on the adaptation of the park to Japanese consumer needs in his socio-anthropological studies of Tokyo Disneyland. Drawing on interviews with Japanese staff members of Tokyo Disneyland and his own visits to the park, Raz compares the structure of the place as well as the employment and management policies to those in Disney parks located in the United States. In doing so, Raz concentrates on the Japanese perspective on Tokyo Disneyland and the recontextualization of the park in Japan, arguing that the success of Tokyo Disneyland is based on the fact that by adapting the theme park to Japanese culture, it has been transformed into something Japanese. This insight will be further extended in order to show that the hybrid, transnational park indeed incorporates both Japanese and American influences and is sustained by this cross-cultural appeal. As a Japanese interpretation of the American park, it reflects the image of America in Japan.

Among the academic studies that understand cultural exchanges between the East and the West as bilateral and interactive is James Watson's *Golden Arches East: McDonald's in East Asia*, which explores the impact of McDonald's restaurants on the Asian market. The book challenges the widespread notion that McDonald's restaurants work only as a global homogenizing force, which destroys local eating cultures and illustrates the locations in which the American fast food restaurants of the McDonald's company are situated in Asia, as well as how they are adapted to local needs. The volume thereby challenges the explanatory value of the concept of cultural imperialism and at the same time suggests a transnational approach.

On the one hand, the growing influence of Japanese consumer products in South-East Asia has been closely analyzed as well, for instance, by Iwabuchi Koichi, Cherry Sze-Ling Lai, Wendy Siuyi Wong, Ogawa Masaki, Mitsui Toru, and Hosokawa Shūhei. On the other hand, and despite both an increasing interest in Japanese popular culture commodities in the United States and the growing world-wide Japanese permeation of the entertainment media, only recently have scholars such as Anne Allison, Christopher Hart, Ken John Belson and Brian Bremner, Steven L. Kent, Tatsumi Takayuki, Sayuri Guthrie-Shimizu, and Ron and Ronald Yates, started to investigate the influence of Japanese culture on the United States. Most scholars who examine the Japanese influence in the U.S. focus exclusively on one topic such as anime (Allison), manga (Hart), Hello Kitty (Belson and Bremner), video games (Kent), cyberpunk culture/literature (Tatsumi), baseball (Guthrie-Shimizu) or Kikkoman, a company most famous for its soy sauce and food seasoning (Yates). In this study, however, examples from different genres will be examined in order to reflect on the complex picture of cultural exchanges between Japan and the United States. Only by comparing the cultural exchanges in different cultural realms is it possible to explain how these exchanges currently work.

In *Japanamerica: How Japanese Pop Culture Has Invaded the U.S.*, Roland Kelts has aspired to create such an overview of Japanese influences on America and the convergence of American and Japanese cultures. After naming different Japanese influences in the United States like sushi, poetry, scrolls, and literature, he focuses on manga and anime. Yet his book, which is more journalistic than theoretical, is based on some daring speculations like the one that Japanese popular culture, especially manga and anime, have become extremely popular in the United States because they "emerged as underground expressions of trauma in Japan" (37) that were caused by the dropping of the atomic bombs on Hiroshima and Nagasaki. According to Kelts, the popularity of manga and anime in the United States nowadays "means that we are finally hearing another voice in our conversations about atomic bombs, Vietnam, the cultural upheavals of the 1960s and 1970s, and the violence, uncertainties, and fears of the twenty-first century" (37). He additionally assumes that Japan "feels a lot closer to us than it used to" after 9/11 because the United States and Japan now share a form of cultural trauma (37). It seems questionable as to whether or not America really "feels closer" to Japan because of the events of 9/11, especially due to the fact that the *Americans* dropped atomic bombs on Japan is hard to ignore in this context.

In order to sort out the different and often contradictory background of Japanese-American interconnections, *Embracing Differences* aims at elucidating cultural exchanges between Japan and the United States in the twentieth and twenty-first century in the context of postcolonial as well as transnational cultural studies. Although the United States is often absent from imperial or postcolonial discussion, as Amy Kaplan examines in "Left Alone With America: The Absence of Empire in the Study of American Culture," it may be highly enlightening to include the United States in the discussion of postcolonial discourses, since colonial patterns are indeed visible in the history of the United States.

The American-Japanese relationship is interesting to investigate through the lens of postcolonial studies since even though Japan was never formally a colony, its relation with the West in general and especially with the United States can be examined in colonial and neo-colonial terms starting with the unequal treaties forced on Japan in 1854 and the Occupation Era which reflect quasi-colonial or neocolonial relations of power and dependence between the two nations. Yet as already indicated above, a postcolonial approach, valuable and elucidating as it may be, is not enough to cover the intricate and contradictory patterns of the contemporary relations between the two nations. Therefore, the second theoretical strand running through this study is the theory of transnationalism.

In 2004 when the American Studies scholar Shelly Fisher Fishkin emphasized the necessity of American Studies as an academic discipline to take a "transnational turn" (17-58), she noted the urgent need for a more inclusive and multi-perspectival approach when discussing American culture and literature. Fisher Fishkin strongly advocated for a turn away from an exclusive focus on Caucasian American culture and perspectives and against ignoring the larger global context. She called for American Studies to locate the transnational rather than the national in its center (21). She urged scholars to acknowledge that the United States is no "static and stable territory and population" (24) and therefore to include perspectives of American Studies scholars from all around the world (38f.). Kaplan described the decentralization of the academic field and the critical interrogation of a unidirectional historicism as significant for American Studies. The influential literary critic Emory Elliott has also demanded of his colleagues that "those of us who study the United States from the inside and those who do so from the outside need to have more dialogue" (6). In the spirit of these critics and many others such as Richard King or Amirtjit Sing and Peter Schmidt, who have tried to shed light on their fixation on the exceptional U.S. position and the interrelations between the USA and the world, Japanese perceptions will be included in order to analyze Japanese-U.S. relationships and follow the theoretical path opened by Peter Hitchcock in his study *Imaginary States: Studies in Cultural Transnationalism*.

## TRANSNATIONALISM

Transnationalism in the context of cultural studies has opened a new way of thinking, of imagining cultural relationships. Perceptions of the self are contested and re-examined by questioning traditional ideas of national identity. Aihwa Ong emphasizes the merits of transnationalism by arguing that the prefix "trans"

[d]enotes both moving through space or across lines, as well as changing the nature of something [...] (it) also alludes to the transversal, the transactional, the translational, and the transgressive aspects of contemporary behaviour and imagination that are incited, enabled, and regulated by the changing logics of states and capitalism. (4)

Ong's definition suggests that transnationalism as a theory offers new perspectives and hints to a new "interconnectedness and mobility across space," a theory that allows to trace "cultural specificities of global processes, tracing the multiplicity of the uses and conceptions of 'culture'" (4). Similarly, Peter Hitchcock describes cultural transnationalism not only as a methodology for cultural studies but as "a challenge of the imagination itself" (1). He emphasizes the importance of "rethink[ing] culture as an object of knowledge beyond its strict and restricting national base" (2-3), reasoning that the "recognition of disjuncture and difference" (3) between cultures is necessary and important and that these differences between cultures do not only need to be acknowledged, but encouraged (3). With this approach to different cultures, "new possibilities to analyze global differences" (5) open up new ways to "imagine difference globally" (1). As Myra Jehlen has argued, in transnational studies the term "difference" replaces the older term "Other" and thus grants the former "Other" identities of their own. The idea of a cultural dialogue is accentuated since "with the substitution of 'difference' for 'otherness', it is hoped that the imperial monologue becomes a two-sided exchange" (42). By imagining situations between different nations "otherwise," transnational cultural studies focus on "representation and non-representation" (Hitchcock 5) and on their possible conditions.

Hitchcock's ideas are based upon the ideas of a new role for the imagination in our time that the sociologist Arjun Appadurai developed in *Modernity at Large*. Appadurai argued that in a world highly dominated by visual materials, the media has to be positioned at the center of the discussion of the global present. According to him, "the imagination is now central to all forms of agency, is itself a social fact, and is the key component of the new global order" (3), indicating that the imagination can be further used as a positive force to imagine alternative modes of the world. Globalization theory has traditionally been more interested in powers "from above," in huge corporations as well as economic elites and cultural hegemonies, and in the interconnectedness and interdependence of the world as the flow and spread of cultural practices, commodities, and people disconnected from nation states. The emphasis on the rising interconnectedness of nation states nourishes the fear of the homogenization of cultures and the decline of the nation state and thus the vision of the loss of distinctive national identities is connected to this theory. Instead of focusing on ideas of cultural homogenization, scholars including Appadurai, Hitchcock, and Jehlen welcome, the new media, mass migration, communication, and cultural interactions as sites where local negotiations take place and create new cultural forms (*Modernity at Large* 6), making hybridization rather than homogenization a process of globalization, and thus focusing on powers from "below."

Hybridity in this context has to be understood as a form of boundary crossing between familiar and exotic elements, which, however, are not completely absorbed, but remain distinguishable. According to Homi Bhabha, the concept stresses interconnectedness and, at the same time, challenges the authority of dominant agencies. Bhabha argues that this "empowering" hybridity leads to the recognition of "Third Spaces," which are defined by him as liminal, ambivalent in-between spaces that can help to overcome notions of exoticism (Bhabha 38). Similarly, Robert J.C. Young refers to Mikhail Bakhtin's concept of hybridity in languages to argue that the nature of hybridity itself is hybrid, "a doubleness that both brings together and fuses, but also maintains separation" (22), thus evaluating hybridity as "the form of cultural difference itself" (23). In a more recent reference to Bhabha, Iwabuchi also used the term and argued that hybridity articulates the dynamic of "cultural interconnection, transgression, reworking and cross-fertilization" (Iwabuchi, *Recentering Globalization* 51), as it is a synthesis of elements from two or more different cultures. All three theorists stress the dynamic nature of hybridity, a concept that also challenges the clearly demarcated boundaries of "us" and "them," or the "West" and "the Rest" (Iwabuchi, *Recentering Globalization* 51).

Though hybridity is a core aspect of transnationalism, it is important to note that the individual cultures and nations are not understood as fusing and vanishing completely in this context. Transnationalism starts from a focus on different phenomena as rooted in nation states, and provides the insight that the nation state is not erased in the global context but imagined in a different way. As Benedict Anderson already described in *Imagined Communities,* nations are always in a state of change (4). Yet, part of their function is to supply all members of one nation with an imagined national affinity, based on shared myths, ideals, and values, nation states simply cannot be annihilated by globalizing processes, dissolved in hybridization.

Since transnationalism shifts away from the exclusively Eurocentric point of view that places the West at the center of cultural exchanges, it may be regarded as an extension of postcolonial studies, which imagined an "Other" as in a binary opposition to a "self" in order to define the self positively. Hence, as transnationalism seeks to reform and even transgress older approaches through which the East was exposed to and defined by a Western gaze, it strives to respect and include Eastern perspectives as well. Transnationalism embraces Appadurai's observation that a permanent tension between the local and the global influences both sides and that the ensuing interactions create "tensions between cultural homogenization and cultural heterogenization" (*Modernity at Large* 32). The theory of transnationalism therefore recognizes existing differences between national cultures and understands these differences as part of a network of power relations. This constitutes an ideal new basis for analyzing cultural exchanges and interactions, with an emphasis on "the in-between and conflictual" (Hitchcock 18) nature of cultural interactions.

## RETHINKING JAPANESE-AMERICAN CULTURAL RELATIONS

Using the insights of transnational and postcolonial studies, the following chapters will investigate Japanese-American interrelations in the fields of theme parks, food, and movies. By following Appadurai's theory and its further specification by Susan Napier and Sylvia Ferrero, seven dimensions of cultural flows across national borders are distinguished in a global context. The first five were named by Appadurai: ethnoscape (the flow of people), technoscape (the flow of technology), finanscape (the flow of money), mediascapes (the flow of images), and ideoscape (the flow of ideas) (*Modernity* 33-37). Two more "scapes" were added to elaborate upon the different spaces where cultural interactions take place: fantasyscape (the flow of play) by Napier and foodscape (the flow of food practices) by Ferrero. As contemporary transnational exchanges are based upon and contextualized by the changing history of Japanese-American cultural exchanges through the last two centuries, a short chapter devoted to this topic introduces the analyses.

The main part of this study is divided into three analytical chapters. The first, "*Yōkoso* Mickey Mouse! Disney in Japan" will focus on the fantasyscape of Disney theme parks in Japan.[6] It will first explain how Disneyland has established itself in Japan and show that Tokyo Disney Resort is an example of how an American 'original' traveled "across distinct cultural boundaries" (Van Maanen 5) and became successful in Japan because of its marked difference from Japanese cultural products. Yet, it has to be acknowledged that the Disney theme park in Japan signifies something different to the Japanese audience than the American Disney parks signify to American visitors. It will be argued that the park is not only popular because it is an American product, but because it was considerably adapted and now reflects an idealized Japanese perception of the United States – and other parts of the world, since the park has expanded to a full-fledged resort, which creates and imagines different European cultures as well. However, the park is neither a form of Japanese cultural imperialism (Brannen) nor an entirely Japanese theme park (Raz). Instead, the originally American theme park has been reimagined by the Japanese owners, who have turned it into a transnational space.

The second chapter "A Taste of Difference: Sushi in the United States," focuses on the influence of Japanese food in general, specifically that of sushi, on American food culture and thereby concentrates on the foodscape in the United States.[7] It explains how Japan and the United States first used food as a cultural marker in order to set themselves off against each other in terms of the food they consumed, and in the process equated strange food with strange people and barbaric eating habits with uncivilized consumers. The conflation of uncivilized people with strange food happened on both sides of the Pacific, since the diets of people living in Japan and in the United States in the nineteenth century were significantly different from each other. However, the idea of what is considered strange or exotic has shifted over history. Today, what was once regarded to be a barbaric eating habit, such as eating raw fish, has become part of the American *haute cuisine*. Nowadays sushi can be found in almost every American supermarket and even Martha Stewart recommends "Japanese Twist Bridal Showers" with sandwiches made of salmon, *wasabi* (Japanese horseradish), and *shiso*

---

6   Parts of this chapter were presented in 2009 at the 36th Annual Conference of the Austrian Association for American Studies, University of Graz.
7   Parts of this chapter were used for a publication in *The Japanese Journal of American Studies*.

(a Japanese herb), or green tea shortbreads (Stewart). Taking sushi as an example and analyzing American Sushi cookbooks elucidates how an originally Japanese culinary product was adopted and adapted by the American foodscape, thereby creating a transnational version of the dish.

From Benedict Anderson's argument that nations are imagined, it follows that different nations are imagined differently. This difference is repeatedly constructed and reconstructed on screen. The final analytical chapter "Could We Have a Geisha in This Scene? Transnational Depictions of Japanese in Contemporary Hollywood Movies," examines the depiction of Japan and the Japanese in Hollywood movies and in doing so investigates the mediascape. With the massive influx of Japanese cultural goods and their rising popularity, American companies felt the need to react to obvious new consumer demands. For example, the enormous popularity of anime in the United States urged big animation corporations such as Disney and Nickelodeon to try to compete with Japanese anime by creating their own anime-style productions. It will be argued that with the increasing saturation of Japanese products and their popularity as well as their "cool" appeal in the United States, Hollywood has started to create new images of Japan and the Japanese. The shift from inscrutable and untrustworthy strangers to civilized allies, from highly stereotyped and often ultimately evil "Others" to individualized and human characters will be shown as importantly connected to the transnationality of the Hollywood film industry. The directors, producers, and actors that made *The Last Samurai* (2003), *Lost in Translation* (2003), and *Letters from Iwo Jima* (2006) came from multiple national backgrounds and brought their cultural backgrounds and knowledge with them. These – in production, consumption, and film-text – truly transnational movies imagine Japan differently on screen.

All these developments in recent cultural exchanges between Japan and the United States reflect how both nations cross-influence each other and thereby create not only new, hybrid, transnational cultural practices and products but also new, hybrid, transnational (imagined) spaces which lead to an altered perception of Japan in the United States and vice versa. It will be demonstrated with regard to Disneyland in Japan, sushi in the United States, and Hollywood representations of Japan on screen that the attraction of these cultural influences lies in their very difference from the recipients' own culture. To Japanese visitors, Tokyo Disney Resort is interesting because it is an American "original," that is, it functions and feels "different" than Japanese theme parks. Similarly, sushi fascinates American consumers because it differs from American food. Hence, although these cultural items need to be adapted to local consumer needs to a certain degree, it is of crucial importance to maintain a sense of "Otherness" in order to keep them interesting. At the same time, movies set in Japan are often considered alluring, as they depict a world often unknown and unfamiliar to the audience.

Since cultural products need to be contextualized within their new surroundings when they are exported, it becomes obvious that in this process, cultural items change their meaning. Cultural goods exported to foreign markets are always re-contextualized and need to be understood in their local context. In "Harajuku Girls," Stefani alludes to this phenomenon by acknowledging that the Harajuku fashion style is a mix of Western and Japanese cross-influences. This challenges the idea that global interconnectedness automatically leads to cultural homogenization and exemplifies the contradictory nature of transnational interactions. While the lyrics signal a creative exchange that results in the creation of new, hybrid styles which incorporate American and Japanese elements, the performance of the song by the American singer with her stereotypically marginalized Japanese girls in the background indicates that this transnational exchange is not at all free from (earlier) cultural imperialist influences. Because national and ideological ideas and histories are attached to cultural commodities and practices, the idea of national stereotypes and supposed national inferiority versus superiority in a world of unequal power relations is exported and imported whenever consumer items penetrate foreign markets.

Yet, as Stefani's expressed appreciation of the "super *kawaii*" Harajuku style makes abundantly clear, the "cultural imprint of the producing country" or "cultural odor" (Iwabuchi, *Recentering Globalization* 27) may further reflect positive associations with the country from which different ideas and goods are imported, even if they are related to its perceived exoticism. Commodities and cultural practices are not only inevitably linked to their countries of origin but are often interesting to consumers from different cultural backgrounds *because of* their distinct national imprints and are often adapted to the different consumer needs. Thus, while globalizing processes may lead to the availability of cultural products outside their original national spheres, a homogenization of cultures is not necessarily implied by these processes. Instead differences can be emphasized and/or goods can be localized in their new surroundings and through these processes new versions of an original are developed. As Gayatri Spivak has phrased it, it is important "to *recognize* agency in others, not simply to comprehend Otherness" (12), in the context of this study that means that differences should not just be noted but also different cultures should be granted agency in the ways they deal with cultural imports.

Contemporary cultural exchanges between Japan and the United States take place within and between the different "scapes" defined by Appadurai, Napier, and Ferrero. The analyses of some of these "scapes" in *Embracing Differences* challenges the simplifying concept of a center-periphery relationship between the cultures involved and shows that they offer instead "building blocks for individuals and groups who create their 'imagined multiple worlds,' spread all over the globe. Thus, these [...] dimensions are powerful enough to subvert a dominant order dependent upon the notion of the nation-state" (Ferrero 196). This does not imply that an ideal equilibrium already exists or has ever existed. Yet today globalization and transnationalism have led to the closer approximation between the two nations and their cultures, especially when compared to earlier Japanese-American cultural exchanges that were marked by immensely unequal power relations, prejudices, anxieties, and suspicions. Nevertheless, *Embracing Differences* will show that the cultural interactions do not make both cultures the same. Instead, differences remain visible and are not only accepted but often appreciated and embraced on the other side of the Pacific. Today's vital cultural exchange is based upon the constant flow of people, commodities, ideas, and images across borders, which leads to the creation of new cultural forms and practices, which then once more travel back to the country of "origin" where they have to be re-negotiated. Thus, transnational cultural products and meanings are created which can no longer be related to one particular country, and transnational consumers embrace these products, which are both familiar and unfamiliar at the same time. However, this does not mean that these transnational practices are entirely free of power relations. This is also evident in Gwen Stefani's song "Harajuku Girls" when she sings, "You got the look that makes you stand out / Harajuku Girls, I'm looking at you girls." The fact that the American singer, "an American girl, in the Tokyo streets" ("Harajuku Girls") is observing and judging the Japanese women in the streets of Harajuku indicates that she is the person who decides, from a Western point of view, what is considered stylish and what not. Although Stefani sings about "a ping-pong match between eastern and western" ("Harajuku Girls") and acknowledges that her own fashion collection was inspired by this Japanese fashion style; she continues with the lines "Just wait 'til you get your little hands on L.A.M.B." ("Harajuku Girls"). By including the adjective "little" to describe the hands of potential Japanese consumers, she belittles them and once more puts herself in a dominant position. It becomes axiomatic that, no matter how much consumers embrace them, transnational cultural practices are never free of power relations and the interactions between cultures have always been and will remain complex and multifaceted.

# "Here Be Monsters": Early Japanese-American Cultural Exchanges

> The mind needs monsters. Monsters embody all that is dangerous and horrible in the human imagination
> - DAVID D. GILMORE (1) -

For a long time, Japan was positioned on many Western maps at the edge to the known and was deemed a place of unbelievable horrors and wonders. Japan was first included on maps on a regular basis as late as in the early nineteenth century as its existence was rendered "unimportant to the world" until then (Black *Maps* 61). Most Westerners did not know much about Japan until the end of the fifteenth century; it is significant to note that "there are only seven known instances of the appearance of 'Zipangu'[1] on western maps before 1500 A.D." (Wood 278). Consequently, one of the few maps that include Japan prior to the nineteenth century, Sebastian Münster's 1558 map of the world, locates the island nation at the Western periphery and shows it surrounded by fierce looking sea monsters.

In the past, explorers who traveled the seven seas developed maps and sea charts not only to provide first-hand navigational data for a safe journey, but also to define geography. Naming and structuring the world according to Western ideologies, map and chart making in Europe and the United States was linked to the colonial process of discovery and expansion and thus was closely related to the conception of a discourse of "the Other." Benedict Anderson names the map among the "three institutes of powers" that "profoundly shaped the way in which the colonial state imagined its

---

[1] Zipangu is an old Western name for Japan which was first used by Marco Polo in the thirteenth century (Perry 5).

domination" (163-164). On some maps, monsters served not only as illustrations and bore the words "here be monsters" on the spaces that designated still uncharted waters to indicate the potentially dangerous, uncivilized nature of the unknown, undefined regions. Monsters have always embodied Otherness and reflected feelings of fear and desire. As Jeffrey Jerome Cohen argues in *Monster Theory: Reading Culture*, "the monster's body quite literally incorporates fear, desire, anxiety, and fantasy" (4) and "the monster is best understood as an embodiment of difference, a breaker of category, and a resistant Other" (x). Therefore, depicting the "Other" as a monster has strong ideological connotations as fear and longing intermingle and allude to a rather ambiguous relationship.

Maps and charts as representations of space; reflect and visualize power relations and depict the world as imagined by those who create them. In his book *The Nature of Maps*, J.B. Harley explains that although maps seem to "present a factual statement about geographical reality," they actually "redescribe the world – like any other document – in terms of relations of power and of cultural practices, preferences, and priorities" (35). This is manifested in different maps of the world from different nations as cartographers locate their own nation at the center of the map, thereby claiming their central position in the world and, at the same time, indicating which nations are considered to lie at the periphery and hence at the verge of the unknown. There is no better representation of Japan's marginal role for the West than these old maps that assign Japan a peripheral position. Concurrently, these spaces at geographical margins were constructed and imagined as monstrous spaces, as map makers frequently filled blank areas on maps with images of monsters (Van Duzer 432), the dangerous unknown.

Early encounters between American and Japanese people were oftentimes accompanied by stereotypes shaped by the representation of the other party. The following chapter will give a short overview of Japanese-American encounters and the early flow of goods and explain how these exchanges shaped early images of "the Other" in both nations. The chapter shall add historical depth to the present study and help to understand the ambivalent nature of Japanese-American cultural exchanges today.

## JAPANESE MONSTERS AND AMERICAN BARBARIANS

In the past, several attempts had been made to map, define, and explain Japan for the West. However, only little was known about the island-nation, and the accounts that were available basically described Japan as completely different from the West. The early images of Japan were highly stereotypical, constructed on the basis of Orientalist ideologies as discussed in Chapter 1 and aroused a keen interest in the "exotic" island nation. Japan, however, was not interested in any exchange with the West. Instead, Japanese people were concerned about the influence of Christian missionaries, who had already converted a considerable number of Japanese people. They viewed the introduction of new religious values as a threat to the harmony of the country as they had already experienced how multiple influences poured into their country and led to tensions which finally culminated in the dissolution of the shogunate in 1868 and the abolition of the official caste system in Japan, thus forever changing the social structure of the country (LaFeber 8). In 1587, as a result, the powerful military ruler Hideyoshi expelled the missionaries, and in 1603, the Tokugawa shogunate closed all Japanese harbors to Western vessels (LaFeber 8; Befu, "Globalization as Human Dispersal" 17-40), while prohibiting Japanese citizens from leaving the country on pain of death. According to the historian Walter LaFeber, at least twenty-seven American vessels headed towards Japan between 1790 and 1853, only to be turned away before landing (10).

Although most Westerners equated the self-imposed seclusion of Japan (*sakoku*) with stagnation, Japan did indeed keep track of developments in the West through their contact with a few Dutch, Chinese, and Korean traders who were allowed to continue trading with Japan, using a small island close to Nagasaki and by reading Chinese books on the West (LaFeber 8 and 15; Buruma, *Inventing Japan* 14-15; Kamei 56). When Shanghai opened to foreign trade after the First Opium War in 1842, American ships frequently travelled past Japan and the United States became increasingly interested in the "impenetrable Japan," as Herman Melville called the island nation in *Moby Dick* (456). Thus, in 1852 Commodore Matthew C. Perry was sent to Japan to "open" the nation for foreign, and particularly for U.S. trade.[2] Since Japan's feudal government was deemed undemocratic by the United States, the political idea of the 'liberation' of Japan was a significant component of Commodore Perry's mission as well (Duus 11). His endeavors resonated with the nineteenth century American belief that "seizing Oriental trade or civilizing Orientals through missionary activity" was "completing Columbus's original mission" (Schueller 9), as the latter's 'discovery' of the Americas was interpreted as "the outcome of a vision to reach the Orient," (Schueller 9) thereby mystifying colonial and imperialist aims as being 'natural' to the American character. The urge of Americans to move further West after the American frontier was largely claimed in the course of the nineteenth century, and a "growing desire to conquer Asian markets" (LaFeber 9) in order to compete with European colonial powers, turned Asia in general and Japan in particular into a new frontier (LaFeber 33).

It never occurred to Americans like Commodore Perry, who "positioned himself as a representative of a higher civilization" (Duus 13), that the Japanese might have identified them as barbarians rather than as saviors. Accordingly, during the Edo Period (1603-1868)[3], the study of the West was known in Japan as *bangaku*, which translates as "barbarian studies" and the central government bureau that translated Western books was named *banshō shirabeshō*: the Barbarian Works Investigation Bureau (Dower, *War without Mercy* 239). Thus, it is not surprising these Western barbarians were often associated with monsters. Basing his findings on Komatsu Kazuhiko's assumption that monsters appear in narratives in times of crisis, Gerald Figal argues in *Civilization and Monsters: Spirits of Modernity in Meiji Japan* that there is a causal relationship between the arrival of Commodore Perry in Japan in 1853 and the increase of monsters or *bakemono* in Japanese texts (22). The Japanese concept of monsters, which are called *bakemono* which literally means "changing thing," connects notions of the unforeseen and unfamiliar to imaginary mystic creatures (Figal 5). As the

---

2   For more information about Commodore Matthew Perry's mission and early Japanese-American history see Walter LaFeber's *The Clash: US- Japanese Relations throughout History;* William L. Neumann's *America Encounters Japan: From Perry to MacArthur*; and Peter Booth Wiley's,*Yankees in the Land of the Gods: Perry and the Opening of Japan.*

3   The Edo Period is sometimes called Tokugawa Period.

arrival of American ships in Japanese harbors was perceived as a threat to the harmony of the nation and seemed to substantiate earlier accounts of North America as "a country cold and large [...] with many lions, elephants, tigers, leopards, and brown and white bears," in which "the natives are pugnacious and love to fight" (qtd. in Dower, "Black Ships & Samurai"). A great number of scrolls from this period visualize the Japanese perception of Americans, showing Commodore Perry closely resembling a long-nosed *tengu*, a traditional Japanese monster (Dower "Black Ships & Samurai").

The perception of the American intruders as monstrous beings was certainly reinforced, as the "strong [American] instinct of conquest" (Dower, *War without Mercy* 239) made them more beast-like than human to the Japanese. Confirming the negative Japanese impressions of the United States, the American commodore threatened the Japanese with his numerous cannons in order to achieve his goals. Thus, he made clear that he did not come as a petitioner but was determined to enforce his country's imperialist policy under the force of weaponry. Perry accomplished his mission with the signing of the Treaty of Kanagawa in 1854, that opened two Japanese ports for foreign trade, "promised eternal peace between Japan and America" (LaFeber 14), and put an end to Japan's policy of seclusion. While Perry's mission was the expression of monstrous power to the Japanese, to Americans it seemed extremely successful.[4]

The next cultural clashes between Japanese and American representatives occurred almost immediately after the signing of the Treaty of Kanagawa, when both parties exchanged gifts to reiterate their new partnership. Among other things, the Americans presented books, clocks, rifles, a telegraph, and a miniature railroad and train to the Japanese. In return, they received gold-lacquered paper boxes, flower holders, paper, porcelain cups, and parasols from the Japanese (Blumberg 127-130) and they were also honored by a sumo wrestling match organized specifically for them. Perry and his men were puzzled and disappointed by the Japanese gifts. They were convinced that their own presents showed "the success of science and

---

4 Many Westerners were not excited about the "opening" of Japan and instead "prophesied the end of 'old' Japan and echoed [Lafcardio] Hearn's lament [that] 'the opening of the country was very wrong – a crime. Fairyland is already dead'" (Wilkinson 123).

enterprise [of] a higher civilization" (qtd. in Wiley 418), whereas the Japanese gifts were merely decorative and, as the official American interpreter of the mission, Samuel Wells Williams, phrased it, came from "partially enlightened people" (qtd. in Buruma, *Inventing Japan* 13). In the same tone, the sumo wrestling match was dismissed by the Americans as "a curious, barbaric spectacle," a "'disgusting display' of 'brute animal force'" (Wiley 417). The Americans used technological inventions as politically charged objects to represent the United States as an enlightened, modern nation (Yoshimi, "The Cultural Politics" 396) which, at the same time, blinded them against the symbolic cultural value of the gifts they received.

The evaluation of unfamiliar customs, food, and behavior as strange and barbaric from a Western perspective reoccurred in later visits as well. Mixed public bathing, a common practice in Japan at the time of the first arrival of Americans, was deemed immoral and uncivilized (Neumann 46, LaFeber 19). Similarly, the use of human excrements as fertilizers was considered unhygienic and led to the conclusion of one American visitor that "the Japanese have no well-developed sense of smell; offensive smell anyway" (G. Johnson 201-202).

Thus, expanding upon early encounters, an American Orientalist discourse developed that deemed Japan overwhelmingly uncivilized and barbaric, the utmost "Other" of the West, while the United States was constructed as a modern nation to which Japan needed to turn (Schueller 12). The fact that the Japanese were neither 'white' nor Christian further made them appear inferior to the Americans. Yet the latter could not ignore the "civilized" aspects of Japan such as the politeness of the people, their "preoccupation with questions of honour and etiquette," and their bravery (Littlewood 3). Therefore, from the very beginning, common Western distinctions between "savage natives and civilized westerners" (Littlewood 3) were hard to apply to Japan. Instead, the image of Japan in the West oscillated between "savage" and "civilized." The early American perceptions of "the self" and "the Other" reflect a binary opposition, according to which Japan was associated either with decorative, female attributes or barbaric behavior, whereas America was equated with science, technology, masculinity, and progress. While it was acknowledged that Japan was not entirely uncivilized, the nation was imagined in a backward, pre-industrial state.

The Japanese, on the other hand, had contradictory attitudes towards the Americans as well as

[...] they fitted the Americans into the xenophobic stereotype of the greedy, wily, and aggressive barbarian, intent on subverting the foundations of Japanese society with their religion and their restless pursuit of profit; on the other hand, since knowing the enemy was the first step toward defense, they wanted to learn more about the Americans and the land they came from. (Duus 17)

Evidently, Japanese people likewise imagined "the Other" to be barbaric and uncivilized. Just as Japan was located at the edge of civilization on Western maps, the world outside Japan was depicted by the Japanese as a dangerous place "populated by strange people and fantastic beings" (Duus 19). Japanese maps of the world located Japan at the center and arranged the other countries of the world around the island-nation, "some close, some distant, according to their degree of 'civilization'" (Steele 9) thereby categorizing "the Other" according to their own, Japanese normative ideologies.

In a similar vein, early Japanese paintings of Commodore Perry and his crew reflect the artists' views that all Westerners look the same. To the Japanese, the Americans were unattractive, "hairy barbarians" (Blumberg 23) with big noses, "bereft of proper morality, uncultivated in manners, and given to wild or violent behavior" (Duus 15). Peter Duus explains in *The Japanese Discovery of America* how "the Japanese ruling elite [...] initially responded to American ethnocentrism with an ethnocentrism of their own" (2). Japan reacted to "the Other" with a counter-Orientalist discourse which has been termed Occidentalism.

Xiaomei Chen has argued in his book *Occidentalism* that the term describes a "discursive practice that, by constructing its Western Other, has allowed the Orient to participate actively and with indigenous creativity in the process of self-appropriation, even after being appropriated and constructed by Western Others" (4-5). Occidentalism, the counter-term to Said's Orientalism, is further defined by Ian Buruma and Avishai Margalit in *Occidentalism: The West in the Eyes of Its Enemies* as a discourse based on the idea that the East and the West are completely different from each other. Within this discourse the West in general, and particularly the United

States, are considered cold, mechanical, shallow, and rootless, whereas Japan is perceived as "spiritual and profound" (3).[5]

These ideas were reinforced after the first Japanese diplomatic mission to the United States in 1860.[6] The Japanese diplomats, who were overwhelmed by their impressions, tried to make sense of the unknown country and culture by observing and interpreting the Americans. Under an Eastern gaze, "fragments of cultural information gathered from direct contact with the Americans had yet to be assembled into an image of what might be called the core values of American society or fitted into new cultural paradigms to replace the old distinction between the 'cultured' and the 'barbarian'" (Duus 28). Even though the Japanese diplomats respected the ideals of liberty and equality promoted in the United States (Kamei 59f.), the growing familiarity with the American culture led to doubts about some aspects of American life. For example, to the Japanese the political model of the United States lacked historical traditions as well as a rigid structure, and they compared the congressional debates they witnessed to "fish sellers shouting loudly in the fish market in Edo" (Kamei 58). Another peculiarity to them was the gender system of the United States, where women had a different social status than in their home country, and the Japanese officials were disturbed when they encountered women at official ceremonies (Duus 24 and 35; Hidetoshi Kato 193f.). Until the end of the Edo Period, the contradictory image of the United States as modern and enlightened, yet cold-hearted and selfish co-existed.

---

5 However, because modern Japan has tried repeatedly to "disrupt, defamiliarize, and queer the conventionally drawn boundaries between Orientalism and Occidentalism" (Tatsumi, *Full Metal Apache* 4), many Asian nations consider Japan part of the Occident rather than the Orient today.

6 This first arrival of Japanese diplomats in the United States was commemorated by Walt Whitman in his poem "The Errand Bearers," which originally appeared in the New York Times on June 27th, 1860. The poem is a response to a parade in Manhattan in honor of the Japanese visitors. In this first American poem on Japanese people, Whitman describes the foreign visitors as "nobels of Niphon" (1) and announces that "Comrade Americanos! To us then at last the Orient comes / [...] / to-day our Antipodes comes" (197). The title of the poem was later revised into "A Broadway Pageant."

Yet, the predominant American image of Japan as being less civilized was not a one-way mirror. Although Japan started to adopt and adapt Western customs and commodities excessively after opening its harbors to foreign influences during the Meiji Period (1868-1912), the American or Western culture was not considered superior but threatening to their own. The Japanese believed that they needed to learn from and keep up with the West in order to "resist total cultural colonization" (Schueller 200).[7] Since "the West" was equated with modernization, Japan started to imitate Western technologies, yet, at the same time, Japan was keen to preserve "an inner core of national culture" (Schueller 200). This policy was referred to as "using the barbarian to control the barbarian" (Beasley 1) or *wakon yōsai*, which can be translated as "Western technology, Japanese spirit." Perry had demonstrated to Japan that the island nation could not shield itself from foreign influences in an increasingly globally interconnected world. Japan's aim after the end of seclusion was to "join the powers, but on their own [Japanese] terms, not the West's" (LaFeber 30). Western advisors and teachers were now invited to come to Japan and instruct them in Western thoughts and technology.

Japanese anxieties about sovereignty were well-justified since, although Japan was never formally colonized, the Treaty of Kanagawa had been forced upon them, and when Japan tried to negotiate its revocation in 1887, they failed since they were not taken seriously by the United States (Wilkinson 65). This unequal treaty not only ended the self-imposed seclusion of Japan by opening Japanese harbors to American vessels by military pressure but also forced Japan to accept a U.S. consul (LaFeber 15), thereby placing the island nation in a semi-colonial position.

This first official encounter laid the foundation for Japanese-American relationships for decades to come and reflected the "double-logic of exoticism, that is, the fascination and hatred of the other" (Tatsumi 125) on both sides. The early perceptions of "the Other" as being less civilized show that both nations, Japan and the United States, believed in the superiority of

---

7   During the Meji Period, Japan predominantly turned to Europe (especially Britain and Germany) in order to learn from the West. The Meiji constitution of 1989 for example was based on the Prussian, i.e. the German model (Duke 363).

their respective cultures.[8] Yet while the United States – on the basis of military and technical might – was convinced that they could export their cultural uniqueness by missionaries or education advisers, thereby enlightening "the Other," Japan assumed that their culture was too unique and thus unfathomable to cultural outsiders (LaFeber 98). Since its beginnings, the historical and cultural entanglement of Japan and the United States was complex and characterized by cultural misunderstandings, prejudices, and economic and cultural power play. Both sides had their stereotypical ideas about "the Other" and considered their own nation to be superior.

In the following decades, the on-going expansionism of Japan in Asia and the increasing number of Japanese immigrants in the U.S. led to malicious sentiments towards the Japanese in the United States. These led to the Gentlemen's Agreement in 1908, the Alien Land Act passed by the California State legislature in 1913, and the Immigration Act of 1924, which put a halt to Japanese immigration to the United States (LaFeber 65f.). American hostility towards the Japanese and Japanese-Americans was further fueled by the Japanese attack on Pearl Harbor in 1941, which triggered anti-Japanese hysteria and was followed by the internment of thousands of Japanese-American citizens under the Executive Order 9066. With Japan as an enemy nation during World War II, Japanese people were depicted by American government propaganda as creatures which enjoyed bloody and cruel battles, and the fact that many high commanders in the Imperial Army were against the war was completely ignored.[9] More differentiated, but not necessarily more positive ideas about "the Japanese" were voiced at the same time, e.g. by Ruth Benedict, an anthropologist who was commissioned by the American government to study the character of "the Japanese" in order to understand them and help to deal with them after the

---

8   The idea of Japanese uniqueness is expressed in the concept of *nihonjinron*, according to which Japan constructed itself in a binary opposition to the West. This notion was visible in its most aggressive form during World War II (see Jarman; Gluck; and Befu).

9   American World War II stereotypes of Japan are discussed in detail in chapter five "Transnational Depictions of Japanese in Contemporary American Hollywood Movies."

war.[10] She describes them in her book *The Chrysanthemum and the Sword* as "the most alien enemy the United States had ever fought in an all-out struggle" (1), and blames their militaristic character on the feudalistic, premodern Japanese government, juxtaposing it with the democratic, modern government of the United States (45f.). Her description of the supposedly ambiguous nature of the Japanese people as "to the highest degree aggressive and unaggressive, both militaristic and aesthetic, both insolent and polite" (2-3) again reflects the stereotypically ambiguous idea of the "oriental Other." Yet, as enemies, the Japanese seemed to be significantly different from other opponents in the war. Unlike the Germans or Italians, who were still considered human, the Japanese antagonists were deemed subhuman. The institutionalized racism of the United States, which made it easy to suppose a non-human character of the Japanese enemy, might also have facilitated the decision to end the Pacific War by dropping atomic bombs on Hiroshima and Nagasaki. As late as in 1981, literary and cultural historian Paul Fussell, a former Marine who fought in the Pacific War, defended in "Thank God for the Atom Bomb" the decision of the American government to use atomic weapons against Japan. He argued that the bombs saved thousands of American lives and that Japan was a barbaric, dangerous and unpredictable nation with the war strategy of "universal national kamikaze" (17). Fussell further claimed that "it is easy to forget [...] what Japan was like before it was first destroyed, and then humiliated, tamed, and constitutionalized by the West" (25). His statements reflect the sentiments of many American soldiers who fought in the Pacific War and who could not understand the Japanese war-time mentality and consequently simply demonized "the Other."[11]

In Japan, American soldiers were likewise portrayed negatively – as depraved, brutal and corrupt cowards (Shibusawa 136). In the Japanese

---

10 It has to be mentioned that Ruth Benedict never traveled to Japan and based her study only on interviews with Japanese Prisoners of War in the United States.
11 For a discussion on the media coverage in the U.S. which defends the use of the atomic bombs on Japan see Uday Mohand and Leo Maley III's essay "Orthodoxy and Dissent: The American News Media and the Decision to Use the Atomic Bomb Against Japan" as well as Samuel Walker's essays "The Decision to Use the Bomb: A Historiographical Update" and "History, Collective Memory, and the Decision to Use the Bomb."

war-time imagination, the Americans only existed as "vivid monsters, devils, and demons" that were depicted in propaganda materials with claws, fangs, and small horns (Dower, *War without Mercy* 9 and 211). Once more setting itself apart from the West, Japan insisted on their racial and cultural "purity" and their upright and strong character (Dower, *War without Mercy* 9) while they depicted "the Others" as monstrous, tainted beings. The concepts of purity and pollution, which are deeply rooted in Japanese religion and the traditional social distinction of Japan from "the Other," were used throughout the war to justify Japan's entitlement to a leading role in the world (Dower, *War without Mercy* 203f.)[12].

The Japanese surrender was followed by the occupation of Japan by American military forces from August 1945 to April 1952. During those years, "Japan had no sovereignty and accordingly no diplomatic relation" to other countries (Dower, *Embracing Defeat* 23). Nearly until the end of the occupation, Japanese citizens were not allowed to leave the country and the Japanese authorities could not make any major economic, political, or administrative decisions without American approval (Dower, *Embracing Defeat* 23). Throughout the Occupation Era, Japan was forced once again into a semi-colonial position. While this might seem a normal, if not even just as a result of losing the war that Japan shared with other defeated nations, John Dower has shown in *Embracing Defeat: Japan in the Wake of World War II* that the Japanese situation was special as:

> [the occupation of] defeated Germany had none of the *exoticism* of what took place in Japan: the total control over a pagan, 'Oriental' society by white men who were [...] engaged in a Christian mission. The occupation of Japan was the last immodest exercise in the colonial conceit known as 'the white man's burden.' (23)

Unlike any European nation, Japan was rendered immature by the United States, and General MacArthur compared the country to a "boy of twelve" (Shibusawa 54f.).[13] This attitude of the American occupying power is re-

---

12 Furuya Jun focuses in "A New Perspective on American History from the Other Side of the Pacific" on a Japanese war-time perspective.
13 The Japanese were offended by this comparison, they were "encouraged, however, by the fact that MacArthur at least has compared them to 'a *boy* of twelve'" since this statement included the possibility to be respected among the

flected in the decision to show "hundreds of educational documentary films to the Japanese people" as part of a re-education policy (Tsuchiya 193-194). The content of the films ranged from "American culture to public hygiene and international relations" (Tsuchiya 193) and demonstrates the assumption that the uncivilized, Oriental "Other" was in urgent need of being re-educated from scratch. This attitude echoed the paternalistic stance already employed 100 years earlier by Commodore Perry, and it reduced Japan once again to a child-like state. In *America's Geisha Alley: Reimagining the Japanese Enemy*, Shibusawa Nabuko traces the history of Japanese-American relationships after World War II. She explains how the American preoccupation with issues of gender, race, and maturity reveals much about the United States during that time, as the portrayal of the defeated enemy as immature "reassured Americans about themselves and their society" (72). However, she argues, despite all racial prejudices it seems as if the citizens of occupied Japan were not the only ones to undergo a learning experience in how to become a democratic society. The Americans who were stationed in Japan also learned to become more liberal and racially tolerant by living among the former enemy; particularly interracial romantic relationships led to a better cross-cultural understanding between the former enemies (Shibusawa 183 and 471f.).

The ensuing relationship between Japan and the USA has been both intimate and complex as the developing "bilateral relationship encompasses not only the military alliance but also close and complex economic and political ties" (Fukuyama and Oh 1). After the end of the U.S. occupation of Japan in 1952, the "patron-protégé relation" (Kanemitsu 145) continued until the mid-1960s. While the U.S. "needed Japan's political and economic stability in the Far East" (Kanemitsu 145), concerning exports and imports "Japan was almost totally dependent upon the United States" (Kanemitsu 145). After the occupation, Japan focused on the development and stabilization of its own economy, which led to a spectacular economic growth of the island nation in the late 1960s and 70s and culminated in Japan's economic boom in the 1980s. At the same time, the U.S. had to struggle with a trade deficit and a slowing growth of its gross national product (Kanemitsu 146-

---

other Western powers one day, whereas "women would always remain women, forever lacking the calm leadership skills, the vitality, the foresight, and the intellect to run a modern society, but 'boys' [...] grow into men" (Shibusawa 57).

147), which led to a rival relationship between the two countries. Nowadays, the situation has significantly defused. The demand for Japanese consumer goods even increased in the 1990s and Japan became "the second-largest foreign investor behind Great Britain in the United States" (Lutz 477), which in turn increased American public anxieties that Japan would challenge the global economic position of the United States (Lutz 477). However, the economic negotiations which preceded the foundation of the World Trade Organization in 1995 led to a more harmonious economic relationship of the two nations that has lasted until today (Lutz 477).

## Reciprocal Cultural Influences

From the very beginning of the Japanese-American relationship, Japan actively incorporated Western commodities and ideas into their culture, thereby enriching and improving it. As expected, Western influences entered Japan after the end of Japan's seclusion politics, during the Meiji Period. The import of Western and American practices and commodities served the purpose of "catching up." Thus the Japanese imported mainly technological devices such as steam engines and telegraphs (Richie, *The Honorable Visitors* 26). Furthermore, Japanese officials and students were sent overseas in the 1860s in order to study Western technologies and institutions as "part of [the Meiji oligarchy's] campaign to develop 'civilization and enlightenment' (*bumei kaika*)" (Guth 4). Thus, hundreds of Japanese visited Europe and the U.S. in order to "inspect and compare their respective military, educational, legal, and cultural institutions" (Guth 4). At the time, foreign practices and products were not so much imposed on Japan, since they were willingly imported, locally adapted and soon considered part of Japanese culture.

One example of a successful adaptation of American culture is baseball, or *yakkyū*, as the sport is called in Japan, which is one of the most popular sports in the island nation today. The history of baseball in Japan is traced in Sayuri Guthrie-Shimizu's book *Transpacific Field of Dreams: How Baseball Linked the United States and Japan in Peace and War*. Guthrie-Shimizu argues that ever since its introduction to the island state by both, American entrepreneurs and Japanese individuals in the late nineteenth century, the game was locally adapted to the Japanese culture. She furthers points out how Japanese influences seeped into the American way of playing baseball, thereby indicating that introducing baseball in Japan was by no means a one-sided, imperialist process but rather a mutual exchange that contributed to an early transpacific cultural exchange between the two nation states. According to her research, the baseball relationship between the United States and Japan throughout the decades "alongside, or despite, formal intergovernmental conduits" (6) has "sustained a myriad of shifting and proliferating social spaces, or contact zones" (6). In her "Introduction," she further explains how the United States and Japan were indeed "intertwined through multitudes of networks,"(7) thus revealing the permeable nature of supposedly strict national boundaries. Before the outbreak of

World War II, Japanese teams traveled the United States and American teams visited Japan to play against each other (Guthrie-Shimizu 140f.). After the end of the war, the sport was revived by the Occupation Forces, who encouraged the Japanese to play it. However, baseball is played with different rules in Japan and emphasizes the idea of team-play much more than the sport in the United States, thereby re-interpreting, adapting, and thus domesticating the originally American sport for a Japanese audience.[14]

In the wake of World War II, Japan once more became interested in adopting and adapting social structures and cultural practices from the West, while in the American mind the image of Japan slowly transformed into that of a model student, eager to learn from the West (Napier, *From Impressionism* 16). At the time of occupation, "Japanese daily life once again underwent an intense westernization – specifically, an Americanization" (Tobin 14). Under the direction of General Douglas MacArthur, reforms concerning the government, education, and industry were imposed on Japan, and Americans promised not to leave "until they [the Japanese] were properly democratized" (Tobin 14). With the American GIs and their families, American English, fashion, and pop-culture was spread. American icons such as Elvis Presley became popular in Japan as the American Top 40 was broadcasted on the Far Eastern division of Armed Forces Radio (Tobin 14).[15] American movies were already popular prior to World War II and were re-introduced in Japanese theaters during the Occupation Era. Furthermore, Japanese movies of this time, such as Kurosawa Akira's 1948 film *Yoidore Tenshi* (*Drunken Angel*), increasingly used "American" movie devices such as close-ups, fast cutting, or expressive camera movements (Richie and Schrader 117-118). Even today, Japan's interest in American cultural products and practices has not lessened and reaches from fast food restaurant chains to music, fashion, movies, and architectural styles.

---

14 Robert Whiting analyzes in his books *The Chrysanthemum and the Bat*; *You Gotta Have Wa*; and *The Meaning of Ichirō* the differences between American and Japanese baseball. This topic is also a central issue in the movie *Mr. Baseball* (1992), in which a professional American baseball player is traded to Japan and has to learn the Japanese way of the game.

15 Warren I Cohen discusses in *The Asian American Century* the American musical influences in post-war Japan.

Albeit these manifold influences, Japan did not adopt everything that came from the United States. Instead, most Japanese continued to maintain what Kumaga Fumie has called their "multireligious cultural orientation" (8), meaning that they defined themselves as both Buddhists and Shintoists. Furthermore, as Kumaga has shown in *Unmasking Japan Today*, from the very beginning, "many practices unworthy of imitation were discarded" and the traditional Japanese family structures remained untouched (3).

Especially telling is the fact that American cars are not very popular in Japan since they do not meet Japanese *expectations* of American cars when compared to some Japanese cars, which obviously feel more American than the genuine ones (Yoshimoto 195). This shows that Japanese consumers are not ineluctably interested in American commodities per se, but in consumer products that have an *American* appeal to them, items which fit *their* imagination of what is American.

By interweaving Japanese culture with Western influences, Japan reacted to globalization in a positive and creative manner. It switched from their former politics of seclusion to an open and flexible mode of interaction that incorporates localized American products without losing its Japanese roots. As Kumaga explains, "Japan succeeded in keeping its ethos and cultural-spiritual traditions intact while assimilating Western knowledge and technology. Thus, Japanese society today has retained its hybrid culture of tradition and modernity" (3). Considering the dominant architectural style in Japanese cities, Bognar similarly argues that

despite its various and significant foreign influences – or perhaps, paradoxically, because of them – the Japanese city remains in(de)finite and continues to constitute both a traditional Oriental and at the same time also a radically new postmodern and, potentially at least, more future-oriented mode of urbanism than its American counterpart. (74)

This perception of contemporary Japan as being simultaneously traditional and modern underlines Japan's ambiguous position as an Asian culture that is open to Western influences without giving up its own traditions. Yet the Japanese were not the only ones who started to import foreign products and adapt them to their needs and taste.

The West increasingly started to regard Japan as a source for "exotic" goods and imported Japanese products. Furthermore, according to Susan

Napier, Japan became a "living and breathing *tabula rasa* onto which Europeans and Americans projected a variety of desires, fears, dreams, and schemes" (*From Impressionism* 9). From the very beginning of Japanese-American relations, the United States had a predominantly decorative image of Japan (Johnson 94ff; Nakashima 246ff; Lee 134). The equation of Japan with ornamental, female attributes helped to reinforce a gendered binarism in which the Orient was considered female and passive, whereas the West was seen as active and masculine (Said, *Orientalism* 206f.) Japanese craftsmanship, which was introduced to the United States by the Japanese at the Philadelphia World Exhibition in 1876, was generally admired by many Americans. Yet while they concluded that a nation which produced such beautiful artistic work could not be entirely uncivilized, Japan remained a strange and mythical place to them. Nevertheless, their first encounter with Japanese art sparked the interest of many American visitors to the fair who subsequently became collectors of Japanese art (Lancaster 48).[16] Shortly after the exposition, interior decorations of privileged families started to include Japanese elements. The resulting Oriental-style rooms reflected the idea that American consumers had about Japan as "a realized fairyland" (Shibusawa 22). Clay Lancester has elaborated in *The Japanese Influence in America* that an increasing number of American artists, architects, and decorators started to include Japanese elements in their work.

As for many passionate collectors of Japanese art, the fascination for Japanese architectural styles started for the American architect Frank Lloyd Wright with the World Columbian Exposition in Chicago, where he encountered Japanese architecture for the first time. He became a collector of Japanese art and visited Japan in 1905, where he gained considerable knowledge about the nation (Bognar 53; Napier, *From Impressionism* 74). Although the influence that Japanese aesthetics had on his work is largely downplayed, since Wright himself insisted that he had never been influenced by it, his admiration for the Japanese architecture can be seen clearly in his buildings. As Botond Bognar argues in his essay "Surface Above All? American Influence on Japanese Urban Space,"

---

16 In her essay "Defining 'Japanese Art' in America" Nakashima Tomoko discusses the varying definition of Japanese art by Americans. According to her, in the nineteenth century, Japanese art was mainly seen as an exotic curiosity and not considered to be "art" in the Western sense.

The [...] Japanese influence in Wright's design is clearly manifested in the horizontal disposition, the multiple large overhanging roofs, the ornamental patterns, the free-flowing spaces, and the intimate relationship with nature characteristic of his so-called Prairie Houses from around the turn of the century. (53)

More Japanese influences are suggested by the fact that Wright never consented to the concept of a room as a box, praised by Bauhaus architects, but experimented with rooms that floated into each other by the use of sliding doors, which are typical for Japanese houses (Napier, *From Impressionism* 74). Wright's references to Japan seem mostly his own idiosyncratic interpretations as he "nurtured a romantic, even exotic, image of this Far Eastern country" (Bognar 54), thus he created his own hybrid architectural style.[17]

The far-reaching popularity of artifacts with a Japanese touch in America not only among architects but also among middle- and upper-class Americans "permitted Tiffany's to make profits from Japanese imports and that prompted the Japanese government itself to open an agency in New York to distribute its native products" (N. Harris 34). Japanese merchants responded to the demand for Japanese commodities by creating special items for the American market, self-orientalizing their image in the West by exporting parasols and pottery to the United States.[18] Yet, not only goods were fabricated to resemble the American idea of Japan in order to make economic profits. The former Japanese Geisha and actress Kawakami Sada, known in the United States as Sadayakko, similarly became a star in the West through the act of self-exotization. She arrived in San Francisco in 1899, just at the time when Americans were keen on seeing a "real" Geisha after having been exposed to Pierre Loti's 1888 *Madame Chrysantheme* and John Luther Long's *Madame Butterfly* in 1897 (Downer, *Madame Sadayakko* 95f.). Although she was "as far as it was possible to be from the fictitious Madame Butterfly and utterly different from Westerners' concep-

---

17 Frank Lloyd Wright was not only inspired by Japanese styles, but his architecture is further influenced by Mayan architecture as evident in his Imperial Hotel, which was opened in Tokyo in 1923 (Bognar 54).

18 Even commodities not explicitly produced for Western consumers were often already influenced by the West. Especially paintings by Japanese artists were oftentimes affected by European painting techniques or subjects popular in Meiji Japan (Guth 115).

tions of Japanese women as docile, submissive, and oppressed" (Downer, *Madame Sadayakko* 3), on stage and to the Western imagination, she was "the very essence of the mysterious East" (Downer, *Madame Sadayakko* 96). Even Sadayakko, the name that made her famous, was invented in the United States by her manager, who insisted that her given name Sada was not interesting enough, and her name as a Geisha in Japan, Yakko, was too unspectacular. Thus, a new label was created by combining the two names – and it proved satisfying enough for the American audience, which embraced the exotic woman just as it had embraced other Japanese products.

Christopher Benfey discusses in *The Great Wave: Gilded Age Misfits, Japanese Eccentrics and the Opening of Old Japan* the Japanese influence on nineteenth century American intellectuals and particularly their fascination with Japanese art, which did not, or did not only result from its artistic appeal. He argues that intellectuals from New England were especially fond of importing Japanese cultural commodities as they sought spiritual fulfillment in art objects from the supposedly pre-modern, exotic island nation. When white upper- and middle-class Americans "developed a nostalgic yearning for an era without the rule of machines and clashes between different classes and races" (C. Chen 216), they were especially fascinated by Oriental art which was so distinctively different from its Western counterpart (C. Chen 228). For them, Japanese art represented the "old" world, which was not yet industrialized and corrupted. The collecting of "Oriental" artifacts turned the Orient into a collectible and consumable object for the West (Kim 384). By possessing these exotic items, the U.S. consumer gained power over the Orient and "publicly represented and celebrated America's expansionist and imperialist power" (Yoshihara, *Embracing* 21). Once brought back by travelers or bought by collectors, the commodity was "interpreted from the collector's rather than the creator's frame of reference" (Guth 167). As Christine M.E. Guth argues in *Longfellow's Tattoos*, the longing for Japanese artifacts and pieces of art unquestionably "implied a degree of respect for the culture that had produced it" (176). Yet, at the same time, within the private realm of the buyer or collector, these artifacts became "fragments of another world employed primarily to tell stories about their owners" (Guth 176) and hinted in particular to their cosmopolitanism. Thus, collecting in this context has to be understood as part of the imperialistic ideology of that time.

The Orient in general and Japan in particular became an interesting motif in American art and advertisings in the nineteenth and early twentieth century as well. European artists such as Claude Monet and Vincent van Gogh were especially fascinated by Japanese aesthetics and woodblock prints, and started to imitate and replicate Japanese themes and styles in their work. This movement called *Japonisme* had an impact on European artists including Renoir, and Henri Rivière, as well as on the American artists Arthur Wesley Dow, John La Farge, and Mary Cassatt who incorporated Japanese aesthetics and motives into their paintings (Benfey 101).[19]

In advertisements, particularly for soap, Japanese women wearing a traditional kimono were frequently displayed as representatives of pureness and cleanliness (Yoshihara, *Embracing* 29). These images were believed to add a "sensual" element to the product, thereby distinguishing it from other Western products of that time (Kim 385). The kimono-clad Japanese was exploited in order to sell mundane American household products as exotic and interesting to American women, the main target group of the advertisements. Mari Yoshihara argues in her study *Embracing the East: White Women and American Orientalism* that American women took part in American Orientalist discourses by consuming "exotic" products, which thereby "functioned as signifiers of aesthetics and therefore class status for women who possessed and consumed them, marking them as sophisticated, refined women" (Yoshihara, *Embracing* 30). The largely ignored aspect of Western women's active participation in Orientalism is further discussed by the feminist critic Rina Lewis, who argues in *Gendering Orientalism* that Said's male-centered discourse on Orientalism needs to be widened by including the female gaze on "Orientalist images *of* women rather than representations *by* women" (3).[20] The possession of Oriental art enabled Western women, who were still considered inferior to men in the realm of politics and economy, to exercise power over the Orient as they could decide which pieces of art were worth collecting and displaying. By decorating their

---

19 For a sampling of materials that reflect the ideas of *Japonisme* see Lional Lambourne's *Japonisme: Cultural Crossings Between Japan and the West* as well as Susan Napier's chapter "Japonisme from Monet to Van Gogh" in *From Impressionism to Anime: Japan as fantasy and Fan Cult in the Mind of the West.*
20 See also Meyda Yegenoglu's *Colonial Fantasies: Towards a Feminist Reading of Orientalism.*

homes with these objects, middle- and upper-class American women could create their own version of "the Orient" or "Japan" at home, thereby defining what was considered Japanese in their household and culture.

However, the increasing number of commodities, most of which were tea, silk, and art, imported from Japan in the nineteenth century triggered anxieties about Japan as a commercial rival. Especially when between 1894 and 1899 Japanese exports to the United States amounted up to $25 million (Iriye, "Japan as Competitor" 75), Americans became increasingly anxious about Japan as an economic competitor. This fear was transferred onto Japanese immigrants[21] who started to pour into the United States in greater numbers from the 1870s on and led to early anti-Japanese feelings among the American population (Iriye, "Japan as Competitor" 77). The image of Japanese immigrants being competitors from "an alien civilization" and constituting a "threat to American society" (Iriye, "Japan as Competitor" 77) was so dominant that it led to the Gentleman's Agreement in 1907, which restricted the number of Japanese immigrants to the U.S. Over the next years, the United States continued to issue laws which further limited Japanese immigration (Powell 160-162). Although not much discussed in the academic discourses thus far, transnational Japanese-American literature that countered Orientalist discourses did exist in the early twentieth century as well. Noguchi Yone's autobiographical fiction *The American Diary of a Japanese Girl* was published in 1902 and describes the Japanese immigrant experience. Noguchi, himself a Japanese immigrant to the United States, describes in a fictitious first-person narrative the experiences of a woman who lives in nineteenth century America as a Japanese immigrant. The novel "counters the romanticized images of Japan" (Franey vii) that were created mostly by American writers. Taking the point of view of a Japanese immigrant woman who frequently comments on American culture, Noguchi introduced a Japanese perspective on the culture of the United States. His cross-cultural, sometime cross-linguistic novel deals with topics of dislocation and border-crossing and already places the experience of Japanese immigrants within the history and literature of the United States.

---

21 In 1908, approximately 103,000 Japanese immigrants lived in the United States (Iriye, "Japan as Competitor" 78).

Likewise, American poets in the 1920s were dazzled by Japanese aesthetics (Benfey xvii): writers such as Carl Sandburg, Ezra Pound, and Amy Lowell were mainly influenced by the Japanese literary style of haiku, sometimes also referred to as *hokku*, a Japanese type of poetry with a distinct stylistic pattern. Traditionally a haiku consists of three lines of five, seven, and five syllables and touches aspects of the season or nature. This poetical style was embraced by imagist writers who "incorporated Japanese poetic devices into the English language" (Schodt 36) and also combined this distinctively Japanese style with American themes and motifs.[22] In the 1950s the literary trend of using the haiku-style in American poetry continued with the writers of the Beat Generation, among them Jack Kerouac and Allen Ginsberg, who were greatly affected and influenced by Zen Buddhism (see Kerouac and Theado) Even today, haiku is popular among U.S. poets, who creatively adapt this style for their work, as the anthology *Haiku Moment: An Anthology of Contemporary North American Haiku*, edited by Bruce Ross, reveals.

Many different Japanese cultural influences have traveled to the United States and have become part of American everyday life. In *Eastern Standard Time: A Guide to Asian Influences on American Culture from Astro Boy to Zen Buddhism*, the editors give an overview of the vast number of different Japanese influences such as Bonsai trees, the art of flower arrangement (*ikebana*), the literature of Haruka Murakami and Kenzaburō Ōe, anime, manga, the Walkman, video games, Japanese music (J-Pop, *taiko* drumming), and sports such as judo, karate, and sumo. The collection indicates the many different realms of American culture that are affected by Japanese commodities. As is the case with American goods in Japan, in the United States most of these products are localized, or rather adapted, in order to meet the tastes of the American consumers. Although some products seem to be "culturally odorless" (Iwabuchi, *Recentering* 24) and therefore are not necessarily conceived as being Japanese (like the Walkman or the video recorder for example), many – such as anime or manga – are appealing to American consumers because of their distinct Japaneseness.

---

22  For further studies of the impact of haiku on American imagist writers see Glenn Hughes' *Imaginism and the Imaginists: A Study in Modern Poetry*; Otake Masaru's "The Haiku Touch in Wallance Stevens and Some Imaginists," as well as Iwahara Yasuo's "Imagist Shijin to Hailu No Kankei."

Thus, Japanese-American exchanges of goods, cultural practices, and images are not a new phenomenon. However, early encounters were dominated by especially inflexible Orientalist and Occidentalist ideas about "the Other," considered to be completely different. Unequal power relations led to one-sided national stereotypes which were often re-enforced by the exchanges. Nevertheless, early negotiations of national differences took place as well and – over time and under changing circumstances that could be only very briefly sketched in this chapter – Japan and the United States not only adapted goods and cultural practices from the respective other culture into their own, but also considered some differences interesting and alluring instead of threatening and repulsive. The balanced mixture of exotic and familiar sights, tastes, concepts, and images also led to the success of Disney theme parks in Tokyo, which are considered to be an integral part of Japanese popular culture today.

# *Yōkoso* Mickey Mouse! Disney in Japan

> Disneyland is dedicated to the ideals, the dreams, and the hard facts that have created America ... with the hope that it will be a source of joy and inspiration to all the world.
> - DISNEYLAND DEDICATION PLAQUE -

Every year, thousands of young Japanese people wrapped in blankets queue up for hours to see a special New Year's show in Tokyo Disneyland, which includes Disney characters clad in traditional Japanese kimonos. Although the New Year's celebration is the most popular event, it is not the only occasion on which Disney characters are adapted to Japanese culture and the park is decorated with Japanese style banners and lanterns. Hence, it is of little surprise that many Japanese children believe that Mickey Mouse and his friends are indeed Japanese. Due to the fact that an enormous amount of Disney merchandising is produced for the Japanese market, and due to the visibility of Disney characters in everyday life in Japan, many Japanese consumers regard Disney as genuine part of their culture. Children, who often grow up with Mickey and Minnie on their *bento* boxes (lunchboxes) and hear Mickey speaking Japanese on TV, do not necessarily understand or recognize that the Disney characters come from another cultural background. Additionally, the two extremely popular Disney theme parks Tokyo Disneyland and Tokyo DisneySea leave a lasting impression on the thousands of visitors, including children, who visit the parks more than once a year. The parks provide a real space as a playground for the imagination and although this space is geographically located in Japan it allows visitors to transcend reality and nationality into a world of fantasy and magic.

The Walt Disney Company is one of America's best-known corporations and it exports its products across the whole world. The major difference between Disney and other entertainment companies like Warner Bros. Entertainment, Universal, or Time Warner is the extent of the influence the Walt Disney Company exerts on popular culture. What started as an American film company, today, has turned into an intermedial, global, transnational, billion dollar entertainment phenomenon. By allowing the audience to re-experience moments from Disney's animated films in theme parks and by supplementing their studio-based activities with countless merchandising products, Disney started to converge different entertainment media and laid the foundation for a media empire. In his essay "Disneyland," Christopher Anderson explains how the 1954 television series *Disneyland* advertised the theme park prior to its opening along with an entertainment program. Walt Disney himself appeared on the show and presented his new park as a novel suburban amusement experience for families. He emphasized the difference between the new park and the dirty, run down parks of the past and thus clearly distinguished his theme park from already existing parks (21). According to Anderson, "television defined Disneyland as a national amusement park, not a park of local or regional interests like previous amusement parks, but a destination for a nation of television viewers" (30). This promise made Americans in the 1950s travel across the country in order to experience a new kind of entertainment.

The same television series was later utilized in Japan to introduce the Disney brand to Japanese consumers. In 1958, it was broadcasted with great success and introduced the American Disney theme park as "one of the most powerful symbols of the affluent society for which the Japanese were earnestly striving" (Yoshimoto 189). The show fostered the wish in many Japanese consumers to open a Disney theme park in Japan and thus, the opening of Tokyo Disneyland in 1983 gave the Japanese a sense of completing the task of keeping up with the West. Surveying the public reaction to the series and to the opening of the park a quarter of a century later, it has to be doubted that Tokyo Disneyland can be seen exclusively or even predominantly as a sign of Western cultural imperialism. Instead it has to be understood as a transnational re-interpretation and adaptation of the American Disney parks in Japan.

In the following chapter the phenomenon of Disneyland in Japan will be analyzed and it will be argued that Disney cannot be reduced to a dominating American force. Mainly keeping with Aviad Raz's argumentation in *Riding the Black Ship: Japan and Tokyo Disneyland,* it will additionally be argued that the perception of Tokyo Disneyland as an emblem of American cultural imperialism does not work since it is difficult, if not impossible, to force popular cultural practices and products on another nation without an asymmetrical power relation. The idea of cultural imperialism underestimates the power of consumers who only spend money on products which appeal to them. In addition, it will be argued that in Japan the park is no longer considered to be 'American,' but is perceived as a Japanese version of Disneyland which is indeed actively appropriated – it is transformed, consumed, and thereby in part a Japanese creation. The chapter will elucidate that the modifications of different rides as well as the relocation of some attractions endow the Japanese park with unique and new meaning, which was generated by the Japanese owners to meet the tastes and interests of a Japanese audience. It will be concluded that Disneyland in Japan serves primarily as a transnational space where Japanese consumers can visit their cleansed and re-adjusted version of America.

The first part of the chapter will give a short introduction into American theme park history in general and then focus on the history of Disney parks in order to situate the Disney park phenomenon in a cultural historical context. The subchapter "The Disneyfication of America and the World?" focuses on the influence of the Walt Disney Company on different cultures. It will be argued that Disney indeed has a major impact on different cultures, but that this influence has to be weighed against deliberate consumer choices and respective national appropriations. The analyses will show how the Japanese parks fit local consumer needs by keeping the parks "exotic" and at the same time making them familiar for a Japanese audience. Tokyo DisneySea, as the second Disney park erected next to Tokyo Disneyland, also contributes to the uniqueness of the Japanese Disney experience. Yet, at the same time it gives a more global touch to Tokyo Disney Resort, no longer only referencing the United States but European countries as well.

## AMERICAN FANTASYSCAPES

According to Dale Samuelson's study *The American Amusement Park,* the "quest for amusement is undoubtedly as old as humankind itself, and almost every form of entertainment that has been tried appears in some form, with varying success, in the amusement park" (9). Long before Disneyland, Europeans and Americans enjoyed their leisure time at parks and World's Fairs. The history of amusement and theme parks in the United States is extensive and looks back on some 3,000 amusement parks, some of which have never been catalogued (Samuelson 6). Early American amusement parks did not necessarily include rides, but were resorts and recreational spaces, where people could spend their free time in a garden-like atmosphere in order to escape the workspace of the city. Later, food and drink vendors were added, followed by attractions like, for instance, shooting galleries and merry-go-rounds. Only in the early 1900s did former bathing resorts in New Jersey and New York start to develop into what we know today as amusement parks (Samuelson 16f). Coney Island, located in the state of New York is one of the most prominent examples of an American amusement park and has become synonymous with early amusement parks. Yet, it has never been one single amusement park but rather a site with a collection of different parks, two of which are the Luna Park and Steeplechase Park. Although a variety of parks opened their gates to visitors over the decades, some had to close down due to poor attendance rates (Samuelson 23f). At the turn of the twentieth century, amusement parks mushroomed in the United States due to three different influences which Samuelson describes as crucial to the growth of the parks: the "natural draw of the seashore, electric railway companies' desire for weekend revenue and ability and willingness to quickly replicate proven success" (Samuelson 37).

In the 1950s, the Walt Disney Company, however, did not replicate previous amusement parks. Instead, Walt Disney envisioned a new, safer and cleaner park which would promote American values he believed in and would be themed around Disney animated movies (Wasko 155). To boost the attendance figures and to influence customers ideologically, Walt Disney aspired the visitors of the park to step literally into the magic world of Disney movies and to become part of the narrative by experiencing the adventures of Disney characters first hand. With his park, Disney offered consumers a new form of entertainment, a new fantasyscape, in a rapidly changing consumer society, where the two-dimensional world of the cinema ceased to be exciting and profitable enough (Yoshimoto 188). This new concept turned out to work very well with the audience. In *Understanding*

*Disney*, Janet Wasko analyzes how the company has been operating and focusing on the public reception of Disney products ever since its inception. Wasko examines how the parks have contributed to the Disney phenomenon and to the shaping of an American culture. She points out that in the United States, visiting one of the American Disney parks has become part of a "family pilgrimage" with the parks themselves becoming "sacred centers" which are visited almost ritually (Wasko 163). According to her, a trip to one of the Disney parks means more than a visit to an entertainment facility, thereby turning this experience into a highly emotional and personal act. Thus, by spending time at the location and consuming Disney products, Disney becomes part of American family rituals, further embedding Disney in the very core of American family values and American culture.

Since Disney advertised his theme park as a three-dimensional extension of its movies, it was crucial to create the illusion that the visitors inside the park had stepped into a world of magic. Thus, the everyday world of work and sorrows had to be carefully shut out by constructing fences and surrounding the area with exuberant vegetation (Imagineers, *Walt Disney* 11; and Anderson 27). In order to realize his dream world of fantasy and magic, Walt Disney invented the process of "imagineering" (Imagineers, *Walt Disney* 11) to be actualized by "imagineers," who work at the subsidiary level of the company. At the same time, although the park was planned as a means of escaping from reality, Disney wanted to "pay tribute to the positive aspects of America's past, and to set out a utopian vision for the future" (Hendry 74). Hence, from the very beginning of the history of Disney parks, national ideologies indeed played an important role, as ideal, imagined versions of the United States and later of other nations were created.

After the successful grand opening of Disneyland Anaheim in California, Walt Disney sought to turn from fairy tales and an idealized version of America to the future and dreamed of an "experimental prototype community of tomorrow" (Epcot), as he called it, to incorporate "the best ideas of industry, government and academia worldwide" (Walt Disney qtd. in Wilson 118). Epcot, originally named Epcot Center, opened in 1982 and consists of two differently themed areas: Future World and World Showcase. It is a self-contained park within Walt Disney World Florida. Company literature describes Epcot as "a community of ideas and nations and a testing ground where free enterprise can explore and demonstrate and showcase new ideas that relate to man's hopes and dreams" (qtd. in Wasko 60).

While Future World accomplished this goal by focusing on ideas of technology and the future, World Showcase "presents the people, places and cultures that make our world special" (Imagineers, *Walt Disney* 75). This part was added to Epcot Center in order to pay tribute to the different cultures of the world - a rather *American* ideal of the future and an *American* perception of the world. World Showcase incorporates different pavilions that represent different nations of the world and are arranged at the shore of a lake. This area is supposed to create a place where people from different parts of the world can interact with each other while visiting the park. This concept closely resembles the idea of early World's Fairs, which served as places where people could encounter different nations and cultures by attending shows or eating foreign dishes. The Disney theme parks owe their conceptual idea and the organized and structured layout as well to prior World's Fairs (Prager and Richardson 205; Nelson 106).[1] The decisive dissimilarity between early World's Fairs and Disney's World Showcase lies in the fact that the fairs pretended to present an authentic world view, yet did not celebrate different cultures. They presented them instead as exotic spectacles of uncivilized cultures by exposing them to the Western gaze of the visitors.

At the Worlds' Columbian Exposition, held in Chicago in 1893, the "concept of racial hierarchy was most symbolically epitomized by the layout of the fair ground: the White City" (Yoshihara, *Embracing* 18). In this layout, a binary opposition was manifested: the main part, the White City, represented only North America and Europe as progressive nations, while all other nations considered "primitive" were put in the entertainment district of the fair, the so-called Midway Plaisance (Yoshihara, *Embracing* 19).[2] There, American visitors could eat exotic Egyptian food in Cairo

---

1  The connection between Disney theme parks and early World's Fairs is referred to with the "Crystal Palace Restaurant" in two of the Disney parks, namely World Disney World, and Tokyo Disneyland. The "Crystal Place Restaurant" in the Disney parks is a Victorian style dining place, which received its name from the first World Exposition which took place in London in 1851 and became famous as "Crystal Palace."

2  Some European attractions like a Germany village were likewise situated at the Midway Plaisance, but Germany as a nation was represented at the State and Foreign Building section of the White City.

Street or listen to exotic music in the Javanese settlement. By geographically distinguishing the "high" cultures from the "primitive" cultures at the fair, a hierarchical order was established, displaying the supremacy of some nations over others.[3] While the fair's overarching theme of unity was reflected in the architectural style and color of the White City, the Midway Plaisance represented diversity and exoticism. As Yoshihara notes in her study *Embracing the East: White Women and American Orientalism*, the "spectacle of the exotic Orient was most vividly played out in the world's fairs of the late nineteenth and early twentieth centuries" (18). In Chicago, people and cultures of non-white, European or other non-American backgrounds were represented as exotic spectacles and displays, which were significantly located at the periphery of the fair,[4] thereby affirming national identities.

Japan had already taken part in the Philadelphia Centennial Exhibition in 1876, where many Americans encountered the Japanese culture for the first time, which they frequently praised and adored for its beauty and high quality (N. Harris 24f). At the time of the Philadelphia Centennial Exhibition, Japan had already undergone some reforms in the Meiji Period and was gaining economic and military power on an international scale. This development and its representation at the previous fair granted Japan a different, more ambivalent position at the World's Columbian Exposition. Its main attraction neither appeared at the Midway Plaisance alongside China, nor in the White City. Instead Japan was located on the so-called Wooden Island and featured one of the most notable exhibits of the fair: the Phoenix Hall also called the Ho-ö-den (Yoshihara, *Embracing* 19)[5]. This building was "modeled after the mid-eleventh century palace built near Kyoto, consisting of three pavilions, each representing the decorative and architectural

---

3 Some nations did not represent themselves but were displayed by their colonizers, who thereby defined these nations for Western visitors of the fair.

4 Judith Snodgrass elaborates in *Presenting Japanese Buddhism to the West* on the power relations between Japan and the USA at the Chicago World's.

5 At the Philadelphia Centennial Exhibition, Japan appeared next to China, reflecting the geographical location of Japan (N. Harris 28). At the World's Columbian Exposition, Japan was present at multiple sites such as the Palace of Manufactures and Liberal Arts, in the Fine Arts Palace, in Agriculture, Horticulture, Forestry, Mines, and Fisheries, and the Midway Plaisance (N. Harris 39).

features of three prominent epochs in Japanese art" (Yoshihara, *Embracing* 20).[6] As Yoshihara writes, the Japanese building "provided visual relief from the overpowering classicism of the White City" (*Embracing* 19) which was based on classical Roman and Greek architecture. Although this was not intended by the Japanese government, which financed the Japanese presence at the fair and strove to make their representation as genuine as possible by constructing its own pavilion, tea house, and garden, "Ho-ö-den reasserted the Orientalist vision of the Japanese as the peculiar Other" (Yoshihara, *Embracing* 20). American visitors of the fair were not only fascinated by the building itself but also by the construction process and the Japanese men who worked at the building. The Japanese carpenters became "objects of the Western gaze, as much as the people displayed in the Midway Plaisance" (Yoshihara, *Embracing* 20) and involuntarily became a living attraction of the fair.[7] It has to be noticed that although Japan was geographically not positioned at the Midway Plaisance among the other "exotic," and by implication less developed cultures, the perception of Japan by American visitors "within the context of the fair's imperial worldview and its representation of nonwhite cultures as spectacles" (Yoshihara, *Embracing* 20) still remained Orientalist.

Early World's Fairs not only showcased the diversity of cultures but commonly celebrated the development of new technologies as well. Hence, Epcot with its focus on technological progress and the celebration of different cultures can be viewed as a kind of permanent World's Fair in Florida.[8] Thus, the fact that only eleven nations are represented, as well as the loca-

---

6 Today the site of the Japanese Pavilion of the Columbian World's Fair is partly turned into a Japanese garden.

7 The Japanese "'almond-eyed' carpenters" (N. Harris 29) similarly fascinated American visitors with their exotic outward appearance at the Philadelphia Centennial Exposition.

8 Walt Disney loved the ideas of different nations and technology and contributed four attractions to the 1964/65 World's Fair in New York. The four attractions he built were: "It's a Small World" at the Pepsi-Cola pavilion, "The Magic Skyway," presented by the Ford Motor Company, "Great Moments with Mr. Lincoln" at the Illinois pavilion, and General Electric sponsored the "Carousel of Progress." The attractions were later partly placed into Disneyland and Epcot (Sklar, *Walt Disney's Disneyland*. 41f).

tion and delineation of these nations in this Disney park are significant as these choices indeed reflect a certain ideology. In Walt Disney World, eleven pavilions, representing eleven different nations, are visible from the entrance to World Showcase and from the front; they all appear to be of the same size. Although some pavilions are larger and contain more attractions than others, to the "imagineers" it was important that no pavilion – not even the American one – looked higher or bigger than another one (Imagineers, *Walt Disney* 68). This shows that in Epcot, unlike at the Chicago World's Fair, no nation is meant to be represented as being "bigger" and therefore, by implication, more important or powerful than the other ones. Yet, due to the central position of the American pavilion "the geography of World Showcase, across the lake, focuses on the American pavilion" (Wilson 122). This can be explained neutrally as expression of the role of the United States as the host of World Showcase, while a more critical reading exposes an underlying Americentric worldview, visualized by the central position of the United States in an arrangement that positions all other nations at the margin. The Epcot center-periphery relationship of the United States' pavilion to the one's of other nations supports Richard Francaviglia's observation that theme parks "embody visions of places – [...] they are [...] three dimensional topographic representations of places, real or imagined, and are thus maps" (157). He further draws attention to the authority of their creators, who have the power over classificatory schemes according to which they define nations and cultures, organizing them on maps/parks matching their ideological understanding.[9]

Planning the World Showcase, Disney's creators of Epcot were aware of the fact that it would be impossible for them to reflect the many different shades of a particular nation (Birnbaum 143). The company decided to react to this insight by simplifying the representation of the nations and hence, the pavilions can be visually easily connected to the nation they epitomize. On the one hand, this helped to stress the diversity of architectural styles around the world, which was meant as reaction to the lament about the homogenization of architecture that globalization supposedly forces upon the world (Imagineers, *Walt Disney* 68 and 77). One the other

---

9  Most theme parks distribute maps at the entry in order to help visitors to orient themselves within the park, thereby determining in which direction visitors should move in order to follow the specific narrative structure of the park.

hand, due to the limited space at World Showcase as well as obvious financial restrictions on what is economically sensible to display in an amusement park, only random bits and pieces of a culture are represented in the resort and the Walt Disney Company decides which aspects of a culture are to be included and which to be left out. In "Simulated Tourism at Busch Gardens," U.S. cultural critic Lawrence Mintz writes that in Epcot "countries of the world are places which are interesting *for us* [the Western audience] to see, charming diversions for our shopping and dining pleasure" (56). He makes it clear that the nations represented at Epcot become Americentric and profit-oriented versions of the "real," mainly targeted at American customers and not at all resembling the everyday culture of the represented nations. Disney turns nations into idealized playgrounds for mainly American audiences. This transformation from real life culture to a simulated state is performed mainly by exotization and nostalgic replacement of the present by the past. Another critic of Epcot, Alexander Wilson, describes World Showcase as a place where "exoticized cultures of the past and present offer relief from what promise to be the urban [or suburban] horror of the future [offered in Future World]" (122). For Wilson, the representation of different cultures in Epcot is a mere spectacle of an exotic "Other" as against the celebration of the glorious American past in the so-called "American Adventure," an attraction at the American Pavilion.

Typically the Japanese Pavilion, like other representative pavilions, only focuses on the past of the nation. A red *torii* gate,[10] a replica of a seventeenth century castle, a pagoda alongside a traditional department store, represent Japan in Epcot and enable visitors to purchase supposedly traditional Japanese souvenirs such as fans, kimonos, samurai swords, and dolls.[11] Recently, anime, Hello Kitty and Pokémon merchandising – strangely out of sync with the nostalgic display - have been added to cash in on the rapidly growing interest in Japanese popular culture products in the United States. In a similar vein, the entertainment program offered at the

---

10 A *toori* gate is a traditional Japanese gate which often can be found at many entries of shrines and temples.
11 According to *The Imagineering Field Guide to Epcot at Walt Disney World*, most of the buildings at the Japanese Pavilion are recreations of specific buildings in Japan as for example the *torii* gate at the Itsukushima Shrine or the pagoda of Horyuji Temple in Nara (The Imagineers, *The Imagineering* 104-105).

Japanese Pavilion is also dominated by Japanese food, which can be consumed at four different restaurants, and by traditional Japanese forms of entertainment: a walk through rock gardens, the display of *bonsai* trees from the Florida Bonsai Society, and a show with *taiko* drummers. Almost everything offered to the visitor at the Japanese Pavilion is a journey to a nostalgic Japanese past and bears little resemblance to the nation's contemporary state. By offering the audience an idealized, safe, and clean(sed) version of foreign cultures, Disney creates myths, which are preferable to reality because they fulfill the expectations of the audience and meet their ideas of how *they* imagine these places to be.

In *Travels in Hyperreality*, Umberto Eco argues – tongue in cheek – that simulations of reality often seem better than the corresponding real-world entities and he exemplifies his argument by describing his trip with a fake Mississippi steamboat on a reproduced Mississippi River in Disneyland. He observes that this river cruise was much safer, cleaner, and more predictable than a trip on the real Mississippi and he describes his disappointment with the real Mississippi, where the promised alligators were missing, while in Disneyland artificial alligators came up to his expectations. Eco concludes that in such moments, tourists "risk feeling homesick for Disneyland" (44). American visitors of Epcot will probably have similar experiences when they visit Japan and realize that not every part of the nation is full of serene rock gardens and romantic temples, but that Japan is a modern nation, with its share of traffic, pollution, and crime as well. In a similar vein, Jean Baudrillard has argued that "Disneyland is a perfect model of all entangled orders of simulacra" (12) as the theme park has to be understood as an imaginary world, a "miniaturized pleasure of real America" (12). Hence, Disney, in an effort to create nations in Epcot that seem better than the real (hyperreal), shapes the imagination of visitors to the park, thus reimagines different nations for a broad audience and often reasserts existing national stereotypes.

## THE DISNEYFICATION OF AMERICA AND THE WORLD?

Over the years, the Disney parks were sometimes praised for their contribution to the reform of the amusement park business but mostly they were criticized by various academic disciplines, ranging from architecture (Warren), urban planning (Bryman, Roost), and history (Ward) to media studies (Booker) and cultural studies (K. Jackson and West), for their superficiality, their selective reconstruction of history and the obsession with control inside the parks. The Walt Disney Company, along with Coca Cola and McDonalds, is one of the best-known trademarks of the United States and serves as a cultural icon of America. While to some consumers Disney is still synonymous with innocent and safe family entertainment; to others Disney constitutes a national threat, homogenizing entertainment by retelling classical fairy tales according to a specific Disney formula. In animated Disney movies, character traits such as strength and weakness, activity and passivity are positioned along traditional gender lines as well as Orientalist ideologies about "the Other," thereby promoting and spreading a white, heteronormative, protestant, middle-class understanding of the world all around the world.

Founded in 1923 as a small animation studio, the company today includes television and radio stations, an ice-hockey team and several theme parks as well as ocean cruise liners and holiday resorts, expanding its influence in the entertainment and leisure industry. The company developed from supplying movie entertainment to supporting an entire lifestyle, including the building of Celebration, a small gated community planned by Disney in Florida (Frantz and Collins).

Because of the immense global popularity and omnipresence of Coca Cola, McDonalds, and Disney many critics use these trademarks as examples in discussions on globalization, homogenization, and cultural imperialism (Ritzer, Bryman). Terms like coca-colonization, mcdonaldization, disneyization, or disneyfication[12] derive from the notion that American brands

---

12 According to Alan Bryman the term "disneyfication" is more generally associated with all cultural products of the Walt Disney Company: "to disneyfy means to translate or transform an object into something superficial and even simplistic" (5). Disneyization, however, describes the way the structures of Disney theme parks influence restaurants, shopping malls, and hotels. In this sense, the

spread their commodities worldwide and impose homogenized beverages, food, logistics, and entertainment on other nations thereby destroying unique indigenous cultures. Originally, the term disneyfication was used as an umbrella term for sanitization, homogenization, and Americanization of the literary sources of Disney movies (Budd 7). Brenda Ayres in "The Wonderful World of Disney: The World That Made the Man and the Man That Made the World" criticizes the process of disneyfication on the following grounds:

> Disney products colonize generations of children and parents to embrace [a white, middle-class, all-American, religious] ideal and to regard divergence as inferior or evil. The disneyfication of our children, then, is empire building, complete with an imperialistic colonizing force that effects either conformity to the ideal or denigration of the Other. (16-17)

The term disneyfication has been broadened and is now used to include processes of the homogenization of culture in general as well. To Ayres, Disney has a powerful impact on consumers first, because the main target group of Disney products is children, and second, because of the number of people who have already visited a theme park or are otherwise familiar with the Disney brand. She criticizes the way the brand sells entertainment by modifying traditional fairy tales and myths from Europe, Africa or Asia, how traditional gender roles are reinforced, and the way those who do not conform are simply made into villains (19).[13]

The discussion of Disney and Mickey Mouse as signs of cultural imperialism is not new. Disney cartoons went global in the 1930s and in the next decades they were followed by other Disney merchandising products,

---

term is more generally connected to the production, display, and consumption of products (1-14).

13 For the disneyfication of fairy tales and classical legends see Robin Allan's *Walt Disney and Europe*, Joseph M. Chan's "Disneyfying and Globalizing the Chinese Legend Mulan: A Study of Transculturation," Donald Crafton's "The Last Night at the Nursery: Walt Disney's Peter Pan," Jane Darcy's "The Disneyfication of the European Fairy Tale," Sheng-mei Ma's *The Deathly Embrace: Orientalism and Asian American Identity*, and Terri Martin Wright's "Walt Disney's Adaption of the Grimms' 'Snow White.'"

reaching international consumers by entering the realm of transnational capitalism (Smoodin, "Introduction" 10). The opening of Disney theme parks in Japan, France, and most recently, Hong Kong intensified the global discourse of Disney as a cultural imperialist force (Smoodin "Introduction," Yoshimoto "Images of Empire," and Van Maanen). The fact that the opening of Disney theme parks, which are dream worlds of leisure and entertainment, arouses debates on cultural imperialism and how the company globally shapes the political as well as social landscapes (see Giroux and Pollock), shows how much this company is associated with America and American popular culture.

In *Dazzled by Disney? The Global Disney Audience Project*, Janet Wasko and other scholars try to understand the Walt Disney Company as a transnational media conglomerate from the point of view of the audience. The project aimed at getting an insight into the reception of Disney products in fifty-three different nations by sending out questionnaires with a total of 1,252 respondents. The questionnaire and an interview focus on different Disney products as well as the values and ideologies distributed by Disney. Participants in the project were also asked whether they perceive Disney as uniquely American (Phillips 31-40). Although the majority of the participants are described as enthusiastic about Disney, their answers nevertheless reflect an overall ambiguity towards the company. About half of the participants thought of Disney as uniquely American, while 28% completely disagreed with this notion. The answers of those who perceived Disney as American can be divided into two categories: those who think of Disney as an American prototype and those who identify Disney as a cultural imperialist. Recipients who do not agree that Disney is uniquely American can be divided into three categories: those who think it is more generally Western than particularly American, those who think it is universal, and those who see Disney as "mine," thus personal (Phillips 50). The respondents who consider Disney a cultural imperialist mostly referred to the "whiteness" in Disney movies and accused Disney of homogenizing European, African, and Asian tales from an American perspective. At the same time, the company was criticized for imposing American economic power and American economic systems on the world. This point of criticism especially refers to the way in which Disney parks are run, the staff is trained, and all processes within the parks are orchestrated. As one French respondent stated:

Disney seems to be one of the best means of cultural standardization throughout the world. Disney takes advantage of the American hegemony over the economical market to spread the values of American society. The notion of national, regional culture doesn't exist. (Phillips 53)

Yet, in contrast to the arguments of cultural imperialism, some participants argued that Disney is not uniquely American since contemporary American culture is often equated with global culture in general. These respondents suggest interpreting Disney more as a representative of world culture than a force of American cultural imperialism. In "The Unification of the World Under the Sign of Mickey Mouse and Bruce Willis: The Supply and Demand Sides of American Popular Culture," Todd Gitlin analyzes the dominance of American popular culture as global culture in terms of both the supply and demand of cultural products made in America. According to his findings, the global spread of goods and services is not only dependent on the supply side which imposes its products and values onto another culture, but also on the consumers who ask for these cultural products and practices. He understands reception to be a key element for the successful export of cultural commodities, since only what is accepted and demanded can be sold. Gitlin suggests that it is easy to spread American culture because America has the advantage of the English language, which is the most common second language in the world, and because America is still associated with modernization. This, he argues, turns transnational corporations like Starbucks or Coca Cola into the "icons of a curious one-world" (23). Gitlin further argues that the defamation of American popular culture as a vehicle of cultural imperialism does not work, since no one is forced to spend money on American products. The demand side willingly consumes what is offered and sometimes even prefers products from the United States to those of its own culture. Thus, he concludes if there is any dominance, it is a soft dominance in "collaboration with the audiences" (25) as the consumer can actively decide what to consume and what to reject.

Hence, it would be too easy to explain Disney's global popularity as simply a U.S. imposition. When analyzing Disney theme parks and movies it is important to pay attention to the ways in which the parks and movies are received by each national audience. Only what is attractive to consumers can be sold to them. The Disney movies are indeed disneyfied according to a specific formula. The simple binary between good and evil, the happy ending of the stories, and values like friendship, compassion, and honesty promoted in the movies are, of course, the reason why not only U.S. but also many parents across the world prefer showing Disney movies to their children. While the original fairy tales are often too cruel and violent for younger audiences, brutal scenes in Disney movies are reduced to a minimum. This reduction of violence is one of the reasons why most consumers consider Disney entertainment suitable and "safe" for children. The same is true for the Disney theme parks which are extremely successful because they offer vacationists exactly what they expect: a day without sorrow, inconveniences, and violence in a clean park with friendly staff members. These are the reasons why Disney is appreciated in Japan and why the movies and the theme park are exceptionally popular among Japanese consumers of different ages. This poses, of course, the same problems as in the American Disney parks as again beautified and hyperreal visions of other nations are created.

## TOKYO DISNEY RESORT

Since its grand opening in April 1983, Tokyo Disneyland has been a magic fantasyscape to most of its Japanese visitors, a place where they seek escape from their everyday life for a few hours. With the extension of Tokyo Disneyland into Tokyo Disney Resort, which consists of a shopping mall, several hotels, and a second Disney theme park, the resort has become the most frequently visited themed space in Japan, attracting 25,366,000 visitors in 2010 (Oriental Land Company Group "Guest Statistics"). The majority of visitors come from Japan and most of them travel more than once a year to the park, some of them own an entrance passport valid for the whole year. In the last decades, Tokyo Disney Resort has replaced historical sites like Kyoto or Nikko for school trips and short holiday destinations,[14] hence threatening to supersede sites connected to Japan and its history, instigating discussions of a cultural homogenization and Americanization of the nation.

---

14 For more information about the popularity of Tokyo Disneyland see BBC News "Disney".

However, the idea of Disney as a cultural imperialist force in Japan has been questioned by Yoshimoto Mitsuhiro in "Images of Empire: Tokyo Disneyland and Japanese Cultural Imperialism." Yoshimoto defines a cultural imperialist power as a hegemonic power "trying to indoctrinate and brainwash the population of periphery regions" (190). However, as cultures are already in flux and exposed to constant exchange and transformation, they cannot stay within national boundaries by definition. Yoshimoto claims that in a relationship of equal power, "the infusion of a foreign culture does not constitute cultural imperialism, destroying native cultures" (190-191). Instead he argues that because of the need of cultures to interact, they do not automatically dominate or become dominated by others. According to his arguments cultural imperialism can only take place when the flow of cultural commodities is accompanied "by imperialism in a conventional sense, the relationship of economic domination between imperial powers and their colonies" (191). In the case of Tokyo Disney Resort, this would have meant that the American Walt Disney Company would have imposed their park on Japan by erecting an exact copy of the American parks there. But Tokyo Disney Resort is operated and owned by a Japanese company which is sensitive to local consumer demands and adapted the park accordingly. Although the American parks served as role models for the first Disney park outside the United States, Tokyo Disney Resort is neither an exact copy of Walt Disney World nor of Disneyland. In Japan, it is mainly the positive representation of America for Japanese visitors that makes the park appealing to the audience. The park thus creates a transnational space, where Japanese visitors have the possibility of experiencing a safe and comfortable version of America; as they mostly get what they *think* is America, without leaving their country. Hence, Tokyo Disneyland works as an exact counterpart to the Disney resorts in the United States with all their positive, but also negatively perceived and ideologically indoctrinating and othering mechanisms.

The image of the United States created in Tokyo Disney Resort is like in Epcot mainly a nostalgic vision of the past, full of friendly staff members and romantic places; and it is more convenient for Japanese visitors than the real America. Like Umberto Eco, who was disappointed when he traveled the real Mississippi, many Japanese tourists tend to be disillusioned when they visit the United States.

## Building a Japanese Dream

For twenty-two years, Tokyo Disneyland was the only existing Disney park outside America. The main difference between the Japanese version of the Disney park and Disney parks in the United States is that Tokyo Disney Resort is not owned by the Walt Disney Company but belongs to the Japanese Oriental Land Company.[15] The company was founded in 1960 with the aim of acquiring the rights to use a newly gained piece of land at the coast of the Chiba Prefecture, which poured sand into parts of Tokyo Bay in order to extend the coast. Yet they restricted the usage of this newly gained land to the leisure industry in order to contribute to the cultural life of the region in particular and Japan in general. Oriental Land Company declares on its official homepage their mission to "create happiness and contentment by offering wonderful dreams and moving experiences created with original, imaginative ideas" (Oriental Land Company Group Homepage). From 1966-1974, the company searched for a suitable idea of a park to build, before finally, in 1974, they came upon the Walt Disney Company. Disney itself was already well known and popular in Japan through the *Disneyland* television show, which was mentioned in the beginning of the chapter, and a contract between the two companies was signed in 1979. This contract determined that the American company would invest 2.5 million dollars into the Japanese project and in turn would get, over the next forty-five years, 10% of all income through the selling of park tickets, 5% of the income of the restaurants and merchandising in the park, and 10% of the incomes from sponsorship contracts (Grover 264). In the same year, it was announced to the Japanese public that a Disney park was going to be built in Tokyo. Most Japanese were pleased by the idea of having a Disney theme park in Japan and Notoji Masako reports in her book *Dizuniirando to iu Seichi* (*A Sacred Place Called Disneyland*) how she found a wooden plaque at a Shinto shrine on which someone had written down the wish that Tokyo Disneyland would really open. Indeed, in 1981 the construction of the park began and within two years, the first Japanese Disney park opened

---

15 Oriental Land Company is a cooperation of two Japanese companies: Keisei Dentetsu and Mitsui Fudōsan. Further, a Disney management team is located in Japan, working as advisors and securing the Disney doctrine in the Japanese park (Van Maanen 16).

its gates. Notoji writes that the opening of Tokyo Disneyland has to be seen as a major event in the cultural life of Japan, since the park significantly changed Japanese popular culture and the leisure market (225-227). She stresses that this change was not imposed by the American company but – starting from the "imagineering" Walt Disney had to offer – rather precipitated by the Japanese. Nevertheless, one has to keep in mind that building a Disney park in Japan was a rational capitalistic investment and a Japanese national project.

Since its opening, a lot of new attractions have been added, some older attractions were replaced and new themed areas have been included. In the following years, Tokyo Disneyland expanded to a full-fledged resort, including Tokyo Disneyland and Tokyo DisneySea, IKSPARI, the Disney Resort Line, and several hotels.[16]

## Occidentalizing America in Tokyo Disney Resort

For Japanese people, the United States evokes first and foremost ideas of freedom and democracy and is further imagined as a materialistic paradise which is associated with adorable technology (Schodt 157). These ideas about the United States were already outlined in Japanese travelogues of the Meiji Period (Hidejoshi Kato 193). Later, especially during the post-World War II era *"Amerika,"* the Japanese term for the United States, has become an idiom that refers to "an imaginary place where the benefits of modern society, such as equal opportunity, personal freedom and material comfort are made accessible and affordable to the masses" (Kurotani 34). All these ideals come together in Tokyo Disney Resort, where visitors are surrounded by friendly service staff and are free to abandon their daily hardships by entering a world of fantasy.

With his theme parks, Walt Disney did not only want to create a fantasy world, but he was also interested in creating a space where people could encounter unknown cultures. As explicitly stated on the official homepage of Tokyo Disney Resort, Disney wanted to give young people "the ability to boldly and openly engage the exotic and unknown." He did so by including an African jungle ride and the attraction "It's a Small World" in the

---

16 IKSPARI is an indoor shopping mall, which contains many American restaurants and stores such as GAP and Planet Hollywood.

U.S. theme parks. Yet, unlike there, the "exotic" in Tokyo Disneyland is derived from the original *American* image. In Japan, Tokyo Disneyland is advertised as something American brought to Japan (Raz, *Riding the Black Ship* 61). It was the aim of Oriental Land Company to let their visitors feel that they in fact were no longer in Japan, but acquiring a piece of North America. With Tokyo Disneyland, to quote Akibo Toshiharu, a spokesperson of the Japanese park, the Japanese company wished to represent "the best America has to offer" (qtd. in Brannen 216). When visitors enter Tokyo Disneyland they enter "America": they can eat American-style food, hear cheerful American music and all announcements are made in American English (and Japanese). Moreover, as American staff members employed in the park are asked to speak only English, these staff members become part of the simulated tourist experience, since visitors can take pictures with them and thus maintain the illusion that they really are in the United States. The fact that there is a European style castle at the center of the park and that the rides are themed around European fairy tales of Snow White or Peter Pan does not disturb the Japanese audience since they were already incorporated in and are part of American popular culture. Therefore, in Tokyo Disneyland the "American" experience includes European elements as well, thus clearly occidentalizing the idea of America.

To maintain the illusion, signs of Japaneseness are kept away from the park wherever possible, a strategy that sometimes lead to interesting results. For example, no vending machines can be found in Tokyo Disneyland, since vending machines are today part of the streetscape in Japan and felt to be totally Japanese.[17] While once seen as a symbol of Americanization and poor etiquette, as drinking directly from a bottle was considered rude, vending machines are now assimilated to such a high degree that they would destroy the American otherness expected in Tokyo Disneyland (Raz, *Riding*

---

17 This was true until quite recently. The devastating 2011 Tōhoku-earthquake that triggered a massive tsunami led to a major catastrophe that affected Japan greatly. Among other things, an increased awareness for safety precautions can be observed. This might also have led to the inclusion of a few vending machines in Tokyo Disneyland and Tokyo DisneySea, which could provide water and tea in cases of emergency. It has to be noted that most vending machines are rather cleverly "hidden" at the side of buildings or are themed as for example the vending machines in front of the "Queen of Heart Banquet Hall".

*the Black Ship* 64). This re-imagining and redefining of the United States in the park shows that in Tokyo Disneyland it is not important to reproduce the "real" United States, where vending machines are an undeniable part of the scene, but to create an environment that meets the image Japan has of America. In Tokyo Disneyland, *"Amerika"* is a country which is as clean, friendly, technologically advanced (Tomorrowland), and derived from a romantic past both in the Wild West (Westernland) and the South (Critter Country). It is also the home of Mickey Mouse and his friends (Toontown) – but all this comes with a Japanese difference.

Westernland, significantly located in the western part of the park, is the part of Tokyo Disneyland that most resembles its American counterpart and is themed – like in the U.S. – around the American West at the turn of the nineteenth century. Attractions like the "Westernland Shootin' Gallery" and the "Mark Twain River Boat" along with the "Trading Post" and "General Store" evoke images of this period of U.S. history. While Westernland resembles Frontierland in American Disney theme parks, it had to be renamed in Japan because nothing resembles the concept of the American frontier in Japanese history and thus, the whole foundational myth of a frontier does not exist. The term "frontier" is either unknown to the majority of the Japanese theme park visitor or it is equated with "the Wild West." Therefore, this section of the park was renamed in order to enable the Japanese visitor to immediately associate the Wild West with this themed area.

Yet the renaming of this area led to some significant geopolitical changes in the meaning of parts of the attraction in comparison to the original Disneyland Park in California, where the "Mark Twain River Boat" is located in Frontierland at the so-called Rivers of America, which surround "Tom Sawyer Island." In the American park, the location of Tom Sawyer in "Frontier"-land makes sense, since the stories of Tom Sawyer and Huckleberry Finn are part of the frontier narratives of American literature. The experience of Huck Finn shaping and being shaped by nature and "to light out for the territory ahead of the rest" (Twain 281) are understood as part of an American initiation process and the shaping of a unique American national identity. By keeping the geographical pattern of the attractions of the American Disney park but changing the name of the themed land from "Frontier"-land to "Western"-land, the meaning of the "Mark Twain River Boat" as frontier experience gets lost in translation and the attraction is put into a completely different context. As is usual in Japan, the narratives of Mark Twain partake geographically and thematically of the American Wild West.

In this context, the "Western River Railroad," an attraction unique to Tokyo Disneyland, is also of interest. Although the name suggests that this ride is part of Westernland, it is indeed located in Adventureland on the park map. This means of transportation, unlike the monorails in Walt Disney World or Disneyland does not run around the whole park. Instead, the railroad in Tokyo Disneyland originally connected Adventureland to Westernland and Critter Country. In her 1992 article, "'Bwana Mickey': Constructing Cultural Consumption at Tokyo Disneyland" Mary Yoko Brannen argued that this railroad visually and geographically cuts off Westernland from the rest of the park. According to Brannen one explanation for this separation could be that Tokyo Disneyland keeps the "exotic exotic" by "distancing the self from the Other" and hence "maintaining the *uchi-soto* dichotomy – the distinctions between inside and out" (219). Brannen argues that by separating Westernland from the rest of the park, by encircling it with railway tracks, Japan secures its own identity even within Tokyo Disneyland and points to its unique culture and national identity, distancing it from the West in general and the United States in particular. Brannen argues that Disneyland was recontextualized and consumed in Tokyo in two ways: "making the exotic familiar and keeping the exotic exotic" (219). While this imaginary mechanism underlies the making and experiencing of Tokyo Disneyland, due to changes in the park, Brannen's reading of the "Western River Railroad" is no longer possible. When Critter Country was added to Tokyo Disneyland in 1992, the "American" part of the theme park was extended. As the "Western River Railroad" starts in Adventureland and passes both Westernland and Critter Country, it rather *connects* ideas of adventure (Adventureland), the Old West (Westernland), and the Old South (Critter Country) than separating Japan from this American part of the park.

Yet, in the overall structure and idea of the park, which work to create the illusion that the visitors are in the United States, Japan indeed is time and again cut off from everyday Japanese experience and exoticized in quasi-American fashion. In "Chiba Traders," a shop that only exists in Tokyo Disneyland and which is located in Adventureland, traditional Japanese lacquer wares with Disney designs on them are offered alongside Japanese dolls, children's toys as well as traditional Japanese items with or without the Tokyo Disneyland logo on them. "Chiba Traders" serves first and foremost the purpose of selling souvenirs and gifts from the region where Tokyo Disneyland is located, the prefecture of Chiba. The shop caters to the needs of Japanese visitors who want to buy regional souvenirs. However, the location of the shop once more helps to set off Japan from America in the park. It is situated in Adventureland, where visitors can enjoy an exotic atmosphere and explore the South American Jungle, visit a Hawaiian Tiki Show, or experience the adventures of the "Pirates of the Caribbean." The shop is advertised on the Tokyo Disneyland homepage as located "in the middle of Adventureland, where people of every color and creed gather" (Tokyo Disneyland Homepage). Locating the Japanese shop "full of crafts and toys created by Japanese artisans" among "people of every color and creed" (Tokyo Disneyland Homepage) can be read as an act of self-exoticism, which makes Japan become part of the exotic experience, reinforcing the idea that Japanese visitors are no longer in Japan.[18]

The importance of a clear differentiation of Japanese and American culture in this fantasyscape becomes further evident with the Japanese owners' refusal to include attractions themed around Japanese fairy tales into the park, or replace one of the traditional themed lands of Disney theme parks with Samurai Land as the Walt Disney Company suggested (Brannen 216). This, similar to the changes from the U.S. design described above, demonstrates that the Japanese are not simply being dominated by Western ideologies but that they actively work to install and uphold an ambiguous distance between Japan and America that is based on exoticizing "the Other" and the self by actively deciding what is included in the park, how it is included and what is kept out. In Tokyo Disneyland it is important to distinguish the local culture from the American culture. What makes Tokyo Disneyland attractive for the Japanese is the perfect symbiosis of the illusion of being in the United States and in the fantasy-world of Disney. Still there are some Japanese aspects to the park which make it easier for Japanese audiences to enjoy them during a visit. While some of these attempts work very well, at least one has failed.

---

18 The shop does not only target at Japanese customers but visitors of the park from Europe and America as well. These visitors are mainly Disney fans who make trips to Japan only to visit Tokyo Disney Resort and are not very likely to see anything else of Japan. For them, the "Chiba Traders" is an opportunity to take something Japanese home.

The attraction "Meet the World," which was unique to the Japanese park, existed from the opening of Tokyo Disneyland in 1983 until 2002, when it was closed down due to its lack of popularity. "Meet the World" was housed inside a rotating carousel theater, and was not a show about different cultures of the world, as the title might suggest. Instead, it focused on the Japanese nation and its interaction with other cultures in a historical context, and thereby situated Japan and Japanese history inside the park. Tokyo Disneyland became a mirror image of World Showcase, positioning Japanese history at the center of attention and offering a similar attraction to "The American Adventure" in Epcot. Presumably "Meet the World" was not popular with the Japanese audience, because it focused on a simplified and sanitized version of *Japanese* history alone, thus interrupting the illusion of being somewhere outside Japan. Even more disturbing to the Japanese audience was the fact that there were no Disney characters involved in the show. Visitors were guided through the narrative by two Japanese child dolls, and an animatronic crane, which severely interfered with the illusion of the visitors to be in a world of Disney's fantasy and magic. For the Japanese audience it is obviously crucial to keep Disneyland purely Disney and American and not to disturb the magic of Disneyland by including too obviously non-Disney, i.e. Japanese characters in the park. Tokyo Disneyland, the idealized, Japanese version of America, includes the ideologies and cute characters of Disney. In this way, it is not only entertainment that is sold to the visitor, but an idea of a Japanese version of the United States.

### Familiarizing America in Tokyo Disney Resort

All Disney parks have some features in common, for example the street which leads the visitor to the Disney castle marking the center of the park. In most Disney parks, this street is named Main Street, USA, yet in Japan it was renamed World Bazaar. In both American parks, Main Street, USA is a nostalgic memory of the American past in rural small towns with romantic old-style houses. It is said to have been inspired by Walt Disney's hometown in Missouri (Birnbaum 102; Salamone 85). Yet, the concept of a main street which runs through a rural town does not exist in Japan and therefore, Japanese visitors have no nostalgic notions about a rural main street. In Tokyo Disneyland, it made more sense to turn this part into a shopping district. Due to Japanese weather conditions and to protect the visitors from the frequent rain showers during the summer months, World Bazaar is completely covered with a glass cupola. This architectural alteration further transforms the original main street into a large indoor shopping mall, reinventing the place as an overt site of consumption and spectacularizing the shopping experience by "giving the feel of a large suburban shopping mall rather than a quaint town center" (Brannen 222). The name World Bazaar gives the shopping district of Tokyo Disneyland a global touch. The impulse runs contrary to Walt Disney's original intention. While he wished to include a piece of his rural hometown, thereby creating a nostalgic memory of an American locality, the Tokyo park emphasizes the idea of the contemporary global world.

This adjustment is meaningful since many Japanese are very fond of products with a foreign touch. This could be easily included in the merchandising of World Bazaar, where visitors are likely to expect goods from around the world. The sales of merchandising in Tokyo Disneyland, which is one of the main incomes of the park, are also increased by specifically Japanese Disney products, like Disney kimonos or special New Year's items which are produced exclusively for the Japanese market.[19]

One reason why merchandising works so well in Japan is the traditional Japanese custom of social gift giving. This practice means that someone who travels brings gifts not only to family members but also neighbors, friends, and office colleagues. These gifts, called *omiyage* are defined as "a representation of otherness that one brings home after a journey to another, often distant and/or mythical place" (Kurotani 28). As a trip to Tokyo Disneyland is considered a journey to another, an "exotic" place, Japanese visitors need to purchase *omiyage* in the park. Traditionally, the most popular item to give as a gift in Japan is food of the region, mainly in the form of sweets (*okashi*). Tokyo Disneyland fulfills this need by offering a great variety of different cookies, chocolate bars, candies, and traditional Japanese sweets like *wagashi* (Japanese confectionery), or *sembei* (rice crackers), all packed in boxes with Disney characters on them. The inclusion of Japanese sweets into the range of products offered makes sense as older people in Japan are often still reluctant to eat Western sweets and thus Japanese sweets in Disney boxes serve as perfect gifts for elderly family members

---

19 According to Aviad Raz, the average visitor spends about $80 in the shops of World Bazaar (*Riding the Black Ship* 66).

and friends. The boxes in which the confectioneries are sold become collectibles themselves, since the design changes from time to time and according to the seasons.[20] The idea to sell Disney sweets in different boxes and cans fits Japanese consumer needs, since these containers are often used in households to store tea, office products, or other little things and do not take much space in the usually small Japanese apartments. Furthermore, it has to be noticed that most confectioneries sold in Tokyo Disneyland as well as Tokyo DisneySea are from famous brands in Japan such as Juchheim, a company specializing in Viennese sweets. This is significant as Western, especially European food labels impart value to the product as they are considered exclusive brands.

The importance of food can be seen more clearly since the Japanese restaurant "Hokusai" was integrated in the World Bazaar. Originally, the restaurants at Tokyo Disneyland served only Western food. Yet, since many visitors complained about the lack of Japanese food, Oriental Land Company decided to add a Japanese restaurant (Brannan 225). "Hokusai" offers Japanese dishes such as *tempura* (battered vegetables and sea-food), sushi, and Japanese lunch boxes. Interestingly enough, the restaurant is advertised on the official Tokyo Disney Resort homepage as "A Taste of Japan in old-time America" (Tokyo Disney Resort) thus once more differentiating Japan from the United States by claiming that dining in this Japanese restaurant is an "exotic" food experience in America.

Also the design of Disney characters themselves contributes to the enormous consumption of Disney merchandising in Japan. Especially many young Japanese women are extremely fond of everything that is *kawaii* (cute). The term *kawaii* most often describes items that are tiny, soft, of round shape and have bright colors such as light pink or light blue.[21] Disney

---

20  This is true as well for popcorn buckets with differently flavored popcorn, available in different sections of the park. The most popular bucket is sold in a cart shop next to the attraction "Pooh's Honey Hunt" and the lines in front of the cart are usually very long and people are willing to wait for more than twenty minutes to purchase a bucket filled with honey flavored popcorn. However, the treat inside the bucket is not of great importance but the buckets themselves, which are collector items, are the main target.

21  For more information about the use of cuteness in Japan read Leila Madge's "Capitalizing on 'Cuteness': The Aesthetics of Social Relations in a New Post-

addresses these demands perfectly as most Disney characters are fluffy with big eyes, round shapes, and bright colors and thus tempt many mature female park visitors to buy Disney products with characters on them every time they visit Tokyo Disneyland. As Donald Richie, an expert on Japanese culture suggests: "This is a passion amounting to near genius of kitsch [...] Japan embraced the biggest piece of kitsch in the West (Disney), broke off a chunk and brought it home to add to its collection" (Richie, *A Lateral View* 43). Hence, "Occidental" products and objects are collected by Japanese consumers, both echoing and subverting the American practice from the nineteenth century to collect "Oriental" artifacts. This further hints to the fact that power relations are not one-sided when it comes to Japanese-American cultural relationships.

The immense popularity of cute products in Japan can be seen in the way several Japanese banks restyled their image in the 1980s by choosing cute mascots and changing their name. Banks started to use cartoon characters as mascots to create a friendlier atmosphere in the rather cold and impersonal banking business. The Asahi Bank for example uses Miffy, a little bunny drawn by the Dutch artist Dick Bruna, and gives little gifts of glasses, plates and other products to its customers. Such mascots attract first and foremost female customers, who are more likely to choose a bank with a cute character, because the checkbooks, credit cards, and gifts have the mascots on them (Riessland 142). More recently, the prestigious French fashion label Louis Vuitton collaborated with the Japanese artist Takashi Murakami and produced a whole product line with bright, laughing flowers on them, which are highly popular among young Japanese women.[22] While cute characters such as Miffy or Mickey Mouse are used predominantly on items for children in the United States, in Japan they are commonly found on items for adults and children alike (Brannen 225).[23]

---

war Japanese Order" and Andreas Riessland's "Sweet Spots: The Use of Cuteness in Japanese Advertising."

22 Takashi Murakmi is associated with the so-called superflat movement in Japan that mixes images from Japanese popular culture with traditional styles or put them in different context (see Looser; Brehm).

23 Yet, a growing popularity of things *kawaii* outside Japan can be seen for example with the increasing acceptance of Hello Kitty products among young adults in the United States.

Depending on the season, visitors to Tokyo Disneyland can purchase merchandising items such as stuffed animals, little figures, pens, and T-shirts celebrating Western as well as traditional Japanese holidays. For example in the spring of 2006, Tokyo Disneyland sold character figures of the Disney animated movie *Lilo and Stitch* (2002) dressed in samurai armor to commemorate Japanese Boy's Day. As an effect of selling Mickey Mouse and Minnie Mouse in kimonos during the Japanese New Year festivities and offering other Disney characters in Japanese outfits, they are familiarized and visually assimilated to Japanese culture. Instead of signifying foreignness they are integrated into the local culture, allowing Japanese consumers to easily create a connection to Disney characters and the Disney theme park, which become part of their life. It can be argued that by adding a Japanese touch to the characters, they become transnational items as they still incorporate American features, yet cannot be regarded as purely American anymore, as they also display signs of Japaneseness and are accepted as part of Japanese popular culture.

Merchandising sold in Tokyo Disneyland usually has images of Disney characters and a tag saying "Tokyo Disneyland" on them. Because of the enormous amount of Disney products available and the changing of items according to the season or special events, Disney goods not only become very expensive collectibles, but the name Tokyo Disneyland itself has turned into a brand of its own. This is particularly important as brand names play a crucial role to young Japanese consumers. In particular the main target group of the Japanese economy, the so-called Office Ladies (young, mostly single women), attaches great significance to brand products. Since most Office Ladies earn a great amount of money while still living with their parents, they do not have to spend their earnings on high rents; they spend a great amount of their income on their leisure time and on expensive brand products. Expensive Western high-quality labels such as Ralph Lauren, Tommy Hilfiger, Louis Vuitton, Gucci, Prada, or Chanel are perceived as exclusive and *kakkoii* (hip) and thus became hallmarks of fashionable Japanese consumers.

This positive image of American and European consumer products is enforced by advertisements in magazines or television, where even Japanese products sell better when advertised by American celebrities. Thus, many Japanese products targeted at a young consumer group, are given names considered "Western" such as for example, Doutor Coffee, Mister

Donut, or A Bathing Ape. However, in Tokyo Disneyland, the brand name is more hybrid. Although the Walt Disney Company is associated with the United States, Tokyo Disneyland is clearly acknowledged as a Japanese brand. Thus the label "Tokyo Disneyland" combines the notion of a Japanese brand with an American touch and is extremely fashionable and popular among Office Ladies, who are the most frequent visitors of the Japanese Disney park,[24] as well as other Japanese consumers.

Another crucial aspect that needs to be addressed is connected to attractions that involve a guide. For example, the conversations in the classical Disney ride "Jungle Cruise" needed to be adjusted since Japan and the United States have a diverging sense of humor. Some of the jokes made in the American version would not make much sense or would even be considered offensive in Japan. For example, when the visitors of the American Disney park have traveled through a mysterious cave during the ride, the tour guide asks the guests to make sure that their neighbor is still sitting next to them and jokes: "Gentlemen, if your mother-in-law is still aboard, you've missed a golden opportunity." This line is taken out from the Japanese version of the ride, since to most Japanese; such a remark would not be considered funny but offensive (Raz, *Riding the Black Ship* 36).[25]

Thus, many different factors contribute to the enormous success of Disneyland in Japan. While some standards of the Walt Disney Company like friendliness, cleanliness, and cute characters directly appeal to the Japanese, others are modified in order to meet Japanese consumer needs. Oriental Land Company is careful to offer enough shopping facilities, special merchandise that can be purchased as *omiyage*, and meets the need of elderly visitors for local food by placing a Japanese restaurant in World Bazaar. Tokyo Disneyland is not only accepted by Japanese consumers, but has become integral part of the local culture. It reflects the idea many Japanese have of a romantic American past, cute characters, and fascinating technologies, mingling these elements and thereby creating a fascinating fantasyscape. Tokyo Disneyland is able to preserve some notions of exoticism, thereby making the park interesting and exciting. At the same time, the

---

24 According to Oriental Land Company, 74.1% of the visitors are female and 68.8% of the visitors are adults (Oriental Land Company Group "Numbers").

25 For a more detailed analysis of the changes in the script of the attraction see Aviad Raz's *Riding the Black Ship* 34f.

place is Japanese enough not to disturb or confuse visitors and to eradicate the negative side-effect of visiting a foreign country, i.e. "culture shock," from a visitor exposed to this Japanese version of America.

Nevertheless, America never was the only center of attention to Japan and while a relative decline in the interest in American culture has taken place since the 1950s, a significant interest in European styles and especially French and Italian design rose in the 1970s in Japan (Tobin 35). Millions of Japanese tourists visiting European cities such as Paris, Heidelberg, and Venice every year, as well as the opening of Italian-style restaurants and French boutiques in Tokyo contribute to this shift in interest. A smaller version of the Eiffel Tower, the Tokyo Tower can be visited in Japan's capital along with an imitated Baker Street and a real Russian Orthodox Cathedral with an onion-dome. The agglomeration of European influences in the cityscape of Tokyo shows how fond Japanese people are of different European cultures (Richie, *A Lateral View* 9). Hence, Disney also provided Japanese visitors with European sites, which was facilitated by the fact that the American Disney parks already included European style architecture, mainly due to references to European fairy tales.

Although not every part of the American Disney parks was adapted for Tokyo Disneyland, the adjustments undertaken changed the meaning of parts of the park which were less adapted as well. For example, Fantasyland is in both the American as well as in the Japanese park dedicated to Disney's world of fantasy. However, the Japanese park includes the "Haunted Mansion," a Western ghost house, which in Disneyland is located in a section of the park called New Orleans Square, a square not integrated in the Japanese park. Furthermore, the architecture of the ride was significantly changed from the "Haunted Mansion" in California, which resembles a southern antebellum mansion to a New England-style gothic brick mansion in Tokyo. This architectural change makes sense as Fantasyland is themed around Disney tales that are set in Europe and the gothic brick mansion evokes idea of European or New England style houses.[26] The ghosts in the

---

26 The façade of the "Haunted Mansion" in Tokyo Disneyland was probably based on the "Haunted Mansion" in World Disney World's Magic Kingdom. Since the Magic Kingdom does not have a New Orleans Square, the ride was placed in Liberty Square, a space dedicated to America's colonial (New England) past.

"Haunted Mansion" are typical Western ghosts and therefore belong to the world of fantasy. This stands in opposition to Japanese ghosts, which are considered to be a vital part of Japanese everyday life. However, in the Japanese Disney park, the Americanized version of originally European fairy tales is expanded by including Western ghost stories.

The acknowledged icon of the park, the Cinderella Castle similarly not only serves as the central landmark of the park, but caters to the Japanese fondness of European castles as well, and once more mingles it with an American version of Europe. While the castles in other Disney theme parks refer to castles from other Disney fairy tales, i.e. *The Sleeping Beauty*, the choice of Oriental Land Company to display a building that closely resembles Neuschwanstein Castle in Bavaria, Germany, is no coincidence.[27] Neuschwanstein, one of the most popular destinations for Japanese tourists, is considered to be the most perfect embodiment of a romantic fairy tale castle. It evokes picturesque ideas of Europe in general and Germany in particular as a beautiful, romantic place.[28] From 1986 to 2006, the castle hosted an attraction unique to Tokyo Disneyland which reflected rather Occidentalist ideas.

The "Cinderella Castle Mystery Tour" included elements of play and entertainment set in a Western context. In *Riding the Black Ship*, Raz argues that this attraction was included because it featured a haunted house, which is – according to him – among the most popular traditional Japanese amusements and by this Disney could be Japanized, once again (44f). Yet,

---

Thus, in Magic Kingdom, the "Haunted Mansion" visually resembles a Dutch Gothic Revival mansion.

27  In Disneyland California, the design of the castle was originally inspired by Neuschwanstein as well but Walt Disney found it too realistic to fit into his world of fantasy and thus the design was altered (Imagineers, *Walt Disney* 57).

28  In Japan this idea is exploited in other recreational facilities as well, the so-called leisure hotels, where Japanese couples or students can escape their everyday life in small apartments. In these leisure hotels, they can watch baseball with friends or share some private time and sojourn together. Most of these leisure hotels resemble little theme parks and feature themed rooms. The "Megurao Imperial" even copies the architecture of the Bavarian monarch Ludwig II. The architecture and decoration of the hotel "create the impression that we are beyond everyday life, in fairyland, never-never land" (Popham 132).

this argument has to be criticized in two points. First, the concept of a ghost house in Japan is significantly different from what was displayed in the "Cinderella Castle Mystery Tour." Traditional ghost houses in Japan, called *obakeyashiki*, have a long historical tradition, are much scarier, and are not considered an attraction for children and therefore would not fit into a Disney park. Second, ghosts (*obake*) indeed play an important role in the Japanese culture and frequently appear in different popular genres such as *obakemanga* (ghost comics), urban legends, and anime movies. However, many different categories of *obake* exist and the rich pantheon of traditional Japanese ghosts and monsters make the concept of *obake* (or *bakemon*) highly complex. The term is used for a range of different characters from dead persons who cannot find peace because they seek revenge for cruel treatment during their life (*yūrei*), demons (*oni*), ghouls, to monsters and goblins (*yōkai*). All the "ghosts" that appeared in the Disney attraction, however, were villains from Disney movies such as the witch from *Snow White* (1937) or the Horned King, a satanic creature from *The Black Cauldron* (1985) and thus did not fit into the traditional Japanese concept of *obake*. Hence, the "Cinderella Castle Mystery Tour" did indeed not Japanize Disney because it featured a Japanese haunted mansion, as Raz suggests. Instead it has to be evaluated as a familiar form of entertainment because it features Japanese concepts of entertainment and role play set in a romantic Western environment.

The attraction started like an ordinary guided tour through any European castle, something highly popular among Japanese tourists abroad. However, the tour was then disturbed and the audience confronted with different villains from classical Disney movies. The dramatic climax featured a fierce dragon-like horned creature which had to be defeated with a magic sword by a person chosen beforehand from the audience. The structure and main storyline of the attraction are universal as they focus on a battle of good against evil, in which, of course, good triumphs over evil.

By actively participating in this role play, visitors of this attraction became part of the Disney magic and illusion in an interactive fashion. Using a dragon-like creature as the final evil to be defeated fit the Japanese culture of play, where dragon-like monsters can be found in many different shapes, as cute Pokémon trading cards, plush toys, and video games or as a fierce Godzilla in movies. Another example is the popular children's series "Ultraman," which was inspired by the American Superman series. In this series the hero is busy fighting monsters, in most cases dragons (Gill 35), while his American counterpart rescues people from burning skyscrapers. Thus, a fight against a monster or dragon is considered a heroic act in Japan, even when acted out in the safe environment of a Disney park. At the same time, fighting dragons is also closely connected to European myths and fables. Contradictory to what Raz claims, in Tokyo Disneyland those who defeated evil were often young men and not children. Especially when accompanied by young women, these men did not hesitate to push children out of their way to play the role of the hero.[29]

However, the staged fight against a monster has an interesting Occidentalist twist added to the narrative. The villains and monsters that Japanese visitors encountered in the castle were all *Western* villains, due to the fact that they are derived from European fairy tales. The idea that villains in Tokyo Disneyland are generally non-Japanese was emphasized by the fact that the Magic Mirror which appeared frequently in the attraction to give some background information, spoke Japanese with a slight Western accent. In most cases, "evil" was defeated by a Japanese hero who was later awarded with a medal and praised by the guide for his bravery and puremindedness, thereby referring to the idea of the "pure" Japanese soul versus the tainted Western soul (see the subchapter "Japanese Monsters and American Barbarians"). The attraction was further clearly marked as an attraction for Japanese visitors since no translations of the dialogues were available, except the idea of the main storyline that good will defeat evil. To visitors who did not speak Japanese very well, the whole attraction remained a great mystery. Among Japanese visitors, the combination of the non-Japanese setting with the familiar adventure structure of fighting monsters/dragons, as well as the fact that the whole tour was guided in Japanese, made the attraction extremely appealing.

Despite its popularity, in 2006 Oriental Land Company announced to the public that the "Cinderella Castle Mystery Tour" was to be closed permanently. Today, the castle hosts "Cinderella's Fairy Tale Hall," exhibiting paintings that tell Cinderella's story of becoming a princess. At the same time, the company declared that a new attraction featuring monsters from the Disney Pixar movie *Monsters, Inc.* (2001) was to open in Tomorrow-

---

29 One has to take into account that in Japan, Tokyo Disneyland is one of the most popular places to invite a woman for the first date.

land in 2009.[30] The replacement of this popular attraction including Western villains by the cute monster characters of *Monsters, Inc.* might reflect an awareness of the underlying Occidentalist ideology of the former ride. While the "Cinderella Castle Mystery Tour" was about the defeat of evil (a Western monster) by good (a Japanese visitor), the forthcoming attraction was advertised by as "capturing the warmth and charm of Boo and the monsters" (Oriental Land Company Group "New Attraction"), thereby focusing on more friendly images of (Western) monsters.[31]

The popularity and success of Tokyo Disneyland encouraged Oriental Land Company to expand Tokyo Disneyland and to open the second Disney park in 2001: Tokyo DisneySea, which includes the Japanese image of Europe (and other regions) even more distinctly. In Tokyo Disneyland images of Europe were already present with the Cinderella Castle and attractions based on the disneyfied version of European fairy tales. However, in Tokyo Disneyland these images remained subordinated to the overall "American experience" that was meant to be created as the main attraction. In Tokyo DisneySea whole sections are clearly outlined as "European" or other regional experiences, no longer directly mediated by America(n popular culture).

## Globalizing Tokyo Disney Resort

The decision of Oriental Land Company to create a second Disney theme park followed the enormous success of Tokyo Disneyland. However, they decided to build a completely new park instead of copying another existing Disney park. Tokyo DisneySea is the only existing Disney theme park with a strong focus on the sea. Both Tokyo Disney parks are located directly at the ocean which has always played an important role in Japanese history and culture, as it has provided the Japanese people with food for centuries, served as a natural boundary to keep foreigners away and, after the opening of Japan connected the country with the world as a trade route.

---

30 To read the whole announcement, see the official homepage of Oriental Land Company. Interestingly enough, this attraction is placed in the building that hosted the rather unpopular ride "Meet the World" until 2002.

31 Unlike in the West, the Japanese concept of monsters is ambiguous since monsters are not necessarily seen as a threat.

Tokyo DisneySea is inspired by myths and legends of the sea, and refers to the mythical seven seas of the world with its seven themed sections: Mediterranean Harbor, Mysterious Island, Mermaid Lagoon, Arabian Coast, Lost River Delta, Port Discovery, and American Waterfront. Like the traditional Disney parks, Tokyo DisneySea features a main entrance that leads to the Mediterranean Harbor, which serves basically the same purpose as World Bazaar in Tokyo Disneyland. The Mediterranean Harbor leads to the center of the park, a volcano called Mount Prometheus, which replaces the castle in the classical Disney park structure. According to the official internet site, Tokyo DisneySea is "a unique combination of atmosphere, live entertainment and state-of-the-art attractions like no other Disney Park in the world" (Tokyo Disney Resort Homepage). While Tokyo Disneyland relates more to classical Disney movies and the original Disney parks, the second Japanese Disney park is more a Japanese version of Epcot, where visitors can marvel at new technologies and encounter different cultures.[32] While Tokyo Disneyland is more popular with young adults and children, Tokyo DisneySea is targeted at more mature visitors,[33] which explains the number of expensive restaurants inside the new park. Throughout Tokyo DisneySea there are twenty-one restaurants, dining facilities, and lounges and in contrast to Tokyo Disneyland, where no alcoholic beverages are available, here beer and wine are sold along with cocktails. The park also includes a very popular Broadway musical review and an expensive five star hotel. The available merchandising targets a more mature consumer as well, as it includes pasta in stylish glass cases, expensive olive oil, sweets sold in boxes shaped like Venetian gondolas, and "Dolce Romanza" chocolate.

At Mediterranean Harbor parts of Old Europe are reconstructed. The center of this area consists of a large lake, where water shows and parades of Disney characters take place during the day. Palazzo Canal displays Italian architecture by reproducing parts of Venice with bridges and gondolas. The area is full of European-style restaurants, shops, and little cafes which are extremely popular with mature visitors, who supposedly imagine Italy

---

32 Port Discovery displays the future of technology and discovery of the sea and the sky.

33 Only one section named Mermaid Lagoon, based on the animated Disney movies *The Little Mermaid* (1989) hosts attractions for smaller children.

to look exactly like this. At "Magellan's," a Portuguese restaurant, a full six-course dinner is served in a wine cellar replica. Visitors can experience a ride in a gondola, eat pasta, and drink cappuccino in a romantic Italian environment before strolling through an ancient Portuguese fortress – all without leaving Japan.

To visitors who are more interested in non-European cultures, Arabian Coast, which refers to the Disney animated movie *Aladdin* (1992), offers an alternative. Arabian Coast evokes images of a mythic Orient with a bazaar-like merchandising store and a carousel inside a replicated mosque. Arabian-style food like couscous and lamb sandwiches along with dried fruits are available in restaurants with Arabian sounding names such as "Sultan's Oasis," "Casbah Food Court," or "Open Sesame." The popularity of this themed space shows that not only Western places are of interest to a Japanese audience, but Arabian countries as well. Furthermore, the relatively "exotic" representation of this part renders Arab countries as different from Japan, thus subverting Western constructions of the Orient in which Japan sometimes is considered to be part of the Orient and thus of Orientalist discourses.

Lost River Delta also displays a non-Western culture as it is supposed to represent the jungle of Central America in the 1930s. The whole area is built to support the main attraction, the Indiana Jones Adventure "Temple of the Crystal Skull." Although a similar ride exists in Disneyland California, there are some significant differences between the two versions of the attraction. While in the American Disney park the ride is set somewhere in Asia, in the Japanese version the story is set somewhere in Central America, hosted by a Latin-American guide who speaks Japanese with a Mexican accent. While the original ride in America features the Asian continent as the exotic, in Japan, Central America becomes a place inhabited by cannibals where unexpected events take place. Thereby once more another region of the world is considered "the Other" in the Japanese Disney parks. This version of the ride even inspired the storyline of the latest Indiana Jones movie *Indiana Jones and the Kingdom of the Crystal Skull* (2008). Hence, a transnational cross-influence can be seen at work: First, an American theme park attraction was brought to Japan, where it was modified before the altered storyline traveled back to the U.S., where it was again altered and turned into an international blockbuster. In this transnational process, the idea of what is perceived as "exotic" shifts from an Asian context in the American versions of the ride to a Central American context in the Japanese version. In both cases, "the exotic" is geographically relocated to settings farther away from either the United States (Asia) or Japan (Central America). These shifts indicate the ideological differences of what or who is considered "exotic."

The most "American" part of Tokyo DisneySea is American Waterfront, which displays the northeastern seaboard of America in the early twentieth century. The section is divided into a larger part called New York Harbor and a smaller part named Old Cape Cod. The area of Old Cape Cod portrays a cozy, romantic, homely little fishing town on the American East Coast, where visitors can buy cookies, jams, teas and country-style household items in "Aunt Peg's Village Store" and take pictures with an altered version of the Men at the Wheel statue.[34] In New York Harbor, the former fish market area hints to New York's past as an immigrant city where European immigrants first landed when they came to the United States. The area is filled with a variety of different food carts and a New York deli, where visitors can buy sandwiches, salads and desserts. New York is imagined as an early metropolis, a multicultural place with exciting shows ("Encore!" – a Broadway theater), business ("McDuck's Department Store"), traffic ("Big City Vehicles"), and a luxurious passenger ship, closely resembling the Titanic. This section constructs an idealized golden American past with all the wonders of New York City, a city of dreams, with an additional Disney touch of magic and harmony: a place where all your dreams can come true. What is completely left out from this imaginary New York City at the turn of the nineteenth century are the dark sides of the metropolis such as crime, poverty, and discrimination of minority groups, thereby reflecting the romanticized, idealized version of New York City popular in Japan. Focusing on the history of *European* rather than *Japanese* immigrants, who mainly entered the U.S. from San Francisco or in Hawaii, replaces the Japanese-American history with European/Western immigration history. Within Tokyo DisneySea Japanese visitors can feel like European immigrants from the nineteenth century by strolling through the streets of

---

34 A Mickey Mouse statue inspired by the Man at the Wheel statue in Gloucester/Massachusetts could be read as a hint to the dangers of the sea. However, the meaning of the original statue is altered in the park, as most visitors relate it to the first animated film with Mickey Mouse: *Steamboat Willie* (1928).

an idealized, reconstructed New York City, thus becoming part of the American immigration narrative.[35] The only marker of Japaneseness in Tokyo DisneySea is located at the American Waterfront as well: the Japanese restaurant "Sakura" However, the restaurant rather adds to the idea of New York as a multicultural city than hinting to the history of Japanese immigration.

Yet, a rather "dark side" of New York City was added by mistake, when a free-fall ride named "Tower of Terror" was placed in this section in September 2006. Although, similar attractions exist in the American Disney parks, they are never located in a New York City context. After the terrorist attacks of 9/11, the location of the "Tower of Terror" in a New York context inevitably adds an extra meaning to the attraction. However, Japanese visitors and the Oriental Land Company do not seem to associate the "Tower of Terror" located in Disney's New York City with the 9/11 attacks, since the story is set in a hotel in New York City in 1912.[36] Thus, Japanese visitors perceive the ride just as a thrilling and entertaining attraction which adds a certain edge and Gothic atmosphere to New York Harbor. Dislocating an American attraction from the United States to a Japanese Disney park leads to cultural mistranslations and once more emphasizes the fact that this park is not an American park.

---

35 The immigration experience of most Asians was different in America from the experiences of European immigrants. While most Europeans arrived in New York and moved westwards, thus becoming part of the westward movement which is considered to be part of becoming American, Asian immigrants mainly arrived in San Francisco and either remained at the west coast or moved eastwards. Thereby, they were excluded from the unique frontier experience and consequently from becoming Americans.

36 The official Japanese "Tower of Terror" homepage gives detailed background information of the attraction. The Japanese version of the ride is, unlike the American "Tower of Terror" attractions, not based on the American TV series "The Twilight Zone" but a unique story was created by Japanese storywriters. In the focus of the Japanese attraction is a selfish and greedy American hotel owner, who was keen on collecting exotic artifacts from Africa. According to the narrative, one of the objects unleashed mythical powers and ever since the hotel owner went missing. Here, an Occidental image of the greedy American is constructed, who is punished for his obsession with collecting "exotic" artifacts.

Tokyo DisneySea as a fantasyscape serves for the visitors not only as a journey to the United States, but to various places in the world. Visitors can hop from Europe to Central America, to Arabian countries and to Disney's fantastic underwater world of the *The Little Mermaid*.(1989) Tokyo DisneySea adapts to current Japanese consumer demands by no longer only focusing on America as an attractive place, but also on other places around the world.[37] According to Angelika Hamilton-Oehrl, the increased Japanese interest in foreign cultures, reflected in the numerous theme parks in Japan with foreign countries as a recurring thematic motif, can be interpreted as an expression of the growing interest in travels abroad (242). Nevertheless, since short, domestic travels are still more popular in Japan than long-term journeys abroad, Tokyo Disneyland and Tokyo DisneySea offer Japanese people the opportunity to visit "Europe," "Central America," "Arabia," and the "United States" within a few hours and without leaving their home country.

## WONDERLAND RE-VISITED

The question still remaining is whether Disney in Japan can be seen as an example of cultural imperialism or not. John Van Maanen starts from the view of Tokyo Disneyland as sign of cultural imperialism in "Displacing Disney: Some Notes on the Flow of Culture":

Tokyo Disneyland is perhaps a glimpse of the coming world culture built on the Coca-Colonizing forces of Western, particularly American, consumer values [...] the apparently asymmetric transfer of meaning systems and symbolic forms give way to an empire of signs ruled by those who produce and export the world's most desirable goods and services. (9)

However, at closer scrutiny, Van Maanen recognizes that the Japanese version of the park functions differently than the American Disney parks. If Tokyo Disneyland would have been exported by the United States as an exact copy of the American Disney parks and if the Japanese had been ex-

---

37 China and other East Asian countries are left out of the park presumably because of the complicated historical relationship of Japan and these countries.

cluded from the establishing process of the park in Japan, Van Maanen argues, it would have been right to describe Tokyo Disneyland as a "cultural bomb dropped on perfect strangers" (9). Yet this would underestimate the self-determination and agency of the Japanese. It was a Japanese company that adjusted the park according to the demands of the Japanese audience and thereby actively incorporated and localized an American cultural phenomenon. Thus, as Raz has also argued, "the selective replication and rearrangement of Disneyland in Tokyo" has to be understood as "an example of a post-imperialist process that suggests a story different from that suggested by other forms of globalization" (*Riding the Black Ship* 15).

The same can be said about the critical discourse of the East's, and in this case Japan's "symbolic domination by the West." As discussed by Frederic Jameson and Jean Baudrillard. The fascination with American popular culture exemplifies more than just the Americanization of Japan, since the interest in American goods is born out of a fascination with America. Tokyo Disneyland is more than "a product of cultureless world capitalism, [which] means the same thing in Japan as in the United States" (Brannen 218). Through the active participation of the Japanese owners who took into consideration the dreams and longings of Japanese consumers, the cultural meanings of the Disney park shift significantly in Japan. The same is true for the cultural meaning of Disneyland. In Japan, the center of attention is the Japanese perception of the United States and the world, thus evaluating the world from a Japanese perspective. By replacing or renaming parts of the American Disney parks a new meaning is created, the United States is exoticized for Japanese audiences and a Japanese ideology is attached to the park. The experience Japanese visitors have in Tokyo Disneyland is, unlike in the U.S. Disney parks, not a nostalgic trip to the nation's past but more a vacation to the United States and other unknown, "exotic" places (Van Maanen 24). Tokyo Disneyland is actively modified by Oriental Land Company and enthusiastically embraced and consumed by the Japanese. Through the changes in presentation and consumption, the theme park focuses on a Japanese and no longer American perception of the world, thus offering an alternative to the American reading of the world, enabling visitors to imagine the world differently.

Disney in Japan has to be understood as a U.S. cultural product, which was voluntarily embraced and transformed into a unique Japanese experience. Just like in the U.S., Tokyo Disney Resort not only sells entertainment to the consumers, but also national cultural experiences. This turns around and appropriates the exoticization of Japan, which had been and continues to be exhibited as an exotic "Other" at fairs across Europe and the United States. Nowadays, Japan itself has numerous parks themed around Western locations, next to Tokyo Disney Resort Canadian World, Glücks Königreich, British Hills, or Parque España (Joy 19). Here, Japanese visitors can travel their idealized, sanitized versions of the West without being disappointed by polluted cities or unfriendly people. Tokyo Disney Resort is clearly a Japanese version of Disneyland in America as well as an idealized image of the United States. When Japan was once perceived as "an exotic Eden" (Wilkinson 112) or "Fairyland" (Hearn qtd. in Wilkinson 125), the Japanese fantasyscape is now turning the United States (and Europe) into playgrounds which can be consumed in the East. In Tokyo Disney Resort, the Japanese owners not only mimic the American Disney parks, but they map and re-map Disneyland according to their own, Japanese ideas.

In his study "Simulated Tourism" Lawrence Mintz writes that "theme park creation is simply another example of our rendering of the world as we see it and/or want it to be" (48). While an American image of Japan is constructed in Epcot, Tokyo Disney Resort offers visitors an image of the United States according to the Japanese perception of America. In both cases, the representation of the unfamiliar cultures is to a great extent restricted to representations of the past. At Epcot the Walt Disney Company did not want to display a highly technologically advanced Japan, as the theme park is meant to celebrate the technological superiority of the United States. At Tokyo Disney Resort the romantic past of America is showcased since the United States and contemporary Japan today are not too different from each other when considering modern architecture and life-style. In the past, it seems, these nations were more distinctly and securely different.

In all of the Disney parks discussed, the "exotic" other – Japan in Epcot and the United States in Tokyo Disneyland – are distinguished from the local culture. Van Maanen suggests in his essay "Displacing Disney," that cultural meanings are changed in different places and lead to the fact that "people on both sides of the border become more aware of their own culture" (24). With this, he indicates that the flow of cultural products and images back and forth can help people "discover new ways to do things" (24), and thus being more open towards alternative ways of life. Japan easily and willingly incorporated Disney into cultural and family rituals such as celebrating the Japanese New Year in Tokyo Disneyland with Mickey Mouse.[38] The import of the "foreign" Disney culture did not lead to sacrificing Japanese traditions for American ones, but it led to an active changing and recontextualizing of commodities and practices, thereby modifying the Japanese culture.

It is not only the Japanese, but customers in many different nations who are attracted by American popular culture products. Americans sometimes tend to interpret the popularity of their culture abroad as a sign of their popularity and superiority in general and sometimes even believe somewhat naively that other cultures aim to become like them. This assumption suggests that these cultures endeavor to attain an imaginary identity with the U.S. and to leave their indigenous identities behind (Yoshimoto 191). Such an assumption disregards the possibility that cultures may embrace certain American products and cultural practices, while at the same time criticizing and rejecting other aspects of American culture. It is highly unlikely that Japan, a nation proud of its unique culture, would hope to become like the United States. Yoshimoto Mitsuhiro even goes one step further, arguing in "Images" that the selection of some aspects of American and Western culture does show a postmodern cynicism: "in postmodern Japan, everything is commodified, including the sense of nationhood. America is, therefore, just another brand name, like Chanel, Armani, and so on" (195).

While Disney is a popular American brand in Japan, Tokyo Disneyland is a transnational, Japanese-American brand and the parks are considered Japanese, a place where foreign visitors are proudly taken to (Notoji 228). By modifying Disneyland for Japanese consumers and putting Disney characters in a Japanese context, they become part of a hybridized Japanese culture. Tokyo Disneyland is "America in Japan and a Japanese view of America" (Raz, *Riding the Black Ship* 13). The Japanese do not celebrate the history and culture of the United States as the American parks do, but with Tokyo Disney Resort they recreate their own idealized version of Disney parks loaded with Japanese ideologies. It can be argued that Tokyo Disney Resort has become more a sign of Japanese nationalism than of Americanization and is a hybrid version of the original Disney parks, and can thus no

---

38 For more examples of the incorporation of Disney by different cultures see Janet Wasko's *Dazzled by Diseny? The Global Disney Audiences Project*.

longer be associated with the United States or Japan only (Van Maanen 22). Tokyo Disney Resort functions as a transnational space where American and Japanese influences come together, thus creating a new, hybrid space. Consequently, Disneyland in Japan has a different meaning than Disneyland in the United States and the Japanese parks have become ambivalent sites, where a panoply of cultural influences are mixed and matched together and create a new space that is in-between rather than clearly American, Japanese or European. In Tokyo Disney Resort, Disneyland becomes a transnational dream, a fantasyscape that is still in a constant flux.

# A Taste of Difference:
# Sushi in the United States

> "I would like to take better care of myself. I'd like to start eating healthier – I don't want all that pasta. I would like to start eating like Japanese food."
>
> - BOB. LOST IN TRANSLATION -

When visiting different cultures as represented by the World Showcase of Epcot in Walt Disney World, visitors have the opportunity to take a break in one of the ethnic-themed restaurants and taste food from various parts of the world. In Walt Disney's Epcot, different cultures are represented and marked as divergent from America by the dishes served in the restaurants, because "food is the principal ambassador of the nations in EPCOT" (Nelson 139). The spectrum of eating options ranges from Norwegian *koldbord* (a buffet-style meal including multiple cold foods), German *Bratwurst*, to Chinese *dàn juǎn* (Egg Rolls), or Japanese *tempura*, and sushi. The idea of defining cultures through food is not new, since food has always been closely connected to national and ethnic identities (Kalcik 44). As food scholar Warren Belasco states in his essay "Food Matters: Perspectives on an Emerging Field," food "indicates who we are, where we came from, and what we want to be" (2). In most cultures food is omnipresent in everyday life and, it seems to be easier to taste food from another culture than experiment with a foreign language or religion, although the idea of eating unknown food can be challenging and in some cases even threatening. However, in Epcot it seems less daring to try new dishes, since in Disney parks foodscapes are created which are considered "safe," familiar places where visitors can access other cultures via exotic dishes without any risk. The

Walt Disney Company decides which dishes are served in the restaurant to represent different nations in Epcot and modifies them to suit the palate of mainly Western visitors.

Epcot is not the only place where people are exposed to a kaleidoscopic flux of dishes from around the world. Because of rapid globalization processes, a great variety of foods from many different countries is available in restaurants and supermarkets around the world. In former times, food already played a crucial role in colonization and exploration processes. Adventurers confronted other civilizations with their food and were themselves confronted with new cuisines, which in turn they sometimes "introduced" to their homeland (Belasco, "Food Matters" 3). However, as Katarzyna Cwiertka argues, also – and especially – when it comes to foodways, the global and local are interdependent. "As a result, not only do global brands spread worldwide diminishing the diversity of local cuisines, but also new hybrid cuisines are created and new identities embraced through the acceptance and rejection of new commodities and new forms of consumption" ("Introduction" 2). Yet, in most cases the "Other" food is not consumed and accepted in its original state, but is modified in order to meet the local palate. As Belasco states, modern eating today is more often than not "compromised, globalized, creolized" ("Food Matters" 14). People adapt dishes according to the availability of ingredients or to their tastes, hence "the majority of dishes that appeared in restaurants and cookbooks, and were claimed to be of foreign origin, were rather products of the imagination of their creators" (Cwiertka, "Introduction" 9). Obviously, food and imagination are intertwined when it comes to cultural exchanges and representations of another culture by means of food.

The following chapter will examine how Japanese food is embedded in and adapted to local tastes in the United States. It will be shown that different attitudes to Asian food co-exist in the United States, ranging from culinary colonialism to culinary tourism and culinary transnationalism. Thus, it will be argued that the term "culinary colonialism" is a crude oversimplification if applied to characterize the whole variety of influences and appropriations of Japanese food in the United States. To contradict notions of sweeping culinary colonialism or simple Orientalizing processes resulting from the creation of new sushi rolls in the United States today, it will be argued that Japanese food in general and sushi in particular participate in a transnational exchange, thereby communicating across culinary and national boundaries. Consumers decide what kind of sushi or fish is demanded or consumed and therefore they determine the popularity of the dish. In the United States as well as in Japan, sushi is not produced by a single company but by multiple sushi chefs from all around the world, who put their individual touch on the dish. My following analysis is based on Sasha Issenberg's economic survey on the globalization of sushi, and his thesis that "in sushi, no one controls all the information" (Issenberg xv) and thus, power relations are decentralized because the "supply and demand are regulated not by moguls but by local ideas about value and taste" (Issenberg xx). Once a traditional, Japanese dish, sushi traveled from Japan to the United States, was modified according to the American palate, and re-entered the Japanese market as American Sushi.

The first subchapter will focus on early clashes and misunderstandings between Japan and America concerning food. It will be argued that fundamental differences in eating habits and the diets of both nations led to stereotypical and hostile ideas about the supposedly "Other." Following a historical overview of Japanese-American food relations, the term "culinary colonialism" as well as the practice of Orientalizing and Occidentalizing a culture via food will be explained in order to verify that these concepts are indeed problematic when applied to Japanese-American culinary exchanges. It will be argued that culinary cultures and dishes are never static but are altered over time. Therefore, re-inventing sushi in the United States should be evaluated as a new way to imagine the dish, which has never existed in only one shape, rather than a form of culinary colonialism or Orientalism.

The second subchapter "Japanese Food in Culinary Texts" closely investigates how notions of "Otherness" are represented via food in fictional as well as non-fictional accounts. This chapter shows how food is used in Cara Lockwood's novel *Dixieland Sushi* to underline the "Otherness" of the Japanese-American protagonist, juxtaposing the eating culture of her and her family against the culinary culture of the American South. In a similar vein, food functions as a marker of Japaneseness and Japanese identity in Linda Furiya's food memoir *Bento Box in the Heartland*, while national as well as gender dichotomies are played out via food in Ruth Ozeki's novel *My Year of Meat*. Finally, the examination of Japanese cookbooks written for and sometimes even by Americans reveals how Japanese dishes are reimagined and adapted for an American palate.

The subchapter "Enter the Dragon Roll: Consuming Sushi in the United States" shows how sushi is modified and familiarized in the United States. Sushi became popular in the U.S. as a health food and a marker of social status as for example evident in Brad Easton Ellis's novel *American Psycho*. Originally eaten as a snack, during the Edo period sushi developed into a food for formal dinners and special occasions. Yet, the more recent influence from America attached a new meaning to the dish, making the consumption of sushi as a snack acceptable and popular in Japan again. When sushi is imported and exported, it transgresses national boundaries and it does not only change its meaning but its ingredients as well. Thus, both cultures, Japan and the United States, take part in a culinary (ex)change and redefinition of sushi as an idea. As Sasha Issenberg concludes in his "Introduction" to *The Sushi Economy,* "the new sushi economy has challenged the way we see the globe" and "food has always been a point of negotiation between people and their environment" (Issenberg xvi).

## OF RICE AND MEAT: A SHORT HISTORY OF JAPANESE AND AMERICAN FOOD RELATIONS

Food and the practice of eating and cooking define all cultures and help to make them unique, distinguishing them from each other. In a global world characterized by increasing mass transnational migration and tourism, a steady flow of people brings a frequent flow of food to different places in the world. In major cities like New York, London, Tokyo or Berlin, a vast number of ethnic restaurants invite culinary adventurers to try unknown, exotic dishes. The variety of different restaurants reflects the multicultural citizenship of those places and thereby "expresses the worldliness" of these metropolises (Murcott 66). Yet ethnic cuisine and exotic food are no longer only available in global cities but spread as well to rural and smaller communities (Corson 132; Matsumoto 36).

The fact that people are exposed to a greater variety of cuisines today does not necessarily mean that consumers are automatically more open and less prejudiced vis-à-vis unknown dishes. According to food writer Leslie Brenner, "we're suspicious of food [...] because we *learn* to be suspicious of food" (166). For example, by explaining to children in Western societies that they are incapable of appreciating the taste of dried grasshoppers, children are already told that they will not like the taste of insects, although they are considered edible in many cultures. Everybody is taught that some foods are not palatable and that people do not like certain tastes because these tastes do not fit their idea of food in his or her culture.

Most consumers are extremely selective and not very open minded when it comes to food and thus, cultural exchanges in the past and today are often accompanied by clashes and misunderstandings over food. This already proved to be true for the initial contacts between Japan and America. When early diplomatic exchanges started between the two nations in the nineteenth century, diplomats from both sides of the Pacific suffered from the difference in eating habits. During the first voyage of Japanese diplomats to America, food was a permanent source of worry for the Japanese travelers, who were not able to cope with the Western diet based on wheat, meat, and dairy products. Feeling weary about the strange food and eating habits of the Americans, which they had observed when Americans visited Japan, they had taken fish and soy sauce with them on the ship. The American sailors, however, threw the unknown Japanese food overboard since they believed that it was tainted and poisonous. With their familiar food gone, the Japanese had no alternative but to eat cheese, meat, and bread for the rest of the voyage (LaFeber 23). One of the Japanese officials wrote back to Japan that "it is well beyond the power of my pen to describe what we, the Japanese, suffer on our journey to a foreign country" (qtd. in Beasley 63), referring to his experience with American food.

Nevertheless, the Japanese were not the only ones suffering from unfamiliar food. American diplomats in Japan made similar disconcerting food experiences. Henry Adams for example found Japanese food inedible and classified green tea as "nauseous" (Benfey 44). In his book *Travellers' Tales of Old Japan*, Michael Wise compiled different impressions of Japan by Western visitors of the island nation and commented on their experiences. One of these travel accounts, for instance, "Hot and Cold Saki" was written by Samuel Wells Williams, the chief interpreter of the 1854 trip of Commodore Matthew Perry to Japan. During the voyage, Williams recorded all events in his diary, among them the visit of some Japanese officials on the American ship. Williams describes how they had a dinner with their Japanese guests during which wine, meat, and pastries were enjoyed by the Japanese and the American chief interpreter appreciated the Japanese "interest in the [American] feast" (15). In return, the American officials were invited to a Japanese dinner which failed to meet the American expectations. They were served tea, sponge cake, raw oysters, mushroom soup, seaweed cooked with sugar and raw ginger among "other unknown matters" (16), none of which were considered delicacies by the Americans. Williams' diary entry reveals the inability of himself and his fellow travelers to accept the unfamiliar dishes and to appreciate the hospitality of the Japanese. While the dishes served might have seemed strange, even challenging or just too ordinary to the Americans, the Japanese considered them delicacies, worthy to offer their guests. While Williams was only ignorant about the Japanese culinary culture, more radical thoughts about Japanese eating cultures were not uncommon. One example is the account of Christopher Dresser, a Western visitor, who wrote about his culinary experience in Japan, in an essay entitled "A Dish So Ghastly." He describes a meal of a raw living fish which is considered a delicacy in Japan as a barbaric eating habit, although he admits that "in flavor and delicacy this surpassed any of the preceding dishes" (Wise 71). Dresser also gives an account of a traditional Japanese tea-ceremony, a highly stylized and complicated form of art, which he completely fails to appreciate or understand.

Indeed, the Japanese were not only interested in Western art, clothing, machines, and weapons; they were equally keen to learn more about Western food. Before their self-seclusion policy, Japan traded with Western, mainly European countries and was already exposed to influences from the West, including culinary influences (Ashkenazi and Jacob 44-45). Many dishes which are nowadays considered to be Japanese indeed have Western roots. *Tempura* for example was introduced in the sixteenth century to Japan by the Portuguese alongside fire weapons and the Bible (Richie, *A Taste of Japan* 26). Even though the Japanese seemed to be fond of Western food, they clearly differentiated themselves from the West by strictly distinguishing the Japanese cuisine from the Western cuisine.

Before the contact with the West, and during the seclusion-era, the Japanese diet was based on fish and vegetables and various taboos against eating meat existed.[1] Animals were not bred for consumption and only on rare occasions were they hunted to be eaten. Eating meat was believed to be impure and barbaric and thus the Japanese distinguished themselves from the

---

1 Edward Washburn Hopkins' essay "The Buddhistic Rule Against Eating Meat" elaborates the religious taboo on meat consumption in Buddhism.

West by the feeling that their "self is to other as rice is to meat" (Ohnuki-Tierney, "McDonald's in Japan"167).

In former times, the term *nanban ryōori*, which can be translated as "barbarian cuisine" was used in Japan to name non-Japanese dishes. The term reveals that although they accepted Western food, the Japanese still considered their food culturally superior to the "Other" eating habits of the Westerners (Slack 152). In spite of the fact that Western food is widely distributed and popular in Japan today, the Japanese still distinguish between traditional Japanese dishes, which they call *washoku* (self), and dishes of Western origin, called *yōshoku* (other) (Richie, *A Taste of Japan* 112).[2] During the Meiji Period, shortly after Japan re-opened its harbors to Western trade, many Japanese started to believe that the consumption of meat was necessary in order to get physically as strong as Western people (Smit and Kobayashi 48-49). Their main concern was that they would be overpowered by the West and that Japan would become a Western colony. Thus, in order to "catch up" with the West, resist colonization, and retain a national identity, meat consumption became a national matter and the Western cuisine started to become a symbol of progress and modernization.

In her study "We Eat Each Other's Food to Nourish Our Body: The Global and the Local Mutually Constituent Forces," Japanese food expert and historian Emiko Ohnuki-Tierney explains how different foods are associated with different concepts in Japan. According to her argumentation, eating rice is about Japanese identity, while consuming meat is about modernity, and American fast food is simply "the Other." In *Rice as Self* Ohnuki-Tierney emphasizes that "food plays a dynamic role in the way people think of themselves and others" (4). Since rice has and always has had a central position in the Japanese diet, it is a symbol of the Japanese identity and plays a significant role in the Japanese culture (Ohnuki-Tierney, *Rice as Self*; Slack 191; Masumoto 140). Theodore Bestor connects Benedict Anderson's idea of "imagined communities" to the foodscape and argues that "food culture equally imagines national cuisines as organized around essential traits" (*Tsukiji* 126). In fact, "as Buddhists, the Japanese were forbidden to eat meat" (Downer, *Japanese Food* 12) and the

---

2   Until today, Japanese dishes are considered special and expensive and therefore, at national holidays or important family celebrations or business meeting, mostly Japanese food is served.

traditional belief that meat was unclean and hazardous thus still remained. Many concerned Japanese tried to "civilize" the consumption of meat by adding a bowl of rice (Ohnuki-Tierney, *Rice as Self* 167). Rice was considered to be "the heart and soul of the Japanese cuisine" (Slack 191) and was used to distinguish the own national identity from others. In comparison to the West, Japan imagines and differentiates itself as a nation of rice consumers, whereas Westerners are declared to be meat consumers.[3] This binary opposition assesses not only the Western cuisine, but Western culture in general and negative connotations with the unfamiliar as well as positive associations with the familiar food were transferred to the culture in general.

Although rice continues to be the most important food in Japan, today food from different parts of the world is enjoyed there. Since 1971, diplomats or tourists from Western countries can retreat to the familiar "Golden Arches" of McDonald's fast food restaurants (Ohnuki-Tierney, "McDonald's in Japan" 162). Yet, the concept of fast food had already existed in Japan for a long time: during the Edo-Period sushi was sold as a snack from carts in the streets of *Edo* and takeaway food was sold at train stations.[4]

Many scholars have assessed the impact of Western food in general and fast food and McDonald's in particular on Asia. Terms like "Mcdonaldization" (Ritzer) echo the concern of some scholars that this fast food company homogenizes culinary cultures around the world in order to satisfy the needs of a capitalist, globalized world (Watson, "Introduction" 5-6). Despite these accusations, the majority of scholars in *Golden Arches East*, a survey of the influence of McDonald's in Asia, conclude that the company does indeed have an influence on local culinary cultures, but that these in-

---

3   Japan differentiates itself not only from the West by juxtaposing rice with meat or wheat. Other Asian countries in which dishes are centered on rice consumption are similarly considered different from Japan. According to the Japanese perception, Japanese rice is considered superior to Chinese rice, or brown rice (Ohnuki-Tierney, *Rice As Self* 10).

4   There was a main difference between Japanese and Western concepts of fast food. While American fast food is uniform in taste, color, and package, the Japanese fast food, especially the *ekiben* sold at train stations vary according to the region and season. Therefore, local differences are emphasized, while uniformity is one of the key concepts of American fast food (P. Noguchi 317-318).

fluences do not erase traditional culinary dishes or eating habits. On the contrary, McDonald's itself is localized by adapting its menus to local eating habits. In Japan for example, the fast food restaurant seasonally offers a *Tsukimi Bāagāa* (Moonviewing Burger), which is only available during the moon viewing season in fall.[5] In offering this special burger, McDonald's acknowledges the importance of seasonal food in Japan. The regular McDonald's menu is also altered in Japan and Japanese consumers can order hot and cold *ōolong* tea (a Chinese tea that is very popular in Japan), or a *Teriyaki* Burger or *Ebi-Filet-O* Burger alongside a Big Mac or Cheeseburger. In general, the Japanese menu contains more seafood items than the American menu, such as the *Ebi-Filet-O*, a very popular shrimp burger. Thus, it can be concluded that in this case, globalizing processes lead to the availability of international food, while transnational processes signify the adaptation to local tastes.

Because of the Japanese pride in their traditional culinary culture and the lack of rice in Western fast food, fast food restaurants such as McDonald's are only accepted since they sell an image of America and promise an "exotic" culinary experience. Indeed, McDonald's in Japan does not regularly sell rice or rice products, yet they have to modify not only the burgers but many more items on their menu to become appealing to the Japanese savor by e.g. substituting jelly in donuts with red bean paste or offering *matcha* (exclusive green tea, traditionally used for Japanese tea ceremonies) ice-cream. As Donald Richie states in *A Taste of Japan*, "nothing, food included, gets into the Japanese world without becoming Japanified" (111). One can conclude that Japan has indeed been influenced by Western eating habits, dishes, and fast food restaurants, but these influences are not passively endured. Instead, Western products are adapted to local consumer needs and consumed according to Japanese tastes. The Japanese culinary culture is hybridized and remains dominated by Japanese traditions and habits thereby clearly differing from the American culinary culture.

---

5   The *Tsukimi Bāagāa* consists of a meat loaf, a fried egg, and bacon, put between two buns, and the egg represents the moon. Traditionally *tsukimi* is a traditional Japanese festival, which celebrates the first autumnal full moon by gathering with family and friends beneath the full moon to write poems, to drink sake and to eat special, round rice buns.

As a result of the popularity and omnipresence of American fast food in the world, the United States has been closely associated with this kind of food and the nation was even labeled by Eric Schlosser a "Fast Food Nation." Since their opening in the 1950s in the United States, fast food restaurants such as McDonald's or Burger King have sold mass produced food items and standardized menus to the world. Hence, more often than not, fast food has been regarded as "one of the most menacing forms of Americanization" (Pells 302), supposedly spreading homogenous dishes and eating habits.[6] However, to assume that fast food was the only national food, and thereby to conclude that it was the only food culture of the United States would not do justice to the American culinary culture as the heterogeneity of the United States is reflected in the diversity of its cuisine.

While the Japanese have clearly defined rice as their national food, there are two possible food tendencies in the United States. As Donna Gabaccia summarizes them in *We Are What We Eat*, on the one hand, Americans are "eating homogenous, processed, mass produced foods" and, on the other hand they are "enjoying the multi-ethnic mixtures of particular regions" (226). Leslie Brenner makes a similar observation and suggests that both fast food and ethnic foods are quintessentially American cuisines. As Susan Kalcik argues, "the plurality of our cooking has been celebrated as itself symbolic of 'Americanism'" (55) and hence, the "real American 'melting pot' is actually a stewpot" (60). The immigrant background of the nation created a variety of mixed, hybrid cuisines, including European (Italian, German, Irish), Asian (Chinese, Japanese), South American (Mexican), and African culinary influences. These influences on the American food culture mostly concentrated on certain regions of the United States, where these immigrants settled in large communities (Root and Rochemont 276-312). Nevertheless, foreign dishes were not simply brought to the U.S. and integrated into the culinary landscape, but in most cases, they are modified due to the unavailability of certain ingredients or in order to adapt to American consumer tastes. In some cases, foreign dishes assimilated so well that they became part of the American food culture and today are considered

---

6   For a more critical survey of the international spread of fast food see James Watson's *Golden Arches East: McDonald's in Japan*, George Ritzer's *The McDonaldization of Society: An Investigation Into the Changing Character of Contemporary Social Life*, and Eric Schlosser's *Fast Food Nation*.

American specialties. One example for such an assimilation is the bagel, an originally Jewish ring-shaped bread, which is today well-known all over the world as a vital ingredient of the New York eating life-style (Gabaccia "What Do We Eat" 36; Brenner 90). Up to this day, immigrants frequently bring cooking utensils, recipes, and ingredients with them in order to ease their acculturation to the unknown environment. A "culture shock is often [a] culinary shock" (P. Harris 12), and "many expatriates can alleviate depression only with the familiar foods of their upbringing" (P. Harris 12). By consuming familiar food, the break-up with their home country seems less abrupt and links people to their ethnic heritage (Kalcik 39). Thus, food plays a central role defining an ethnic identity and creating a bond with one's cultural background.

Like many other ethnic cuisines, Japanese food was introduced by Japanese immigrants in the New World. The first Japanese restaurants were opened by Japanese expatriates longing for a familiar taste. While in the last decades many Japanese dishes such as sushi or *tempura* have become increasingly popular, in the past, Japanese food in the United States was mainly consumed by Japanese immigrants within Japanese immigrant communities. Although living in a nation of immigrants, Americans were reluctant to consume unknown food from the Far East and, like the Japanese in Japan; they preferred to consume familiar dishes. Japanese food became more accepted among Americans only with a rising health consciousness and the promotion of Japanese food as truly healthy.[7] Today, authors like Moriyama Naomi use this image of Japanese food to introduce new diets to Americans. In her books *Japanese Women Don't Get Old and Fat* and *The Japanese Diet*, Moriyama offers a new way of eating at home by focusing on typically Japanese dishes, most of them based on rice, vegetables, fish, and soy products rather than on meat, instant products, fat, and sugar. By encouraging Americans to literally turn Japanese when it comes to eating habits, she promises that this diet will lead Americans to a healthier and slimmer life. The promise of the Japanese cuisine to help reduce weight and become healthy made many American consumers curious about the "exotic" Japanese cuisine.

---

7  Even in visitor guides to Disneyland, Japanese food and restaurants are listed under the "vegetarian/healthy" section.

## Japanese Food in Culinary Texts

As it has become clear in the account of the historical encounter, American people as well as Japanese people were at first suspicious of the foods from the other culture. If we are what we eat, the logical conclusion would be that we are not what we do not eat (Belasco 2). Analogous to the creation of binaries in Orientalist and Occidentalist theories, both nations defined themselves as different from the other via food. The Japanese self, symbolized by rice, was opposed by the West, symbolized by meat or wheat.

In the United States, Asian immigrants were deemed to be "the Other." Compared to European immigrants the outer appearance of Asian immigrants already marked them as different from the dominant Anglo-American. Additionally, since most Asian immigrants from China and Japan arrived in the American West, the group did not participate in the Westward Movement which is considered an important part of American identity. Henry Yu suggests in his study *Thinking Orientals* that Asians experienced their own frontier, which can be understood "as a sort of anti-frontier myth" (5) since such an Asian-American frontier narrative could be a "powerful way [...] of subverting Frederick Jackson Turner's thesis" which places "the white European-American at the center of history" (5). Yu suggests turning to Asian immigrants, who mostly arrived in the West (California) and crossed the Pacific instead of the Atlantic, thereby creating "their own eastern frontier-myth" (5) and welcomes an approach "corrective to Eurocentric American history" (Yu 5). Yet, the different frontier experience was not the only thing that differentiated Asians/Japanese from Anglo-Americans. The food that was imported by these Asian immigrants was very different as well.

In the United States "foodways are an especially significant symbol in the communication of statements about ethnic identity" (Kalcik 55) and therefore food choices become important beyond personal matters. "Food is never just food" (Heldke 46), but it is always connected to cultural practices and national identities. Therefore, when guests from foreign countries are invited, they are most likely to be exposed to the national or regional specialties of the hosts. If food can reflect the identity of a person by what he or she eats or refuses to eat (Gabaccia, "What Do We Eat" 40), it is not only capable of revealing the ethnic identity of the consumer, but can communicate something about a person's social status as well. Some foods such as caviar and lobster, or dining in an expensive restaurant are considered markers of social class and status. This significance of food in cultural and social exchange, demonstrates how food can help to define oneself and others.

Already in the 1970s, the anthropologist Claude Lévi-Strauss stated that food was not only important in terms of nourishment, but was also of great cultural importance. Different cultures have different, sometimes even diametrically opposed rules about how food has to be prepared, served, and consumed. The notion of what is considered edible and therefore food and what is deemed inedible varies. By classifying food into categories of edible and inedible, a binary is created. Such classifications seldom reflect a differentiated point of view but rather echo nationally coded norms of one particular culture. Thus, a categorization always is based on ideas and values of a certain nation, which are then used to judge other cultures. Lévi-Strauss classified different forms of food preparation, relating them to ideas of civilization and wilderness. He used the concept of the "raw" versus the "cooked" to set up a dichotomy of the uncivilized, natural and the civilized, cultural.[8] According to his definition, natural ingredients only become a dish, and thus part of culture, when they are cooked – "the cooked is a cultural transformation of the raw" (Lévi-Strauss, "The Culinary Triangle" 29). Hence, civilized human beings are distinguished from uncivilized human beings or animals on the basis of their diet and eating and cooking habits.

This act of categorizing people and dishes as being either civilized or uncivilized on the basis of their culinary culture is not new. Because most cultures consider themselves to be civilized, consumers tend to apply their culturally defined culinary norms to other people. A clash between cultures and their rejection of the unknown frequently takes place in the realm of food. Westerners tend to apply their standard of differentiating between the civilized and uncivilized, between "us" and "them," as Lévi-Strauss showed in his structuralist approach of inclusion and exclusion via the cooked and the raw. Therefore, cultures consuming supposedly raw food are often condemned as uncivilized. This Eurocentric definition of civilized or uncivilized food collides with the definition of food by the Japanese, for whom "raw or uncooked food is food, while in other cultures food usually

---

8   Issenberg makes a similar argument in *The Sushi Economy*.

means cooked food" (Ohnuki-Tierney qtd. in Issenberg 94). Disregarding the difference in Japanese culinary culture, in the U.S. Western eating practices are frequently set up as the norm against which everything that does not fit is seen as strange and suspicious. Therefore, even if Japanese food becomes more and more a part of the American cuisine, "the most exotic foods, or those with ingredients that are unusual in American foods may not appear on menus for fear of offending customers" (Keller Brown and Mussell 4).[9]

Roger Abrahams lists negative stereotypes that are related to food under "deep stereotypes" and defines them as "general characteristics by which people throughout the world talk about strangers and enemies" (22). Because "foods enter into the dynamic of culture – a dynamic that involves motives of acceptance and avoidance, attraction and repulsion, celebration and rejection" (Abrahams 29), derogative terms about "Others" are often connected to food. Germans are called "Krauts" and Italians "Maccaronis" (Murcott 50), reducing national identities to dishes associated with a nation. Such crude terms "reduce[s] entire ethnic group[s] to a single dish from their cuisines, turning good food into bad feeling" (N. Harris 61). Japan is frequently associated with sushi and the Japanese food culture is reduced to the consumption of supposedly raw fish, thereby simplifying and generalizing Japanese culture. This is utterly wrong, because although the fish used for sushi is raw in the sense that it is not transformed by heat (cooked), it is prepared and altered from its natural state and thus cannot be defined as "raw" even in Lévi-Strauss' sense. Indeed, different kinds of sushi exist, the most common of which is *nigirizushi* which consists of vinegared rice with a slice of fish on top. In the West, sushi is often equated with *makizushi* which is, because of the small quantity of fish used, a less expensive form of sushi. In *makizushi*, or rolls, as they are called in the West, the filling is rolled up in a sheet of *nori* (seaweed) (Hosking 90). Thus, the supposedly "raw" food is indeed thoroughly prepared. By imagining Japanese food to

---

9   This is reflected in the representation of food in the media as well. For example, the eating of rice balls in the original Pokémon television series was substituted with eating donuts in the series' version broadcasted in the United States. Because the eating of rice balls seems strange to most Americans (Allison, *Millennial Monsters* 46), the U.S. network feared that the strange eating habit would distract a Western audience.

be exclusively raw fish, and thereby imaging Japan to have a monolithic food culture, a stereotypical, Orientalist discourse of "the Other" is created.

The field of postcolonial studies explains how in the past weaker nations were dominated economically, politically, and culturally by colonizing nations. Based on the belief that the morals of the colonizing nations were superior to those of the colonized, Western nations believed they helped civilize and enlighten undeveloped nations in the world. In order to justify their interference, colonialists frequently created an imaginary Orient that was construed as less developed and less civilized than the West. The Orient, as an unknown and exotic place, always fascinated many Westerners and just like Oriental art fascinated the fantasy of Western art collectors in the past, today many people are fascinated by – more or less – Oriental dishes. Consumers are often curious about new dishes because they promise to be different from the mainstream food and therefore interesting. Like other ethnic products, food that seems to be different from the known and available attracts the interest of people exactly because of its difference from the norm. As bell hooks argues "within commodity culture, ethnicity becomes spice, seasoning, that can liven up the dull dish that is mainstream white culture" (21). The image of Oriental food being special and exotic is used by chefs in restaurants who, for example create a *Salade Orientale* to cash in on the exotic allure of the name. The *Salade Orientale* is just a salad with shrimps, crabmeat, white wine, celery, onion and cucumber (Beard 161). The only "Oriental" aspect of it is the addition of rice, since normally this ingredient is not added to salads. The rice exoticizes the dish because it is closely associated with the East, the "Orient" and used in an uncommon context.

For similar reasons, in 2003, McDonald's added the Asian Chicken Salad to its menu in the United States to satisfy the consumer demand for healthier food. The salad is marketed first and foremost as a new, exotic, and healthy alternative to burgers and French fries. On their official homepage, McDonald's gives a detailed description of the salad "A harmonious blend of crisp greens, warm orange-glazed chicken (grilled or crispy), snow peas, *edamame,* mandarin oranges and toasted almonds. Add the Newman's Own Low Fat Sesame Ginger Dressing and we're talking pure inspiration" (McDonald's). Most of the ingredients listed above are associated with the East, the "Orient." They come from different nations in the East, as for example mandarin oranges from China, or *edamame* (a Japanese side dish made of immature soybeans) from Japan. These different ingredients tossed together create an 'Oriental' salad which is supposedly different from Western salads. Additionally, the notion of a "harmonious blend" and adjectives such as "crisp greens" emphasize the idea that this salad will be fresh and healthy. In order to give the salad a mysterious touch, uncommon ingredients like snow peas and *edamame* are used while the slogan "seek flavor – find harmony" (McDonald's) evokes the idea of finding harmony via food, alluding to the Asian concept of Zen. The name and advertisement of the Asian Chicken Salad elicit curiosity in the potential consumer and promise to be an ideal way to relieve oneself from the stress of a hectic work day, hence creating an alternative foodscape for Western consumers. Some familiar ingredients such as chicken and greens are used to reassure the consumer and provide him/her with familiar aspects of a salad. This menu item not only promises to be a healthy food choice, but it also transfers ideas of up-to-date-ness and a touch of modernity with its Asian ingredients, since nowadays Asian movies, perfumes or clothing styles are *en vogue* in the West. McDonald's uses old images and stereotypes of the Orient in order to sell a new product. They present consumers a salad that diverts very little from the food they are used to and has nothing to do with salads eaten in any Asian country. The Asian Chicken Salad is an Oriental dish, constructed and imagined by American fast food chefs for American consumers.

Yet while McDonald's Asian Chicken Salad may be a poor attempt to ride on the wave of Asian health food, most ethnic food consumed in the U.S. today is closer to the original food. Still, Lisa Heldtke calls the preparation and consumption of all ethnic food, which she points out is mainly from so-called third world countries, "food colonialism" (xv). She argues that the choice to eat different, exotic food is often "strongly motivated by an attitude with deep connections to Western colonialism" (xv). Even when consumers endeavor to be respectful towards other cultures and their cuisine, according to Heldke they are not likely to overcome their colonial culinary attitude. Already in the nineteenth and early twentieth century, adventurous Europeans used different, uncommon ingredients in completely new contexts and thereby created new dishes that were meant to be "exotic" and therefore interesting. Sometimes it "even seem[ed] desirable, instead of risking the addition of a foreign dish to the American repertory, to invent instead an American dish with a foreign name and a vague resemblance to a foreign creation" (Root and Rochemont 276). Some dishes with a supposedly exotic background such as Chop Suey or Vichyssoise were inspired by foreign food cultures and indeed were invented in the United States (Ross and Rochemont 277). Heldke accuses such culinary adventurers as merely using foreign cuisines as "raw materials to serve their own interest" (7) and she claims that such people are less likely to be interested in the authentic cuisine of another culture.

However, if people are exposed and have access to a great variety of new tastes, this does not automatically mean that they are obsessive about exotic food and indifferent to the original cultural context of the dishes. Instead, the intake of interesting new dishes can also signify openness toward culinary experiments. Lucy Long suggests the term "culinary tourism" in her essay "Culinary Tourism: A Folkloristic Perspective on Eating and Otherness," instead. Her choice of terminology seems to be more appropriate since Long defines culinary tourism as follows: "culinary tourism is about food as subject and medium, destination and vehicle, for tourism. It is about individuals exploring foods new to them as well as using food to explore new cultures and ways of being" (20). This approach takes into consideration that it is not wrong if people open themselves to a new and unknown cuisine. Like other tourists, people who decide to go on vacation and choose a certain place in order to learn about other cultures, culinary tourists want to learn about new cuisines unknown to them (21). Indeed, some tourists may have colonialist attitudes, but by choosing to take part in a new (culinary) cultural experience, they show openness towards different (eating) cultures. Unlike culinary colonialists who "regard a colonized culture *not* as a culture in the full sense [...] but as a source of materials to be extracted and used to enhance our own cultures" (43), culinary tourists are interested in different cultures and their culinary heritage. Culinary colonialists think of their food culture and eating habits as the universal standard, against which other food cultures are measured. They seldom question their own habits but tend to think of deviant culinary customs as "the Other." Quite on the contrary, culinary tourists use food as a "contact zone" (Pratt) with other culinary cultures and do not judge or categorize food that is unknown to them. Their interest lies in the difference of the exotic food and this difference is recognized and appreciated, not judged. Mary Louis Pratt defined contact zones in *Imperial Eyes: Travel Writings and Transculturation* as "social spaces where cultures meet, clash, and grapple with each other, often in contexts of highly asymmetrical relations of power, such as colonialism, slavery, or their aftermaths as they are lived out in many parts of the world today" (7). It is important to note in this context that Pratt understands that the local and the global have to be seen as inextricably interconnected as nowadays local cultures are set in global contexts and vice versa. One result of the interactions of the local and the global are new hybrid cultural formations. Thus, when talking about the influence of Japanese food in the United States, the idea of culinary colonialism or Orientalism is not the only theoretical framework that should be used. Although there are examples such as McDonald's Asian Chicken Salad, which have to be seen as an Orientalist appropriation of foreign foodways, many American consumers of Japanese food today are curious culinary tourists, genuinely interested in new dishes. By choosing to consume a culturally different dish, consumers engage in a culinary dialogue and thereby cross culinary boundaries.

## The Raw and the Cooked: Food Writing Against Orientalizing and Othering Via Food

In Japanese-American literature, food often serves as an indicator of difference between Japanese and Americans. In many novels, memoirs, and autobiographies, food is shown to be used by Japanese immigrants as a form of resistance to Americanization and as a connection to their national identity and heritage (Ho 3). Additionally, some stories show how Japanese are Othered by Americans by means of food. In most cases, unknown food is differentiated from familiar food as suspicious, inedible and often, at the same time, as exotic and alluring. People consuming these "weird" foods do not belong to one's own group, but are always "different." As Susan Kalcik puts it, "strange people equals strange food" and consequently "not-so strange people equals not-so strange food" (37). Defining some food as weird, strange or inedible, people determine those who are like them as well as those who are not, in the case of Asian food this creates an Orientalist discourse.

One example of the "Othering" of Japanese or Japanese-Americans by food can be found in Carla Lockwood's novel *Dixieland Sushi*, which highlights the narrow-mindedness of food-based racial bias. The protagonist of the novel, Jen Nakamura Taylor, recalls her childhood, growing up half white, half Japanese in a small town "known for fried pickles, an annual barbecue cook-off, and a higher than average teen pregnancy rate" (7) in the South of the United States. *Dixieland Sushi* is not only a geographical journey from the North of the United States to the South, but it is also a journey back in time, as Jen frequently recalls her childhood as a Japanese-American in Dixieland. At the beginning of the novel, Jen remembers her tenth birthday party at the local roller rink. What starts off as a wonderful day in her life ends in a disaster when her Japanese mother unpacks "a giant Tupperware tray full of foul-smelling sushi and pickled vegetables" (4) and scares the boy Jen has a crush on. She admits that "in the privacy of my own home, away from the questioning eyes of Kevin Peterson, I would gladly have devoured the sushi and pickled treats" (5). In front of her American friends, however, she was not able to appreciate or touch the food. Especially "under his [Kevin's] gaze, as I saw the look of horror and surprise" (5), Jen is unable to eat her favorite food. As the text suggests, here the Japanese-American girl is exposed to a gaze which renders her different from the American mainstream. The fact that her Japanese mother offers rice and fish as a birthday meal in a place that is famous for meat and a barbecue cook-off further emphasizes the difference between her family and the American community they live in. Jen is treated as different by her friends because they suspect her of eating strange food at home. In this situation, Jen, a girl born and raised in the South of the United States, celebrating her birthday at a roller rink and dreaming her own dreams, including marriage to Kevin Peterson, is no longer part of her American environment. Instead, she becomes an outsider and suspicious to her friends.

In contrast to the stereotype that all Japanese people eat sushi all the time, as an adult Jen herself cannot handle to eat "gruesome raw varieties" (35) like squid, eel, or octopus which are usual for original Japanese sushi. Instead, Jen reveals that she is "strictly a cooked-meat only sushi eater" (35). Her preference of sushi substituting fish with meat shows how much Jen, as second generation Japanese-American, is Americanized. At the same time, she has the very Japanese notion that "sushi is a gourmet delicacy that shouldn't be consumed casually like French fries" (36). Despite her Japanese heritage, Jen does not feel very Japanese and she sometimes even forgets that she has Japanese roots. This becomes most obvious in her childhood wish to become a country western star, "it didn't occur to me that I had two major stumbling blocks to my Nashville dreams: namely that I can't sing and that I was half Japanese. There were no Asian people in Nashville" (121). Throughout the book, Jen frequently questions her identity as a Southern-Japanese-American girl or woman. Although she considers herself an American, she cannot and does not want to completely deny her ethnic heritage and food. As Jen grows up and works as a producer for a popular television show in Chicago, she recognizes that "sushi these days is as common as hot dogs" (35). Over the decades the Americans seem to have embraced sushi and the dish has become rooted in the American culinary culture. It is consumed on a regular basis and has become part of everyday life.

Thus, the image of sushi shifted from a strange, uncivilized, Oriental dish to a common, trendy fast food snack. The supposedly "raw" sushi in Lévi-Strauss's sense is no longer completely rejected by the American mainstream and the boundary between what is considered civilized and what is considered uncivilized is transgressed. At the same time, sushi in the United States is consumed as a snack, comparable to hot dogs and French fries and thereby transformed from a special high-class dish for upper-class consumers to a fast-food dish affordable for everyone. The portrayal of sushi in *Dixieland Sushi* reveals that among other things, the idea of food in a culture is never fixed but is permanently in flux.

A similar sense of un-belonging and being different is evoked in the food-centered autobiography by Linda Furiya. In her food memoir *Bento Box in the Heartland*, food shapes the Japanese identity of the author and her Japanese parents, who immigrated to the United States after World War II. Linda, like Jen in *Dixieland Sushi*, feels different from other children of her community because of the food she consumes.

Linda Furiya grew up in the only Japanese family in Versailles; a homogenous small town in the American Midwest, and like Jen, Linda refuses her familiar Japanese dishes in front of her American friends. In order to fit in, she expects her mother to make her "a classic elementary school lunch of a bologna, cheese, and Miracle Whip sandwich and a bag of Durkee's potato sticks" (5). Her mother, however, insists on making her a classical Japanese *obentō*, including "three round rice balls wrapped in waxed paper" (5).[10] Realizing that her "*obento* lunches were a glaring reminder of

---

10 In her article "Japanese Mothers and Obentōs," Anne Allison discusses the cultural relevance of *obentōs* in Japan.

the ethnic differences between my peers and me" (5), Linda refuses to touch them in front of her friends. Instead, she eats "cookies and apples with [her] friends and consumes the rest of [her] lunch in the stall of the girl's bathroom" (11). Linda eats her Japanese food in secrecy, as if it were something forbidden, because she knows that in order to fit into her American community, she has to eat American food. As Kalcik puts it, "a group's eating habit is one clue to which side of the boundary the strangers should be placed" (47) and Linda wants to belong to the American side.

The fact that Linda's mother refuses to make her an entirely American lunch reflects the effort of her parents to preserve their Japanese eating habits. By clinging to their familiar food, which gives them a sense of home, Linda's parents separate themselves from their American environment. While many Japanese immigrants have indeed changed their eating habits to adapt to their new homeland, some immigrants like Linda's parents do not want to give up their heritage.[11] For them, food serves as a connection to Japan and the kitchen becomes the center of her mother's memory. Linda's mother defines herself through food and she vividly remembers her last meal in Japan before she left for the United States to marry Linda's father. In *Bento Box in the Heartland*, most stories evolve around food and the struggle Linda's parents face while trying to find proper ingredients.

The author recalls how her parents "devoted their time, heart, and energy to maintaining their Japanese diet" (85) and shows how "ethnic or regional identity can be acted out within the home by eating certain foods prepared in special ways" (Abrahams 20). One of the main concerns for Linda's parents is not to run out of Japanese ingredients which they need for the familiar taste. Linda remembers how her parents were "carefully eyeballing the remaining fish shavings and kombu[12]" and how her mother would "calculate exactly how many ingredients remained before doomsday" (94). For her parents, Japanese ingredients are important to make familiar food which helps them to acculturate into their new environment. They need the taste of Japanese food in order to feel comfortable and to find relief from their daily hardships and thus, running out of their Japanese provisions equals doomsday for them. Of course they would not starve

---

11  For more information about the eating habits of Japanese immigrants see Katarzyna Cwiertka "Eating the Home Land."
12  *Kombu* is edible kelp which is widely used in Asian cuisine.

without the Japanese ingredients, but an important part of their life would be missing. Once Linda's parents take their children to a trip to Florida not, as the children hope, to visit the newly opened Disney World, but to buy fresh seafood in order to refill their stock in time. *Bento Box in the Heartland* illustrates how identities can be strongly connected to food by showing how Linda tries to assimilate to her environment by eating American food while her parents continue to define themselves as Japanese by consuming Japanese food.

In the novel, Linda also learns that being different from her friends is not necessarily a weakness. The author describes the 1960s town in the Midwest where she lived as a child as "a meat-eating town where pork constituted seasoning, whether it was a couple of slabs of bacon cooked with canned green beans or bits of ham in pea soup or bacon grease baked in cornbread" (87). Linda's best friend Tracy Martin is a girl that seems to embody the perfect American girl – with "the blond June Cleaver mom, the bedroom spun in pink and white, and the red barns of the family farm" (65) – and who perfectly fits into these surroundings. Linda envies Tracy's Americanness and desperately wants to be like her. She is afraid that her parents will embarrass her with their Japanese behavior and thus will prevent her from being a real American girl. She recalls that "the differences reflected at my home were glaring. We had to take our shoes off at the door. My parents spoke a foreign language. In our kitchen, a wok was poised on the burner instead of a cast-iron skillet. A jelly jar hosted chopsticks" (69). However, Tracy wants to spend a day with Linda's family and to Linda's surprise, she is fascinated by the Japanese family. She is willing to try Ms. Furiya's Japanese omelet with rice, vegetables, and *tonkatsu* (Japanese deep-fried pork cutlet) sauce without hesitation and the next day at school, "instead of making it sound freakish, she spoke with the enthusiasm of someone who had spent the weekend at Disney World" (79). Obviously, for Tracy, who becomes a culinary tourist, the day with Linda's Japanese family resembles a short voyage to another culture and the difference of the Japanese culture from the American culture turns out to be not threatening but interesting, exciting, and fascinating. By entering the transnational foodscape of Linda's family, she is able to enjoy and appreciate this foreign culture.

At the same token, Linda recognizes that differences within a culture can enrich any culture and that she as an American with a Japanese heritage can educate people about Japanese food and culture (70). With her book, Linda Furiya not only recalls childhood memories, but she also attempts to make Japanese food more familiar by seasoning her memoir with Japanese recipes of dishes she refers to in the narration. Furiya encourages her readers to try to cook these dishes themselves and presents her stories and the recipes as part of Japanese-American history and culture. Tracy's reaction to the unknown food shows that Lévi-Strauss's idea that unknown or "raw" food has to be classified as uncivilized is not necessarily true. The boundaries between different cultures, as he suggests them, are not always clear. Instead, these supposedly clear and stable boundaries are constantly transgressed and blurred. Like Tracy, many consumers take a more transnational approach to food and are interested in and open to new tastes.

## Consuming Gender: Distrusting the Dichotomy of Masculine Meat and Female Fish

America has always been and still is a nation of predominantly meat-consumers (Root and Rochemont 192) and a vast quantity of meat is consumed annually in the United States (Pillsburg 24). Beef in particular is closely connected to American identity, and evokes romantic notions of an agricultural past and of cowboys herding cattle. Thus, according to Christopher Schlesinger and John Willoughby "for reasons of geography, history, and cultural identity, beef has become the emblematic food of our country" (35) and as "America's self-image was largely formed in and around the cattle drive" (36), beef symbolized and still epitomizes "an indigenous American life style" (Root and Rochemont 194)[13]. The majority of Americans prefer beef to other meats and a large variety of different beef dishes such as burgers or steak are frequently associated with American food. The consumption and preparation of meat is regarded as a male domain, especially the barbecue (P. Harris 17-19). While conjuring up a meal in the kitchen remains the duty of the housewife, outdoor cooking is predominantly done by men. Leslie Brenner connects the desire of men to grill meat at a barbecue with "the incipient pyromaniac boy in every man" (31) and sus-

---

13 The use of the term "indigenous" is problematic in this context as Weaverly Root and Richard De Rochemont refer to Caucasians and not Native American life styles.

pects that a sense of adventure and freedom is still attached to barbecues (31). Fish, however, was seldom considered appropriate masculine food in the West, as Murcott argues, because it has to be consumed in small portions (57). In the West meat, especially red meat, is considered masculine food, whereas fish is considered female food, thus attaching gender norms to food (Lupton 107).

In Japan, however, fish is part of the national cuisine and the consumption of sushi is not only considered appropriate for both men and women, but sushi bars are still considered a male space. Meat being acknowledged as masculine and a symbol of America and fish being a marker of femininity and symbol of Japan reinforced Orientalist ideas of a female East and masculine West. This is reflected in Japanese-American literature as well. In *Dixieland Sushi*, Jen's hometown is described as being famous for the annual barbecue cook-off, and Linda in *Bento Box in the Heartland* lives in a "meat-eating town" (87). In both books, the protagonists feel misplaced in these meat-centered communities because their cuisine is dominated by rice and fish, the traditional foods in Japan.

Ruth Ozeki's transnational novel *My Year of Meat*, plays with this idea of the masculine West represented by meat and the feminine East represented by fish and Japanese dishes. The main characters relate to each other on a transcontinental, transnational level and national identities are constructed via food. The story trails the life of two women who live in different worlds and create a transcontinental bond.[14] Jane Takagi-Little, a Japanese-American woman living in the United States, gets the commission to coordinate a documentary series for a Japanese audience. Meanwhile Akiko Ueno, a Japanese housewife, struggles in Tokyo to please her abusive husband, who happens to be the Japanese producer of the show. The only connection between these two different characters is the documentary series entitled "My American Wife," which is meant to increase the popularity of meat in Japan. The documentary is financed by an American meat company and thus, according to the Japanese producer, it is of great importance that each episode of the show should "culminate in the celebration of a featured meat, climaxing in its glorious consumption" (12). In order to encourage

---

14 Shameem Black discusses the topic of transnational feminism in *My Year of Meat* in her article "Fertile Cosmofeminism: Ruth L. Ozeki and Transnational Reproduction."

Japanese housewives to emulate American meat recipes, and to make them "feel the hearty sense of warmth, comfort, of hearth and home – the traditional family values symbolized by red meat in rural America" (12), the documentary should "bring the heartland of America into the homes of Japan" (14). Ironically, although promoting "My American Wife" in Japan as authentically and typically American, the Japanese producer Joichi Ueno only accepts *his* ideas of America on screen. He refers to market studies revealing that "the average Japanese wife finds a middle-to-upper-middle-class white American woman with two to three children to be both sufficiently exotic and yet reassuringly familiar" (17-18). In contrast to Joichi, who aims to recreate a *Japanese idea* of America on screen, claiming this version of the U.S. to be "authentic," Jane, who lives and works in the United States, tries to represent America as more multicultural. Ironically, as a consequence, she frequently receives memos from her Japanese superior of how to depict the U.S. accurately to a Japanese audience as Joichi's notions of America does not match Jane's version, instead reducing the country to a homogenous nation of happy meat eaters. The aim of the Japanese executives is to sell an *image* of the United States in order to sell meat. However, Jane does not limit her selection of American housewives according to the guidelines of the show and confronts Joichi with an African American family, a Southern patchwork family with twelve children, of whom ten are adopted from different parts of the world, and a lesbian, vegetarian couple. Joichi is outraged by her selection and laments that the show has a "solid program concept, and the Americans are ruining it" (51). Because of her choices, Jane's production has to undergo severe editing by the Japanese producer and in the end, when she starts to uncover criminal production methods of the meat industry, she is fired. To make things worse, Jane is sexually harassed and almost raped by Joichi, who is represented in stereotypical terms as a sexist, lascivious Japanese man.

On the other side of the Pacific, Akiko Ueno, the wife of the Japanese producer, faces a similarly hard fate. She has to cook all the recipes from the show for her husband and she has to give feedback by filling in a questionnaire. However, Akiko has a different idea of the United States than her husband. Whereas Joichi believes that one episode perfectly represents the United States, Akiko does not feel that this particular episode is authentic at all. Instead, she favors the episodes featuring the African American family or the lesbian couple, preferring those shows which her husband has dismissed. The problems of Joichi and Akiko are not limited to a different evaluation of the shows. Akiko is repressed and mistreated by her husband, who frequently abuses her, until the domestic violence escalates in her rape. At the end of the novel, she frees herself from her sadistic husband by leaving him and Japan to start a new life in America with the help of Jane. Thus, the transnational female bonding of Jane and Akiko helps them to cope with the patriarchal and sexist behavior of Joichi.

At the beginning of the novel, Japan is represented by the stereotypically submissive Japanese housewife Akiko, who does not like to eat meat and instead prefers vegetables, rice, and fish. Her husband Joichi believes that it is his duty to eat beef since he equates America with beef and he does not allow any other meat recipes. In the novel, he has the power to decide how the United States is represented in the TV show and he chooses to represent it as a country of beef eaters. Joichi connects his masculinity to the consumption of beef, and his attitude towards women reflects that he considers himself to be very masculine and powerful. Thus, he is outraged when his wife confronts him with a report that reveals that the consumption of too much meat might endanger his potency. The fact that *his* potency and not his wife's anorexia might be the reason why Akiko and he cannot have children enrages him and he tries to save his threatened masculinity by beating and raping his wife.

Additionally, *My Year of Meat* criticizes globalizing forces and homogenizing effects like the dominance of the meat industry with its criminal and dangerous producing methods, as well as the potential of transnational media to represent different cultures according to the sketchbook of the producers. However, on the other hand, transnational media shorten social and geographical distance, thereby making a friendship and bonding between Jane and Akiko possible. Additionally, Ruth Ozeki's novel questions what America really is like and what kind of food represents America. Jane Takagi-Little is torn between her Japanese and American identity, as even her hyphenated surname Takagi-Little reveals. Takagi, the Japanese part of her name literally translates as "high tree," an image that is countered by the American part of her name, Little. What is more, the juxtaposing meanings of the two parts of her name reflect her own in-betweenness, as she herself voices in the novel "being racially half" she is "neither here nor there" (13). While working on the documentary, Jane learns much about the country she is living in and finally comes to terms with her own hyphenated identity. As she recalls,

During my Year of Meat, I made documentaries about an exotic and vanishing America for consumption on the flip side of the planet, and I learned a lot: For example, we didn't even have cows in this country until the Spanish introduced them, along with cowboys. Even the tumbleweed, another symbol of the American West, is actually an exotic plant called Russian thistle, that's native not to America but to the wide-open steppes of Central Europe. All over the world, native species are migrating, if not disappearing, and in the next millennium the idea of an indigenous person or plant or culture will just seem quaint. Being half, I am evidence that race, too, will become relic. (20)

Jane is thrilled by the diversity of the United States, and tries to reflect the multiple ethnicities of the country with different meat recipes, including poultry and lamb, thereby celebrating different styles of meat.

Food is only one area in which cultural complexities appear in the book. Jane's hyphenated name additionally subverts Orientalist ideas of a dominant, masculine West and a passive, feminine East. Jane explains that the hyphenation was a "thrust of pure superstition" of her mother, who was stricken by the idea that her child would bear "an insignificant surname like Little through life" (13) and she believed that "the stature and eminence of her lofty ancestors would help equalize Dad's Little" (13). Thus, Jane's Japanese mother considers her own cultural roots superior to that of her American husband, at least when it comes to the surnames and she insists on adding something "big" to the belittling surname of her husband.

The idea of an active, masculine West and a passive, feminine East is further challenged in the novel by the title of the documentary "My American Wife," which is an allusion to the title of a novel written by Clive Holland in 1859, *My Japanese Wife*. Holland's Orientalist novel portrays the Japanese female character Mousmé as a submissive and decorative object to the Western gaze. In Ozeki's novel, none of the women is a decorative object which needs to be patronized by a male protagonist in former Hollywood movies, where an abused Japanese woman had to be saved by a Western hero. Akiko and Jane liberate themselves form their patriarchal environment and save each other with a female bond. Additionally, the show defines and exposes American women to an Eastern, Japanese gaze, thereby objectifying them as according to the ideas of the show these women are "Meat Made Manifest: ample, robust, yet never tough or hard to digest" (12). This statement equates American women with meat, or cattle, turning them into consumable objects for a Japanese audience.

The multiple recipes and ethnicities shown to be representative for the United States once more question the idea of America as a dominantly masculine and culturally unified country. The recipes in the show are cooked and presented to the audience by American *women*. If beef is the symbol of America in the novel, this status is questioned because the beef-industry is criticized for its corrupt and hazardous (company) politics, which are unveiled by Jane. Japanese businessmen like Joichi Ueno, who have fixed, outdated, and static images of America are criticized for their narrow minded attitude. Ueno tries to act as he expects an American to behave by excessively consuming beef, considering the consumption of lamb "un-American" (196). Trying to pass as American, Joichi further decides that he wants to be called John Wayno since he was once told that his Japanese family name Ueno sounds like "Wayno." He believes that the name gives him an American appeal and connects him to the actor John Wayne, an icon in the Western movie genre (52). His attempts to "turn American" seem ridiculous because he obviously does not understand American culture at all as he is blind to the multicultural heritage of the country. Instead, he rather clings to a stereotypical image of the United States which equates it with the "Old West."

Ozeki, however, deconstructs this romantic vision of America and warns her readers that randomly copying American meat production practices may lead to serious consequences such as miscarriages, impotence, and physical handicaps, resulting from the usage of synthetic hormones which are fed to cattle. Finally, Jane's insight that the cow is not an indigenous animal to the United States but was imported by the Spanish emphasizes the idea that the American identity is ethnic and immigrant.

### Recipes for Japaneseness: Exoticizing and Familiarizing Food in Cookbooks

In the novel, America is represented to a Japanese audience via recipes. The fact that Japanese producers evaluate which recipes are suitable to present the U.S. hints to the importance of cooking directions. If it is true that "cooking is a language of self-representation," as Meredith Abarca has stated ("Los Chilaquiles"120), cookbooks are a form of self-representation as well. Different people from inside and outside a culture write books about the cuisine of a nation (see Appadurai, "How to Make"). Cookbooks can be read as cultural texts since recipes reveal a lot about a culture through the ingredients used and dishes cooked. They often celebrate special holidays and include native ingredients and thereby represent a distinct culture. Additionally, cookbooks set the standard for a cuisine and preserve the culinary heritage of a country and, at the same time, make culinary traditions accessible to people from outside the culture.

However, cookbooks can also "reinforce stereotypical assumptions that are further diluted by the imperative of the marketplace" (Keller Brown and Mussel 4), for example by decorating recipes with pictures considered representative of or typical for the cuisine or by using ingredients associated with a certain region. Arjun Appadurai argues in "How to Make a National Cuisine" that cuisines are social and cultural constructs and therefore cookbooks are always selective in that they either include or exclude dishes (4). Culinary stereotypes and sometimes Orientalist notions of "the Other" can be created and standardized in cookbooks (Appadurai, "How to Make" 7). Cookbooks written by cultural insiders are often regarded as more authentic and less stereotypical than cookbooks written by cultural outsiders. In *Exotic Appetites* Heldke even criticizes ethnic cookbooks written by authors who do not belong to the culture they are writing about since she suspects them of exoticizing and defining the cuisine. As Heldke puts it, "ethnic cookbooks have long relied on stock descriptions of the mystery, culture, and exoticism of a land and its people to describe a cuisine" (122) and "many cookbooks take you to an imaginary tour of the country or countries in question, attempting to create in words the experiences the traveler allegedly experiences first hand" (122). These cookbooks are seen by Heldke as another example of colonial attitude and they are said to "almost invariably flounder in clichés and stereotypes" (122). It can be indeed argued that these cookbooks fabricate a hyperreal fantasy-foodscape as they create a false reality that is supposed to be consumed as real as, according to Umberto Eco there are "instances [...] where the American imagination demands the real thing and, to attain it, must fabricate the absolute fake" (8) that surpasses and improves the original, "real."

It can be, however, argued instead that recipes stemming from so-called outsiders merely offer a different way into a culinary culture. While "a Western style of dominating, restricting, and having authority over the Orient" (Said, *Orientalism* 3) might be executed by writing cookbooks which represent a culinary culture by a selected canon of dishes that define the (culinary) culture along the line of a discourse of gastronomic Orientalism, this need not be the case. Outsiders writing cookbooks may also broaden the idea of a culinary culture and, as culinary tour guides, offer their interested readers another, maybe more transnational view of an unknown food culture. Japanese cookbooks written by Western authors may wield authority over the cuisine by including and excluding recipes and dishes, yet this is also true for cultural insiders.

Most Japanese cookbooks in the United States create an image of Japan via food but they seldom reflect a colonial attitude. In the 1970s macrobiotic cooking became popular in America. Many Japanese cookbooks of that time written in English and intended for an American market, such as *Introducing Macrobiotic Cooking* (1978) or *Macrobiotic Cooking for Everyone* (1980), reflected this trend. These books introduced Western readers to a supposedly healthy, Japanese cuisine. The authors of these early Japanese cookbooks popular in America discerned the necessity to modify certain recipes to make them more accessible to the American consumer. The target groups of the majority of Japanese cookbooks written in English are either Japanese-Americans or Americans who are curious about or already fond of Japanese cuisine. Today, Japanese food is less unfamiliar in the United States, yet most Americans would seldom try to cook Japanese dishes themselves since the preparation seems complicated. Therefore, many Japanese cookbooks aimed at Western audiences emphasize simple recipes. In order to demystify the preparation of Japanese dishes, Japanese cookbooks for American users combine elements of traditional Japanese cooking techniques and ingredients with American elements, thereby blending culinary traditions from both sides of the Pacific. By mixing the exotic with the familiar, the dishes no longer remain strange and, Japanese food becomes part of the American food repertoire. Food, like other cultural commodities becomes familiar when the exotic ceases to be disturbingly exotic and the task of cookbook writers is to familiarize the reader with ethnic food *without* totally erasing the exotic (Heldke 102). The dishes need a certain degree of exoticism in order to remain interesting for the consumer.

The American journalist, food author, and lecturer on Japanese food culture Elizabeth Andoh uses American and Japanese ingredients in order to create hybrid dishes like her bi-cultural pasta made of fresh tomato sauce and Japanese buckwheat noodles. In her first cross-cultural cookbook *An American Taste of Japan* she presents "a collection of delicious recipes that make the most of what's best from two worlds: America and Japan" (Andoh 15). As "an American trained in a Japanese kitchen" (15) who frequently travels back and forth between Japan and the United States, Andoh is keen on sharing her experiences with Japanese food and endeavors to make Japanese food less exotic and more familiar to American consumers.

Similarly, Russ Rudezinski, an American owner of a Japanese restaurant in San Francisco, collected Japanese home-style recipes in his *Japanese Country Cookbook*. Rudezinski not only provides the reader with recipes but also with the historical background of the dishes, thereby making them familiar to a Western cookbook user. Additionally, he changes ingredients of some dishes or puts them in an American context, since in his opinion, "there is little harm in rearranging a Japanese menu so that it is more suited to American tastes and eating habits" (21). Even though sushi might be the best known Japanese dish in the West, Rudezinski does not center his book on sushi but instead focuses on cooked dishes like *yaki tori* (grilled chicken), *sakana-no shutū* (fish stew) or *gyū-niku dango* (beef patties). These dishes resemble the American idea of food while the cooking styles, ingredients, and names keep them exotic.

Another common method he uses to familiarize uncommon dishes is to compare them to familiar foods. He equals, for example, the great variety of sushi with the array of Western sandwiches (106). By comparing unknown food to known food, like sushi to sandwiches, and by substituting some Japanese ingredients with more common Western ingredients, the former seemingly inedible becomes edible for Americans. Again, it can be argued that in the *Japanese Country Cookbook*, written by an American, the Japanese cuisine is defined and altered by a cultural outsider. However, another perception would be to acknowledge Rudezinski's effort of explaining Japanese culture to American readers and seeing his cookbook as his way of re-imagining the Japanese culinary culture and making Japanese food more accessible to an American audience.

When recipes are seen "less a formula than general model, less an axiom of unchanging law and more a theory of possibilities" (Debra Castillo qtd. in Abarca "Authentic" 19), they are open to interpretation and to being reimagined in new ways. Recipes, like foods, are not static but are in a constant flux and will always be altered when cooked by different chefs, whether they come from different cultural backgrounds or not. When it comes to food, there are no fixed recipes nor are there definitions of what is considered civilized or uncivilized, edible or inedible, exotic or familiar.

## ENTER THE DRAGON ROLL: CONSUMING SUSHI IN THE UNITED STATES

Time after time, "the discovery of any food system starts with the shock of the unknown as it crosses one's sensory facilities" (Ashkenazi and Jacob 5). This is also true for the consumption of sushi in the United States. Among all dishes and Japanese flavors which seeped into the American culinary landscape, sushi was the most challenging. Sushi, once seen as the epitome of strangeness and otherness of Japanese food, entered the United States first at the end of the 1950s. The first Japanese restaurants serving sushi were opened in the 1960s by Japanese expatriates for Japanese businessmen, who sometimes introduced their American clients to the dish. However, despite the growing number of Japanese restaurants, most Americans were still inclined to believe that the consumption of raw fish was a sign of a lack of culinary skills and proof of barbaric eating habits. Dishes like *teriyaki* (a dish of meat or fish seasoned in a marinade), *tempura*, and *sukiyaki* (a Japanese stew pot) were consumed by Americans instead of sushi or *sashimi* (bite-size slices of raw fish).

The most daring and adventurous thing about sushi for a Western consumer is the fact that the dish is frequently considered to be raw fish only. "Through the 1960s, to most Americans fish was something that could be canned, battered, fried, grilled, steamed, broiled, roasted – but certainly not served raw" (Issenberg 94). However, although raw fish is processed for sushi, so are vegetables. Additionally, most of the fish used for sushi is prepared in some way, either being smoked, salted or pickled, and therefore cannot be considered to be "natural" or "raw" in Lévi-Strauss's sense. "The distances that matter in sushi are personal, not geographic" (xvii), as Issenberg observes in the introduction to his survey *The Sushi Economy*, since the *idea* of eating raw fish is still unfamiliar to many Westerners. However, globalizing processes made sushi widely available outside Japan and what Sasha Issenberg labeled the "sushi economy" contributed to an intercultural exchange (Issenberg xvii). The availability of sushi even in American supermarkets familiarized the exotic dish and it became increasingly fashionable to combine different ingredients and cooking styles in a new, creative way and to thereby create new Western versions of the originally Japanese dish without completely erasing the exotic flair.

With a rising health consciousness in the United States during the late 1970s and 80s, the American interest in sushi rose. The *Dietary Goals for the United States*, which "blamed fatty high-cholesterol foods for the increasing incidence of disease" (Issenberg 47) were issued in 1977 by the United States senate. Almost simultaneously, health experts started to promote "the benefits of omega-3 fatty acids, abundant in fish" (Issenberg 47). The Japanese cuisine, which mainly uses fresh vegetables, fruits, and soy products rather than meat or sugar, was seen as the reason why Japanese people have the lowest obesity rate and longest life expectancy in the world (Moriyama 4).

Today, the consumption of sushi is no longer special to Americans and it is widely considered "cool" and stylish (H. Kato, *Taberu Amerikajin* 154). What started in the 1970s as a foreign dish has developed into a part of American mainstream food culture and Japanese food authors like Kato Hiroko wonder whether Americans are addicted to the dish and love sushi more than Japanese consumers (*Sushi Purizu!* 155). Although the healthiness of sushi may have helped to spark an interest in the dish, the main reason sushi was successful in the United States was the idea that consuming sushi was sophisticated and a marker of high class. The fact that sushi was first expensive and served only as a delicacy made it easier to convince Americans that it was indeed a culinary delight.

Exotic dishes sometimes indicate aspects of class as well, since uncommon dishes with ingredients which are hard to get are considered a luxury, available only for those who can afford the price. By consuming these exclusive foods, "desirable because of their foreign origin" (Van der Veen

406), status and economic wealth are expressed.[15] In the United States, sushi started as one of these expensive dishes. The West Coast Movement, led by Alice Waters in the 1960s, stressed the importance of fresh food, and a new beauty ideal stressing thinness led to a diet craze. Therefore, light food was preferred to dishes using heavy sauces or red meat. During this time, sushi started to become "a diet food with social cost" (Issenberg 97). Through the decades until today, sushi continued to "represent the taste of the elite snob, as evidenced by the inclusion of tuna sashimi in *The Yuppie Handbook* on a list of 'Things Yuppies eat for lunch'" (Issenberg 98-99). With the rise of the popularity of Japanese food as health food, sushi became the signifier of class and status, thereby turning from "an exotic, almost unpalatable ethnic specialty [...] to haute cuisine of the most rarefied sort" (Bestor, "How Sushi Went Global" 56-57). Unlike Chinese food, Japanese food and sushi were never considered "cheap" food (Issenberg 93). While American fast food is often associated with a lower class life-style, expensive restaurants offering healthy food like sushi signify an urban upper-class such as the type represented in Brad Easton Ellis' novel *American Psycho*.

The novel revolves around the eccentric and upper-class yuppie life-style of the New York bachelor Patrick Bateman. His life is dominated by expensive clothes, brand-name products, high-tech entertainment gadgets, and frequent visits to expensive, *en vogue* restaurants. Japanese food in the story, which is set in the 1980s, is part of the upper-class life-style of the protagonist and the consumption of Japanese food emphasizes Bateman's high social status. The protagonist describes himself in one scene as "standing at the island in the kitchen I eat kiwi fruit and sliced Japanese apple-pear (they cost four dollars each at Gristede's) out of aluminum storage boxes that were designed in West Germany" (28). Here, the globalization and homogenization of exotic food becomes obvious. Fruits from different nations, like kiwi from New Zealand and a Japanese apple-pear, are contained in aluminum storage boxes from West Germany. The protagonist

---

15 The idea of what is considered a luxury good often changes over time and the status of some former exclusive foods such as lobster, coffee or tea changed "from being desired by many but possessed by few, to becoming widely available and, ultimately to being deemed social necessities" (Van der Veen 409). See also Leslie Brenner and George Lewis.

does not even comment on the taste of the fruits. Their consumption just indicates his class status, which proves that the consumption of exclusive food does not necessarily mean that the consumer appreciates the taste. Patrick Bateman's case proves that "in our culture, an appreciation of gastronomy indicates a certain level of sophistication. We equate being knowledgeable about food and wine with being well-traveled, cosmopolitan, urbane" (Brenner 162).

Evelyn, Bateman's girlfriend, uses food for similar purposes: to create an image of her own cosmopolitanism and status, she attempts to impress her guests with a dinner at her home. Evelyn is very interested in Japanese food and especially in sushi because she believes the dish to be part of a high-class life-style. Her cooking ambitions at her Japanese dinner reveal that she has not the faintest idea about the food she is preparing. She simply re-heats some bought *tempura* in a microwave, thereby destroying the crispy batter coating and freshness of the dish. The purchased sushi is arranged by her in the middle of a "glass table from Zona that Evelyn's father bought her like some mysterious apparition from the Orient" (12). In her desire to impress her friends and to host an exclusive, exotic dinner, she explicitly arranges the sushi in an "Oriental," mythical context. But her guests are ignorant and disrespectful to the food and one of them even sticks a chopstick in his yellowtail sushi, insisting that it moved (13). This behavior reveals the guest's narrow-mindedness as it arises from the common Orientalist prejudice that sushi is raw fish. Patrick, Evelyn, and their friends cannot be considered to be real food lovers, but seek to exploit the image of certain dishes. Throughout the whole novel, sushi is just another expensive commodity which is consumed as a marker of class. John Watters comes to a similar conclusion and argues in his essay "The Manners of Mass Murder: Eating Fear" that Bateman consumes food according to fashion trends (91). Watters argues that for the protagonist, "food serves as a purpose other than physical substance, just as fashionable clothing serves a purpose over and above covering the body" (Brenner 162). Ironically, in his desperate attempt to secure his social status, the protagonist consumes food formerly associated with people who are different, ethnic, "the Other." Although some of the characters openly state that they dislike the taste, they frequently visit sushi bars and restaurants. Food becomes part of a life-style, a public indicator of class and status and, as evident at Evelyn's dinner, no longer creates a familiar atmosphere or any bonds among friends.

The importance of food and the concern of the characters in the novel about food reveal how the upper-class "convert[s] their economic capital into symbolic capital, as a way of acquiring or maintaining prestige" (Van der Veen 420). Japanese dishes and ingredients are only used because they symbolize status, and the consumers are not interested in the cultural context or background of the dishes. Like any other brand, sushi and other Japanese foods are consumed for their image, thereby attaching a new Orientalist meaning to the dish. This consumption and digestion of food as a commodity is neo-colonialist, since Americans now give new meanings to exotic food that is imported to the United States.

*American Psycho* shows how upper-class life-style exploits sushi and other "exotic" dishes as markers of class. Yet, foreign dishes such as sushi can also become integrated into local foodways and enjoyed for their freshness, texture, and – yes – healthiness. Localization according to the taste of the consumers makes them less exotic and high-class. Re-interpretations of sushi are embraced for their taste and can be understood as transnational varieties of an originally Japanese dish.

## Fusion Cooking

In order to familiarize sushi and make it appealing to a broader consumer audience, many new, Western sushi versions were created and became part of the so-called California Cuisine, which puts great emphasis on the use of local ingredients such as avocado and embraces Asian and Mediterranean influences (Brenner 124). The idea of this kind of cooking, also called fusion cooking, is to bring different ingredients and cooking styles together and the result can be called transpacific, transcontinental, transnational dishes. The *Academic Dictionary of Cooking* defines fusion cooking as "a style that incorporates ingredients and/or methods from at least two different ethnic/regional cooking styles. Originally combining western and Oriental culinary art but now includes all ethnic cuisines" (171). The new creations of fusion cooking do not only cross national but culinary borders as well, thereby enabling new, hybrid eating experiences.

The main focus and appeal of these dishes is their difference: different ingredients from different cultural backgrounds are consciously combined in a new, daring way. The exotic touch of the dishes that contain unknown ingredients or the unusual usage of ingredients makes them especially interesting for Western consumers who want to make new culinary experiences in a familiar environment. The new creations are no longer part of a specific national cuisine, but a hybrid mix of Western and Eastern eating cultures and rely on the differences on both sides of the Pacific.

Examples of such fusion dishes are beef *teriyaki* or American Sushi. However, the concept of fusion cuisine is not new, since immigrants always tended to add familiar ingredients to the cuisine they found in their newly adopted country. Japanese immigrants to the United States added soy sauce, fish broth or *miso* (fermented soy paste) to Western dishes like spaghetti and omelet. This adding of a familiar taste to an exotic, unfamiliar dish helped them to cope with the new, unknown, often hostile environment. On the other hand, fusion restaurants helped to familiarize the 'old' American palate with the new ethnic foods.

One example for the latter is Rocky Aoki's Japanese steakhouse franchise Benihana, which first opened in New York City in 1964. The restaurants offer steaks prepared on Japanese grills in a Japanese farmhouse interior. Furthermore, Japanese chefs prepare the dishes at the table in front of the guests, thus adding the aspect of entertainment to the dining experience. The concept of the restaurants is to mix Japanese and American influences in order to offer the guest exotic but familiar dishes in an "exotic" yet familiar environment. Additionally, the preparation of *teppanyaki* (Japanese-style grilled beef) directly in front of the guests combines delicious food and entertaining elements and thereby makes the restaurants unique and popular (Belasco, "Ethnic Fast Foods" 5).

Ongoing globalization processes and the use of new transportation and preserving systems made fresh fish available and affordable almost everywhere in the United States. With Japanese food and sushi becoming chic, a great number of sushi cookbooks and food guides such as *Sushi for Dummies, The Connoisseur's Guide to Sushi, The Encyclopedia of Sushi Rolls* or *A Dictionary of Japanese Food* flooded the market. Apart from these books, which intend to explain sushi to a Western audience and familiarize them with the Japanese dish, the California Sushi Academy helped to integrate sushi into the American foodscape.

## The California Sushi Academy

Founded in 1998 by Sugiura Toshi, the California Sushi Academy offers different sushi classes for anyone, regardless of gender and ethnic background, who is interested in the preparation of the dish. Sugiura, "the pioneer of American Sushi" (Corson 4), realized that the rising demand for sushi led to an increased need for sushi chefs, since many fusion restaurants wanted to offer sushi on the menu and turn a profit with the sushi boom. He concluded that the traditional education of a sushi chef, which is based on a long apprenticeship, takes too much time and that it would make more sense to train new sushi chefs in only a few months. Many of his fellow Japanese sushi chefs, who are very protective about their profession, disliked the idea of introducing outsiders to the world of sushi and some of them even considered Sugiura to be a traitor (Corson 4).[16] These traditionalist sushi chefs reinforce the boundary between original, Japanese sushi and its preparation techniques and the new American Sushi. For them, a clear distinction is of central importance because they want to ensure that this national dish is prepared and defined by Japanese chefs in the future.

Sugiura, however, is convinced that "America had already embraced sushi, and it would be foolish not to train American chefs" (Corson 4). For him, the education of sushi chefs in a short time is a logical consequence of the sushi-boom in the United States and necessary in order to secure the good reputation of the dish. He observed how an increasing number of untrained chefs started to produce sushi on their own, often lacking the most basic knowledge about hygiene and proper technique. At the California Sushi Academy, students learn in different classes how to prepare traditional Japanese sushi, the proper usage of Japanese cooking utensils, and the meaning and history of Japanese food. Since most of the graduates are likely to work in the United States, the academy also encourages their students to create their own *American* rolls. In the United States, American sushi rolls are the most popular version of sushi, so that "most sushi rolls in America have never been served in Japan" (Corson 81).

---

16 In Japan, producing sushi is traditionally considered to be a masculine realm. Some sushi chefs even believe that women should not make sushi at all, since their hands are warmer than male hands and thereby more likely to spoil the fish.

The best example of such a popular American roll is the famous California Roll, which is a Western form of *makizushi*. Invented by Mashita Ichiro in the 1960s in Los Angeles, it has become synonymous with sushi in the West. Although the roll turned out to be a tremendous success, it was not consciously invented to offer Westerners a roll without fish. Mashita had problems with the tuna supply and therefore substituted the fish with the readily available avocado, a fatty fruit that has a similar texture in the mouth as tuna (Corson 82; Ikezawa 38). Even though it was not first and foremost created to adapt sushi to the American palate, today the California Roll is "considered the key innovation that made sushi accessible to Americans" (Corson 81). Ever since its introduction, many different American sushi rolls are being invented and are entering the international foodscape. Students of the California Academy, for instance, are specially trained to create California rolls particularly for American consumers. They learn, for instance, that most Americans are reluctant to have black food like seaweed and therefore invented inside-out rolls, where the rice coats the roll, hiding the black seaweed inside the roll (Corson 82; Ikezawa 38).

American sushi rolls are larger than Japanese rolls and use fatty ingredients absent in the Japanese version. American rolls, with pork, mayonnaise or even ice cream are no longer a healthy alternative and "a sushi takeout box from an American supermarket could easily contain as many calories as two slices of pizza, and the rolls served in restaurants are often worse" (Corson 27). Sushi, formerly appreciated for having low calories, is now no longer necessarily a health food and American Sushi has become more an exotic version of finger food and is often used as an appetizer at parties.

## American Sushi Cookbooks

The first great wave of books about Japanese food and Japanese food preparation appeared in America already in the late 1970s. More recently, a shift to promote the Japanese diet in general and sushi in particular as fancy food for stylish parties and as a supposedly healthy alternative to heavy meat dishes has taken place. Sushi is no longer positioned among other exotic dishes in contemporary cookbooks. This reflects how much it is familiarized in the American culinary culture. One example is *Sushi for Dummies*, a book from a whole series of instruction books. By introducing formerly exotic sushi alongside topics as American history (*U.S. History for Dummies*) or online market places (*eBay for Dummies*), the dish becomes part of American mainstream culture. *Sushi for Dummies* explains the basics of sushi, dispelling the "*huge* misconception that sushi means raw fish, when it really means vinegared rice" (11). The two authors Judi Strada and Mineko Takane Moreno introduce traditional Japanese sushi but also add recipes for fishless varieties. Using ingredients such as avocado, hot chili sauce, mayonnaise, sweet barbecue sauce, or mango they give sushi a familiar context and further assure their readers that making sushi is easy and that it will soon become as much second nature to every American as "building a cheeseburger" (15). Strada and Takane Moreno explain that there are many different types of sushi today and that the origin of most of these variations is not clear anymore (13). They do not restrict sushi to the Japanese original but instead recommend using leftovers to make sushi "using what's on hand" (163). Expanding the opportunities to serve sushi in the United States, the authors include a selection of "Glamorous Sushi" for parties with sushi variations in matching colors and a recipe for a birthday cake sushi. With their innovative and sometimes daring recipes, the authors make sushi a less expensive and exclusive food which is primarily consumed in restaurants but they also offer it as a fashionable party food easily prepared at home by any American host.

Tracy Griffith, an American chef and graduate of the California Sushi Academy takes a similar approach in her cookbook *Sushi American Style*. Griffith focuses on the preparation of sushi without the use of raw fish in order to offer alternatives for those who would like to try sushi but feel weary about eating raw fish. Her sushi rolls, like the Thanksgiving Roll containing turkey and sweet cranberries, blend in perfectly with the American dining habits and she also suggests sushi rolls for "Monday night football gatherings" to be served alongside potato chips and beer (77). Suggesting a new use of sushi for typical American family gatherings or national American holidays like Thanksgiving, she integrates sushi into the American culinary culture. Following her credo that "whatever you roll up with this [seasoned rice], you are making sushi" (California Sushi Academy), Griffith recommends, as do Strada and Takane Moreno, the use of leftovers for making sushi rolls. Since many Americans crave sweet deserts, she offers recipes for American sweet sushi rolls such as the Elvis Roll made of peanut butter and bananas, thus resembling Elvis Presley's favorite sandwiches.

Most recipes in her book have little in common with the original preparation of Japanese sushi and clearly give the dish more than an American twist. Griffith caters to the demands of American consumers, who prefer the American versions of sushi to the original. Because of the extreme popularity of localized American Sushi in the United States, most restaurants, especially fusion cuisine restaurants, offer a large variety of rolls made of avocado, cream cheese, or roast beef. When comparing American sushi rolls to Japanese sushi rolls, it is evident that the ingredients used are culturally and locally specific.[17] Not only are the ingredients changed for the American market – the rolls themselves are given names that position the rolls within a familiar, American context by referring to American cities (New York Roll, Boston Roll, Philadelphia Roll, Seattle Roll) or by using names that are reminiscent of American history (Crazy Horse, Mayflower, Titanic). Other names allude to exotic, Japanese roots (Samurai Roll, Bonsai Roll, Happy Sumo, and Tokyo Sunrise), thereby keeping the exotic exotic and reflecting a culinary colonialism.

## IMAGINING SUSHI OTHERWISE

Many Japanese sushi chefs are extremely reluctant to prepare American Sushi. In Japan, the altered American versions of sushi are not considered to be sushi but rather a new American dish, sushi as *imagined* by Americans. Japanese food writers like Kato Hiroko, Matsumoto Hirotaka, or Ikezawa Yasushi acknowledge the popularity of sushi in the United States and do not criticize the modification of sushi in the West. Instead they understand that sushi can have different meanings in different countries (Matsumoto) and thereby they reinforce the idea that the meaning of a cuisine is never fixed. Kato Hiroko explains in *Sushi Purizu!* to Japanese readers the difference between the Japanese idea of sushi and the American idea of sushi. She does not criticize the American way of consuming sushi made using

---

17 In his *Encyclopedia of Sushi Rolls*, Ken Kawasumi introduces readers to 180 different rolls, most of them made of Western ingredients to be served as party food.

avocado and mayonnaise and drinking Coke, since she acknowledges that Japanese consumers prefer their pizza with squid while drinking ōolong tea, thereby consuming pizza in a Japanese way (73). Kato observes that much more sushi is consumed in the United States than in Japan (7) and suspects that the Americans are not only fond of their taste of sushi, but that the originality of the dish and the entertainment in American sushi restaurants contribute to a positive image of sushi and Japan in America (68). Indeed, in the United States, sushi is frequently served in an entertaining surrounding were popular music is played and sometimes even karate shows add to the entertainment for the guests. These restaurants see "Japanese food with an American taste of entertainment" (Issenberg 89). In Japan, however, sushi is normally consumed in silence to appreciate the taste (H. Kato, *Sushi Purizu*) and "the sushi experience is a matter of getting to know the chef at your neighborhood sushi bar, visiting frequently, and letting him choose what he thought you would like" (Corson 101). Thus, it is not only the ingredients of sushi which are changed in the United States, but the context in which the dish is consumed and altered as well.

In Japan the preparation of sushi is traditionally considered to be a male realm and the same is true for most traditional sushi bars. However, the more recent trend of serving American Sushi in Japanese sushi bars with Jazz music playing in the background increasingly attracts young Japanese women (Corson 54). American Sushi restaurants such as Rainbow Roll Sushi in Tokyo are less traditional and offer a more modern ambience. Rainbow Roll Sushi advertises itself on its official homepage as a place for "casual dining" (wdi.co.jp) and the menu is full of sushi and rolls that would "scandalize traditionalists" (Issenberg xxiii). Nevertheless, not all American rolls are reproduced and served in the restaurant, but only "rolls that can be served in Japan" are offered (H. Kato, *Sushi Purizu!* 220). The Japanese owners of the restaurant acknowledge that sushi, like other cultural commodities, changes when it travels across national and cultural borders.

The history of sushi shows that the dish was always in flux, changing over time and "remaking itself over centuries due to shifting pressures of economics and culture" (Issenberg xxi). Sushi was "invented" in the eighteenth century as a means to preserve fish with vinegared rice. In the nineteenth century, it was mainly sold in *Edo* as a street snack, before it was served as an upscale, formal dinner. Today, it is served in different variations not only in the United States, but also in Japan, where the usage of a conveyer belt in some sushi stores to deliver sushi to guests, as well as the invention of a sushi robot that processes sushi, made eating sushi for a light lunch or snack popular again. This informal form of consuming sushi paved the way for American Sushi in Japan. Nowadays, the so-called New-York-Style Sushi is an established genre in the Tokyo restaurant culture (Issenberg xxiii). Yet, American Sushi is not only imported to Japan. In some cases, it is again modified to make it more appealing and palatable for the Japanese consumer, (H. Kato, *Sushi Purizu!* 220) thereby localizing American Sushi in Japan.

Sushi, traveling from Japan to the United States, is modified and made into American Sushi and then travels back to Japan, thereby contributing to a transnational globalizing process. Both culinary cultures influence each other's eating habits and challenge their own ideas about the "Other" food by openly engaging in a culinary exchange. Although the diet of the United States is centered on meat, sushi has helped to popularize fish. On the other side of the Pacific, the Japanese started to consume meat and dairy products after regular contact with the United States, and today they even eat sushi rolls containing beef. Cookbooks and restaurants help to familiarize food by explaining and adjusting it for the target audience without erasing too many exotic features.

Mixing different ingredients or cooking styles is not a new phenomenon in the United States but "is rather a recurring theme in our history as eaters" writes Gabaccia in *We Are What We Eat* (3). Nevertheless, since food is "linked to overall social hierarchies and power relations" (Counihan and Van Estrik 3), the question of whether using or not using and mixing different ingredients and different culinary styles in American Sushi might or might not be a sign of culinary colonialism and disrespect for different culinary cultures cannot be conclusively answered. It could be argued that using Japanese techniques to create an American version of sushi for an U.S. market is a violation of Japanese culinary habits because this new version could be consumed as just another exotic, Oriental dish, modified to meet the Western taste preferences. Yet, at the same time, Japanese and Japanese-American sushi chefs take part in the creation of American sushi versions, as for example Sugiura Toshi and his students at the California Sushi Academy. Additionally, the creators of these new rolls do not claim at all that these creations are Japanese originals. Instead, the blending for Japanese techniques and the modification of sushi can be judged as an appreciation of the Japanese dish. Eating habits are culturally learned and dishes are constructed, i.e. imagined, by those who prepare them. Therefore, they are not only frequently changed when transferred to another culture but also when prepared by another chef.

Theodore Bestor argues that the availability and popularity of sushi and the modification of the dish do not mean

> that sushi has lost its status as Japanese cultural property. Globalization doesn't necessarily homogenize cultural differences nor erase salience of cultural labels. Quite contrary, it grows the franchise. In the global economy of consumption, the brand equity of sushi as Japanese cultural property adds to the cachet of both the country and the cuisine. (Bestor, "How Sushi Went Global" 61)

According to his argument, the fact that sushi is still considered Japanese and works as a brand of its own adds to the attraction of the dish and therefore the national character of the sushi is indeed preserved despite all modifications.

The example of American Sushi shows how intercultural, transnational exchanges take place when a dish travels from one country to another, where it is modified to travel back to the country of origin. Transnational and cross cultural exchanges of food lead to a larger variety of food and eating styles in both cultures and do not necessarily lead to a homogenization of tastes and foodscapes. By crossing and re-crossing Japanese and American culinary borders, mixing cooking styles from both cultures, and giving them new names that are both familiar and exotic, a new hybrid eating culture has been established that no longer primarily belongs to one culture. Sushi changes its meaning when consumed in another culture: by producing American Sushi, a new meaning is attached to the dish. American Sushi is based on Japanese sushi, but the preparation techniques and ingredients are altered significantly.[18] The dish is a fusion dish and even if it might hold Orientalist ideas for some, it is open to new interpretations and cannot be regarded simply as a form of culinary colonization or Oriental-

---

18  In *Osushi Chikyū O Mawaru* (*Sushi Around the World*), Matsumoto Hirotaka has written about the different meanings attached to sushi when the dish travels around the world.

ism. American Sushi is an American dish with a Japanese twist and vice versa.

What makes American Sushi appealing in both cultures is different in both cultures. While for Japanese consumers the mixture of uncommon ingredients with familiar cooking styles proves to be an appealing combination, for American consumers it is the uncommon cooking style combined with familiar ingredients. Seen in the light of Benedict Anderson's and Peter Hitchcock's ideas that nations and communities are constructed and created through the act of imagination, American Sushi can be regarded as a new way to imagine eating differently. The story of sushi traveling from Japan to the U.S. and back tells of culinary connections that do not reduce but allow the variation and multiplication of culinary differences. If sushi used to be part of the food that had the power to keep Japanese and American culture separate, new codes in eating and preparing American Sushi helped to bridge cultural differences in eating patterns. Thus, "the acknowledgement of differences has led to a birth of new cultural forms, one that is not [sic.] American nor Japanese but a fusion of the two" (Matsumoto 142). National culinary differences were needed to make the dish interesting for American and later Japanese consumers.

The American ingredients give Western consumers the reassurance of something familiar, while Japanese techniques and ingredients like seaweed or vinegared rice provide a point of identification for the Japanese consumers. Therefore, American Sushi did not generally displace Japanese sushi, but became an alternative, a transnational possibility to enjoy sushi differently both in Japan and in the United States.

# Could We Have a Geisha in This Scene? Transnational Depictions of Japan in Contemporary Hollywood Movies

> "See, they love black toe over in this country. You got a sharp knife? Gotta be, you know, in this country – somebody's gotta prefer a black toe ... or we should probably hang around until someone orders it."
>
> - BOB, LOST IN TRANSLATION -

Since food frequently works as a cultural signifier, several movies explicitly show a clash of different cultures taking place whilst consuming food. As discussed in the previous chapter, the acceptance or rejection of food from another culture may indicate the acceptance or rejection of the other culture itself. In Sofia Coppola's movie *Lost in Translation*, Bob (Bill Murray), one of the protagonists, articulates his disdain towards Japanese food culture by suggesting that the Japanese are uncivilized barbarians, consuming everything, even a black toe. This stereotype is ridiculed in the context of the film and underlines the message that Bob's ignorant behavior is unacceptable nowadays. Throughout the movie, it is obvious that the American actor, visiting Japan to shoot an advertisement for a Japanese whiskey, is not open for new cultural experiences, let alone for assimilating to the unknown environment. With his comment on Japanese eating habits, Bob creates binaries and thereby others a supposedly uncivilized East versus a civilized West, reflecting the Orientalist attitude that is criticized in the movie.

Orientalism is a key concept that has been instrumentalized in Hollywood for a long time to represent the unknown East. The majority of Hollywood productions from the 1920s to the 1990s depict Japan closely following this pattern, thus reflecting ethnocentric prejudices by representing the Japanese culture and people as fundamentally different from the West. In the past, Japan was portrayed either as an "Oriental Eden" with submissive, beautiful women, or as a land of fierce, inhuman warriors and kamikaze pilots. As Jacob and Aviad Raz state, "as a monster and a model, Japan has long captured the Western imagination" (153). While earlier renderings of the Japanese in Hollywood were only highly stereotypical and monolithic, more recent images of the Japanese in Hollywood films distributed around the world have gradually become more nuanced.

A correlation between the altered image of Japan and the popularity of Japanese cultural products in the West as well as the influence of Japanese popular culture on Hollywood can be observed. Though sushi has now become a standard light dish to be found all over the United States, other items of Japanese culture have also become extremely popular over the last twenty years. Especially among the younger generation Japanese video games, Pokémon trading cards, manga, and the animated movies of Hayao Miyazaki such as *Mononoke Hime* (*Princess Mononoke*) (1997) or *Sen to Chihiro no Kamikakushi* (*Spirited Away*) (2001) helped to create an image of "cool" Japan. Douglas McGray closely investigates this increasing cultural power of Japan in the global marketplace in his article "Japan's Gross National Cool," in which he argues that the "cool" appeal of Japanese commodities has first been appreciated only among subcultures of anime, manga, and science-fiction fans in the United States. However, today Japanese popular culture commodities reach a wider public.

The following chapter will scrutinize how the image of Japan has become more refined in the mediascape of Hollywood productions of the twenty-first century by shifting from an outright Orientalist mode to a more transnational approach. After a short sketch of the history of Orientalism in the American entertainment industry, the rising Japanese influence in Hollywood productions will be discussed. Even movies that are not noticeably connected to Japan such as *The Matrix* (1999) or Disney's *Lilo and Stitch* (2002), reveal that American Hollywood directors borrow elements from Japanese visual traditions such as manga and anime, and use Japanese movie techniques (see for example Feng "False and Double Consciousness"). American movie remakes like *Shall We Dance* (2004), based on the Japanese *Shall We Dansu?* (1996), *Godzilla* (1998), reimagining the Japanese monster movie *Gojira* (1954), or *Hachi: A Dog's Tale* (2009), an American remake of *Hachi-Kō Monogatari* (1987), proved extremely popular with the American audience. The attraction of horror movies based on a specifically Japanese concept of horror shows how readily a Western audience embraces a new Japanized genre of horror movies, which includes American remakes of Japanese horror movies as *The Ring* (2002), based on the Japanese horror movie *Ringu* (1998), *The Grudge* (2004) based on *Ju-On* (2002), *Dark Water* (2005) based on *Honogurai Mizu no Soko Kara* (2002), or *One Missed Call* (2008) based on *Chakushin Ari* (2004).

Additionally, a number of recent American motion pictures such as *The Last Samurai* (2003), *Lost in Translation* (2003), *Kill Bill: Volume One* (2003), *Memoirs of a Geisha* (2005), *Into the Sun* (2005), *The Fast and the Furious: Tokyo Drift* (2006), *Babel* (2006), *Letters from Iwo Jima* (2006), *The Ramen Girl* (2009), or *The Harimaya Bridge* (2009) reflect an increased interest in Japan as a cultural setting for American movies. The analyses of three of these contemporary motion pictures, namely *The Last Samurai*, *Lost in Translation*, and *Letters from Iwo Jima* will explain how Hollywood turns to Japan for inspiration and thereby opens itself to new perspectives on differences on screen. The movies reflect the multi-layered meaning attached to Japan by American directors for an American audience and show how the historical images of Japan and the Japanese are creatively rewritten in contemporary Hollywood and how these images reach beyond Orientalism.

Yet an extended fascination with Japan and Japanese culture does not mean that Orientalist, exoticized images of Japan in Hollywood cease to exist. Instead, it will be argued that supposedly "exotic" elements make these movies captivating and appealing for a Western audience. Although today Japan is still considered to be different from the West, and is therefore depicted as different from the Occident, these notions of difference arise from more complex interpretations of the country which are more manifold than mere strategies of Othering that emerge from cultural anxieties.

## FLASHBACK: ORIENTALIZING JAPAN IN MOVIES

Movies allow their audience to travel to distant places through the medium of film. Without actually leaving their home country, movie viewers can catch a glimpse of another culture, thereby "'deterritorializing' the process of imagining communities" (Shohat and Stam, "From the Imperial Family" 145). As movies have the power to construct an image of a culture on screen, and thus to define the culture for the viewer, the central position of Hollywood, the main distributor of movies in the world, is indeed dangerously hegemonic. Spreading and controlling images, Hollywood does not only literally imagine other cultures on screen but sets norms of what is acceptable and what is undesirable about these cultures. Images can be used and misused to shape attitudes and foster stereotypes which show "Others" either as role models or as a threat in the popular imagination. The fact that representations of "Others" as barbarians have the power to even serve as a justification for colonialism and control cannot be denied either. In this context, Japanese stereotypes in movies lead a Western audience to grasp the unknown culture by essentializing and reducing a complex society to selective core ideas and images. Stereotypes, comprising shared fears and desires, are often used to ridicule characters in movies (see Lester and Ross). Most dominantly, propaganda movies like for instance *My Japan* (1945) or *Know Your Enemy: Japan* (1945) employed stereotypes and turned invasions "into an act of self-defense" and sometimes even "prepared [their] audience for the acceptance of genocide" (Engelhardt 481). Scholars such as Gina Marchetti, Sheridan Prasso, and Jun Xing have written about the construction of an Oriental "Other" in Western cinema and they explain how stereotypes were used in order to create an either hostile or submissive image of Asian and Japanese characters on screen.

This close relation between power and representation calls for an increased "critical media literacy" (Kellner 335) since the process of reception is of great importance. When Hollywood movies represent cultures on screen, it is actively decided which details are included or excluded, often distributing subjective, Eurocentric images, thus encoding them with Orientalist ideology. Already Edward Said pointed to the power of representations. According to him, representations, "because they *are* representations, are embedded first in the language and then in the culture, institutions, and political ambience of the representer" (*Orientalism* 272), implying that those who have the power to represent another culture have the power to define this culture as well. Furthermore, Stuart Hall explains in "The Spectacle of the 'Other'" that differences are of great importance when it comes to representations since it is only possible to define one's own identity in contrast to "Others" (234 f.). Images of such "Others" frequently project Western anxieties and desires and function as mutual images. Binaries of a normative, modern, civilized West against a traditional, uncivilized East have long been employed in motion pictures to make it easier for the audience to identify with the (Western) protagonists and to create "a logic for Western intervention, because [they] construct a view of modernity as a corrective to tradition" (Grewal and Kaplan 268) thereby juxtaposing an inferior "Other" with a superior West. In this sense, the West has the power to define the East visually for the broadest possible audience and "media spectacles demonstrate who has power and who is powerless" (Kellner 2).

Japan has been of great interest for American movie makers for a long time and "Hollywood has created a system of discourse which constituted the 'Japanese' [...] as 'imaginary other' who were simultaneously categorized [...] excluded and included within the Western framework" (Raz and Raz 154). In the Orientalist mode of image construction, Japan and the Japanese people have been dominantly depicted as exotic, Oriental, unpredictable, sometimes even vicious and dangerous "Others." These stereotypes are subject to change and are oftentimes adapted and developed. In *Yellow Future: Oriental Style in Hollywood Cinema*, Jane Chi Hyun Park further investigates the influence of techno-oriental representations of Asians in Hollywood movies that depict the East and its inhabitants as dangerous, dehumanized cyborgs. By closely analyzing movies from the 1980s, 1990s, and 2000s, she traces the history and "process of racialization of East Asians in the United States" as well as the function of these created "aesthetic products" (ix) in movies. Park argues that these created images are important as they shape American perceptions of East Asia in the twentieth and twenty-first century (ix) and thus reveal much about the Western gaze on Japan.

Indeed, Hollywood's production of Japan's otherness has always been embedded in the historical relationship between Japan and the United States and reflected fears and desires of the particular period. In numerous movies, the Japanese landscape was used as an exotic backdrop for a Western narrative which focused on Caucasian protagonists, reducing Japanese characters to minor roles. Japanese characters were mostly limited to one-dimensionality and they were either helpless victims or evil aggressors. In this context, Jun Xing distinguishes three narrative traditions according to which Asians were represented on screen in Hollywood: the Madame Butterfly narrative, the Charlie Chan stories, and the yellow peril formula (55). However, the Madame Butterfly and Charlie Chan stereotype are often merged, as they either represent female or male rather passive and powerless "Others." Together with the image of an outright inscrutable, dangerous, uncivilized enemy (yellow peril), these stereotypes are part of the discourse of Orientalism on screen. The representation of the Orient as submissive to and different from the Occident is further closely connected to the gendered discourse of Orientalism which uses the fantasy of a passive, submissive, female East as the binary opposite of a supposedly active, dominant, masculine West.

## Submissive Butterflies of the East

The most prominent example of a female East versus a masculine West on screen is the highly exoticized and stereotyped image of the Japanese Geisha, personified in the renowned character Madame Butterfly. This concoction of Western male fantasy, made famous by Puccini's opera *Madama Butterfly*, which was first performed in 1904, serves as a basic construction of the Orient as a sexualized space with an exotic lure of the foreign which demands to be conquered and civilized (Heung 160).[1] This colonial desire, which is "concerned with forms of cross-cultural contact" (Young 3) has to be understood as an active, sexual desire for "the Other" (Young 3). Such Western sexual fantasies were projected onto Japan and led to an eroticized encounter of East and West on screen. Ian Buruma's book *A Japanese Mirror* criticizes the image of Japanese women in general and the Geisha in particular, created by the West as being problematic and he states that the figure of the Geisha is a "much misunderstood symbol of Japan" (72). Indeed the Geisha is often employed in movies to create a female *Asian* stereotype that "epitomizes an exoticized and subservient femininity that is leavened with a tantalizing mix of passive refinement and sexual mystique" (Heung 160). This dominant Western representation of Japanese women includes the idea of a sexual availability of Japanese women for Western men (Heung 160), hereby creating a "double colonization" of Japanese women.

---

[1] Many scholars have already discussed this female screen representation of Asians in Hollywood (see Peter X. Feng, Sheridan Prasso, and Shibusawa Naoko).

Both concepts, imperialism and patriarchy, are based on a supremacist, phallocentric ideology, which conquers and exercises control over its subjects. Especially in the post-World War II Occupation Era, Japanese women were not only discriminated against on account of their status as subjects to occupation but also on the basis of their gender and within this colonial context, national stereotypes were projected on gender divisions.

The constructed image of the Japanese woman as the perfect, hyperfeminine lover persistently prevails also due to novels such as Arthur Golden's *Memoirs of a Geisha* and the movie based on the novel. The image of Japanese women as sexual toys and ideal lovers is echoed today in books with titles such as *The Japanese Art of Sex: How to Tease, Seduce, and Pleasure the Samurai in Your Bedroom* or *Sex Secrets of an American Geisha: How to Attract, Satisfy, and Keep Your Man*. The authors of these guidebooks claim that by following "the feminine and sexy secrets of the bedchamber" that Japanese women supposedly possess (Conant 14), every woman can have a better sex life and thus "will bond [her] Good Man to [herself]" (ibid. 14). Western women are encouraged to act more feminine and submissive and thereby to follow the example of Japanese women as constructed by the West. In a similar vein, numerous Hollywood movies such as *The Teahouse of the August Moon* (1956) and *The Barbarian and the Geisha* (1958) have helped to set the still prevalent image of the stereotypical Geisha.

Indeed, the majority of female Japanese characters in Hollywood movies are part of the classical Madame Butterfly narrative. In this "quintessential Orientalist narrative[s]" (Yoshihara "The Flight" 975) Japanese women are portrayed as powerless, submissive women who fall in love with the first Western man they meet, only to be abandoned, and eventually commit suicide in the end. This interracial East-West romance between an Eastern woman and a Western man became one of the most enduring Hollywood narratives and was retold in various movies (Xing 59) as for example in *The Teahouse of the August Moon, Sayonara* (1957), *The Barbarian and the Geisha* (1958), *The Yakuza* (1974), *Shogun* (1980), *Karate Kid Part II* (1986), and *Come See the Paradise* (1990). The Madame Butterfly narrative suggests an unequal power relation with the East being depicted as weak and dependent on the West (Yoshihara; Heung). This dominant image of Japanese women as exotic and devoted to Western men "represent[s] a symbolic conquering of Japan and indeed of the Orient itself by the West"

(Xing 60), and turned Japanese women into metaphors for the dependent nation (Marchetti 179), thus linking sexuality to the idea of conquest (Dower, *Embracing Defeat* 138).

According to Karen Kelsky, most Madame Butterfly narratives followed the pattern of a cross-cultural relationship "between a grateful, gracious, and feminized Japan in thrall to the American military men who had liberated her" (70) which, as she argues convincingly, reflected symbolically the post-World War II relationship between Japan and the United States.[2] Especially in the 1950s and 1960s, narratives of a romance between an American soldier and a Japanese woman were popular (Marchetti 158). In the historical context of the Japanese occupation, Japanese men had not only lost a war and consequently control over their country, but they also had to witness many Japanese women entering relationships with American men. While the love of local women reassured Western men of their masculinity, Japanese men were twice humiliated and emasculated. Sabine Frühstück outlines in her study *Uneasy Warriors: Gender, Memory, and Popular Culture in the Japanese Army* how the Japanese Army was dismantled after the end of World War II and how the new Japanese Constitution forbade the formation of another army. When in the 1950s, the institution was reinstated as the *Jieitai* (Self-Defense Forces) it had a highly ambivalent status, especially related to gender questions, as Japanese men felt emasculated by the fact that they were denied military agency. Unlike soldiers of the Japanese Imperial Army, who "had fought to establish, maintain, and defend the Japanese empire in Asia," (Schneider 61) the soldiers of the *Jieitai* only engaged in non-combat operations until 2004 and were thus rendered less masculine.

The symbolical representation of Japan as female and the West as male employs what Hamid Naficy has termed "gendered binarism of space" (211). This binarism weakens Japanese men and essentializes the Japanese culture into an unthreatening, female core, while the West is associated with vital masculinity. These ideas are underlined by the fact that there are only few movies where an interracial romance takes place between a Western woman and a Japanese man, as this concept seems less attractive, since

---

2   This binary was not intended to empower white women. Although they were considered superior to the "Other" women, they nevertheless remained subordinated to white men.

it subverts the idea of the powerful, masculine Western space. Instead, to preserve power relations in Orientalist discourses, Asia is feminized and romances only seem possible between Asian women and Western man. This idea is summarized by the protagonist, opera singer Song Liling, in the movie *M. Butterfly* (1993), which was based on the eponymous anti-Orientalist play by the American writer David Henry Hwang:

It's one of your favorite fantasies, isn't it? The submissive Oriental woman and the cruel white man. Consider this: if a blonde cheerleader falls in love with a short Japanese businessman and he goes home for three years, she learns that he has remarried and kills herself - you would think that she is stupid. Only because it is an Oriental who kills herself for a Westerner you think it is beautiful. (*M. Butterfly*)

Yet, the movie (like Hwang's play) subverts the fetishization of Japanese women and the idea of ensuring Western masculinity by affairs with an Eastern woman. This stereotype is reversed in the 1993 version of the Madame Butterfly narrative that deconstructs older variations of the story. The narrative relocates the Madame Butterfly narrative from Japan to China, where the French diplomat Rene Gallimard (Jeremy Irons), who is assigned to Beijing, falls in love with a Chinese opera singer. However, Gallimard, the personification of Western, masculine imperialist arrogance, is ignorant of the fact that all roles are performed by men in traditional Chinese opera. His obsessive longing for Song Liling as well as his own idealized visions of the passivity of Eastern women prevents him from discovering that Liling is a man who uses the diplomat for his own ends, for most of the plot. When Gallimard finally, after twenty years unveils Liling's identity, he is deeply ashamed and disillusioned and commits suicide, thereby reversing the Madame Butterfly gender plot. Although by substituting the Japanese setting with a Chinese setting, hence assuming that Japan and China are, at least visually, interchangeable on screen, this narrative twist nevertheless is significant as it empowers the Asian character while, at the same time, revealing how the French man constructed the perfect imaginary woman in order to feel fully male. Thus, the Orientalist notion that desirable, but sexually depraved and too active Asian or Japanese women are dangerous to Western males is reinforced and it is stressed that the sexually and economically empowered female Japanese character threatens Western patriarchal paradigms (Prasso 71f.).

Additionally Asian/Japanese men have rarely been "depicted with traditionally masculine traits" (Prasso 103) but were frequently emasculated by representing them exclusively as domestic servants and as "nonassertive, devoid of all the traditional masculine qualities associated with Anglo-American males" (Xing 61). This so-called Charlie Chan stereotype goes back to Earl Derr Biggers' Charlie Chan mystery novels, which were published in the late 1920s in America and the forty-seven Charlie Chan movies that were produced in Hollywood and made the stereotype widely popular (Benshoff and Griffin 120). It is further striking that the character of the Chinese detective on screen was never played by an Asian actor. Instead, white actors used "yellow-face" make-up and played the role (Benshoff and Griffin 120), thus reflecting the bias of early Hollywood movies against employing Asian actors.

The harmless Chinese-American detective figure of Charlie Chan can be applied to many Asian characters and was most famously embodied by the character of Mr. Miyagi in the Karate Kid movies or Mr. Yunioshi, the bucktoothed Japanese neighbor in Breakfast at Tiffany's (1961). These Japanese characters are prime examples of degraded men who, due to their mysterious behavior were either rendered childlike and inferior or just untrustworthy, yet not dangerous. Sean M. Tierney argues in his article "Themes of Whiteness in Bulletproof Monk, Kill Bill, and The Last Samurai" that the inferiority of Asian characters is subtly visible in martial arts movies in which the white protagonist is able to master Asian martial arts within a very short time period. Tierney explains how the role of Asians in these movies is limited to either being "helpful or defiant" (615) and observes that "those Asians who are defiant or question the white person's presence are defeated, killed, or overcome their 'inappropriate' resentment and, realizing their 'mistake' befriend the white person" (615).

The non-threatening Asians that belong to the category of Charlie Chan stereotypes are not threatening the masculinity of Western characters as they are either very old or just too different to be attractive for white women. Thus, Charlie Chan characters are often perceived as rather "positive" by Western audiences. Nevertheless, depicted as having slant eyes, being pudgy, always speaking only broken English, and giving wise advices (mostly to white characters) that sounds like fortune cookie sayings, the passive, sometimes funny Charlie Chan character is offensive. As Charlie Chan characters often wish to serve and please their white friends or colleagues they are perceived as "yellow Uncle Tom" (Huang xvi) characters and are seen as counter stereotypes to the more powerful, yet aggressive, yellow peril stereotype.

## The Yellow Peril

Already established in American detective novels of the early nineteenth century, the yellow peril stereotype has been used in literature and movies ever since (Jarman 78). The most dominant Japanese yellow peril stereotype in Hollywood, however, is that of inscrutable Japanese soldiers during World War II, especially embodied by *kamikaze* pilots.

The historian John Dower elaborates in *War without Mercy* how the Japanese were demonized and dehumanized by Hollywood and the American press during World War II. According to him, the war in the Pacific has to be understood as a race war (4) in which America used Hollywood to produce propaganda that was utilized to educate Americans about their enemy (15f.) and to "dramatiz[e] the international conflict and mobiliz[e] the populace to renewed fighting" (Benshoff and Griffin 124). These movies as well as many war propaganda posters portrayed the Japanese as yellow monkeys, rats, apes, or monsters (Dower, *War without Mercy* 81 and 84f.). According to Dower, people wished "good luck, good hunting" to American soldiers sent on missions to Japan (*War without Mercy* 90) and the practice of desecrating bodies of Japanese soldiers in order to collect trophies fed this hunting metaphor that helped to dehumanize the enemy. The frequent use of flamethrowers, a weapon normally used for rodent exterminations, against the Japanese in combat mirrors the attitude that the enemy was hardly recognized as human. The monstrous features attributed to them as well as the denial of their human qualities made it easier for American soldiers to kill their Japanese opponents in combat and by depicting the Japanese as monsters, their ideology was deemed to be outside the acceptable norm. "American propaganda inflamed emotions – particularly against the Japanese, who were portrayed as an evil, inferior and barbaric race lacking all sense of decency" (Piehler 42), a prejudice that was later reflected in numerous Hollywood movies. Even as late as 2001, in movies like *Pearl Harbor* or *To End All Wars* (2001) the Japanese, especially *kamikaze* pilots, were depicted as "half-man, half-machine, an incomprehensible human torpedo bringing doom from the peripheries of fanatical animate existence"

(Engelhardt 482) and their lives were rendered less valuable than that of American soldiers, thus justifying actions against them.

The depiction of the Japanese as dangerous and emotionless was not limited to war movies. In the 1980s, the Japanese yellow peril stereotype took a new twist and the economic competition of Japan and the United States was turned into an analogue to World War II battles on the screen (Xing 58; Hartwig 147ff.). Movies such as *Gung Ho!* (1986) and *Rising Sun* (1993) present Japanese businessmen (to different degrees) as employing inhumane, unfair business practices in order to take over the American economy. The movies echo the fear of an economic invasion in the United States during the 1980s, when Japanese entrepreneurs increasingly bought American corporations and real estate and when the technological advancement and manufacturing capabilities of Toyota surpassed the sales of General Motors (Hartwig 157).[3] The decline of the American car industry in the United States in general and Detroit in particular led to local protest with car holders putting bumper stickers with the slogan "Buy American," "Made in America by Americans" (James 218), or "Honda, Toyota – Pearl Harbor" (Zia 58) on their cars. This domination of the American auto industry by the Japanese is the main topic of *Gung Ho!* The movie depicts how the Japanese get control of an American automobile company in a small town in Pennsylvania and try to enforce their draconic working practices on the local workers. Although the movie reflects the American fear of being dominated by the Japanese car industry, it ends on a positive note, as in the end the American workers are able to prove to the Japanese that the "American way" can be more effective than inhumane Japanese business practices. The movie hence suggests that initial cultural differences can be overcome and that both cultures can learn from each other, working as a "good team" (*Gung Ho!*).

In contrast, *Rising Sun* lacks this idea of cultural exchange and understanding. The domineering and aggressive economic power of the Japanese is already indicated by an impressive Japanese company headquarters in Los Angeles which dominates the city skyline. In this movie, the Japanese

---

3   Japan already became a threat to the West in the 1920s and 1930s, since the Japanese alone were increasing their exports despite the Great Depression in America. Their expansion triggered accusations of unfair and manipulated business methods (Wilkinson 129, 135f).

Nakamoto Company, is about to take over an American microchip company. Furthermore, *Rising Sun* fortifies the stereotype of Japanese men as being sexually depraved and potentially dangerous for American women. The Japanese character Eddie Sakamura, who is the son of the director of the Nakamonto Company, surrounds himself with blonde, Caucasian American women who insinuate that American women can be equally dominated as the economy. Shown eating sushi from the naked body of one of his American girlfriends, Eddie is also the main suspect in the investigation of the murder of an American woman from Kentucky. It can be concluded that the hyper-masculine, yet emotionless character of Eddie poses not only a threat to American women who are abused and even killed by him, he is also a serious rival to American men, since he is able to attract and debase American women. Furthermore, Eddie shares some characteristics with the Japanese businessmen in *Gung Ho!* as he is a very cold and calculating person who lacks humane qualities.

The depiction of such dehumanized Asian characters was discussed by David Morley and Kevin Robins, who coined the term "techno-orientalism" to refer to this anti-Japanese sentiment in the context of a Japanese economic growth. They explain in *Spaces of Identity* how American media created stereotypes of Japanese as half-human, half-machines. The fact that the supposedly backward Oriental was flooding Western markets with new technological products fostered the fear of Japanese invading the American market and culture. Morley and Robins argue that Japan had challenged "the supposed centrality of the West as a cultural and geographical locus for the project of modernity" (160), which made former binary distinctions of the West and the East problematic. In order to maintain this dichotomy it was thus necessary to deem the Japanese modernity as abnormal and monstrous. Japanese technological advancements were embedded in the Orientalist discourse, creating dehumanized, dystopic, futuristic spaces in movies such as *Blade Runner* (1982). This "association of technology and Japaneseness" helped to reinforce the stereotype of the Japanese culture as "cold, impersonal, and machine-like" (Morley and Robins 169).

Thus, while a powerful, aggressive, masculine Orient was depicted as dangerous to the United States, the submissive female Orient remained a non-threatening place for exotic adventures of Western men. Thus, American Orientalism on screen was rooted in the belief in the sexual difference of "the Other" either as being "submissive femininity," "emasculated man," or "aggressive masculinity" (Browne 241).

## SUBTITLES AND SUBVERSION: TRANSNATIONAL CINEMA

Despite ongoing media globalization and an opening of the U.S. mediascape to foreign influences, which offer new platforms to represent different cultures with greater diversity, some directors as well as scholars see media globalization as a threat rather than a possibility. Because "the media are located at the center of the culture of the capitalist West" (Tomlinson 34) and most of the industrialized East, they dominate everyday life and leisure, "shaping political views and social behavior, and providing the materials out of which people forge their very identities" (Kellner 1).

The theory of media imperialism, which is often closely linked to theories of globalization, accuses the media of working as a cultural imperialist power by imposing values on other cultures (Tomlinson 34). Yet, as Shohat and Stam have argued, the idea of media imperialism underestimates the role of the audience in actively "reading" the Hollywood products, as images have the capacity to create, interfere with, and even trouble common conceptions since "spectators can also return the gaze through critical comments or hostile looks" ("From the Imperial Family" 158). Even though audiences can be drawn into the narrative of a movie and sometimes use media imagery to construct their own reality (Tomlinson 61), the consumer can still actively decide which movie he/she wants to see and how he/she wants to decode the messages encoded in the movie. Additionally, the influences in movies not only come from a "center" (Hollywood) which economically and culturally shapes the "peripheries," but the "peripheries" in turn influence the "center" as well.

More often than not, in academic discussions transnational cinema becomes synonymous with diasporic or Third World Cinema. However to limit transnational cinema to these genres would not be just. Ezra and Rowden widen the term and see transnational cinema as an extension of the postcolonial realm of media culture, since the postcolonial is often not flexible enough as a tool when cultural exchanges and relationships are examined. They argue that "Third Worldism" and the related notion of Third

World Cinema "have become increasingly problematic in a world no longer marked by the sharp divisions of discursive resistance to cultural imperialism" and that "because of the hybridized and cosmopolitan identities of so many contemporary filmmakers, it could be argued that binary oppositions and tertiary relations have lost even their heuristic value in the complexly interconnected world-system with which even the most marginalized of them must now contend" (4). Indeed, postcolonialism remains too much tied to "particular conditions of imperial oppression" (Ezra and Rowden 5) and thereby excludes nations that have never been colonized such as Japan. Transnational cinema, on the contrary,

> offers a more multivalenced approach to considering the impact of history on contemporary experience owing to the fact the issues of immigration, exile, political asylum, tourism, terrorism, and technology with which it engages are all straightforward readable in 'real world' terms. And increasingly, this real world is being defined not by its colonial past (or even its neocolonial present), but by its technological future, in which previously disenfranchised people will gain even greater access to the means of global representation. (Ezra and Rowden 5)

This approach to transnational cinema allows broadening the term while having a closer look at all cross-cultural movements in movies regardless whether they are set in a former colonial terrain or not.

A transnational turn in Hollywood is visible on many levels. Firstly, an enormous amount of capital is needed to shoot films and therefore, today, the majority of movies are internationally financed. The American remake of the Japanese horror movie *Ju-On, The Grudge*, for example was financed by an American film studio, owned by a Japanese corporation (McRoy, *Case Study* 176). The American remake was shot entirely with American actors but was co-produced by the original Japanese director Shimizu Takashi and combines American horror film aesthetics with visual and narrative elements from Japanese horror movies. Such complex, multinational productions blur the boundaries of national cinemas and lead to "hybridizing tendencies" (Ezra and Rowden 2) since the result cannot be assigned to one specific nation.

The fact that contemporary film business has increasingly become a global business with a multicultural, global audience was also reflected in the 2007 Academy Award nominations. The movies *Letters from Iwo Jima*,

*The Queen* (2006), *The Departed* (2006) and *Babel*, all nominated in the category "Best Picture" incorporate different cultural influences and employ a multinational cast. *Letters from Iwo Jima*, was directed by American director Clint Eastwood and focuses on a dark chapter of Japanese history, *The Queen* is a British drama film shot by the British director Stephen Frears, starring British and American actors, and *The Departed* is an American crime thriller, with a screenplay based on a Hong Kong film, directed by Martin Scorsese – an American director with Italian roots. Finally, *Babel* was directed by the Mexican film director Alejandro González Iñárritu and is set in Morocco, Japan, and the United States, employing actors from these nations. Likewise, nominees for "Actresses in a Leading Role" as well as "Actresses in a Supporting Role" came from multiple backgrounds such as Japan (Kikuchi Rinko), Australia (Cate Blanchett), Mexico (Adriana Barraza, Penelope Cruz), and Great Britain (Helen Mirren, Kate Winslet).[4]

Obviously, the media in general and movies in particular have become "more multicentered, with the power not only to offer countervailing representations but also to open up parallel scapes for alternative transnational practices" (Shohat and Stam, "From the Imperial Family" 145). Furthermore, American directors and screen writers increasingly borrow from and are influenced by other cultures as for example the Hong Kong cinema (see Hunt; Yau), Bollywood, or Japanese visual traditions (Park 61).The cross-pollination of elements from American and foreign cinemas are by no means a recent phenomenon. For example in 1961, Kurosawa Akira's *Yojimbo* (1961) inspired the run of so called Spaghetti Westerns like *Per un Pungo di Dollari* (*A Fistful of Dollars*) (1964), starring Clint Eastwood whose character "was modeled after the samurai character of Mifune Toshio" (Littlewood 187-188). Kurosawa, famous for his samurai movies, was also influenced by and affected American director John Ford.[5] Many American directors, especially in the Western genre, borrowed from Kurosawa as well, like the American director John Sturges, who remade Kuro-

---

4   Interestingly enough, the nominations for male actors in a leading role and supporting role were more homogeneous.
5   For more information on the influence of Kurosawa on Ford and vice versa see Stephen Prince "Genre and Violence," The Cinema and Donald Richie Japanese Cinema.

sawa's samurai epos *The Seven Samurai* (1954) as the Western *The Magnificent Seven* (1960). Kurosawa in turn adopted different styles from the American cinema in his movies *Nora Inu* (*Stray Dog*) (1949) and *Tengoku to Jigoku* (*High and Low*) (1963) (McRoy, *Case Study* 177).[6]

The frequent mutual borrowing of aesthetics and narratives in Western and samurai movies can be explained by the fact that both genres share some elements. Being "national" genres, incorporating the national core values, they both deal with "men of violence who are defined in terms of their weapons, yet the character and stories are embedded in networks of different social structural values, which firmly separate the two classes of film" (Prince 14-15). This reveals the existence of some shared values and popular narratives that work in both nations. As Kevin Decker and Jason Eberl argue in *Star Wars and Philosophy*, even the American science-fiction movie saga *Star Wars* draws heavily on the samurai culture and ethic, adapting for example the idea that the sword is the soul of a samurai, or adapting the samurai clothing to the Jedi culture in the movie (55 ff.).

Similarly, Quentin Tarantino incorporated aesthetics and narratives from Japanese samurai and *yakuza* (Japanese gangster) movies in *Kill Bill: Volume One*, referencing for example many ideas and visual styles from the Japanese director Suzuki Seijun, famous for his movies that reflect his "aestheticized, absurdist worldview, depicting the boundaries between reality and dream that constantly shift as the code of the tough guy devolves into choreographed grotesquerie" (Schilling 95). More specifically, the use of silhouette in numerous fight scenes in Tarantino's *Kill Bill: Volume One* directly quotes Suzuki's *Tōkyō Nagaremono* (*Tokyo Drifter*) (1966) which itself is a mixture of different movie genres and influenced by Hollywood Westerns (Vryzidis 282). Another influence of Suzuki in *Kill Bill: Volume One* is "the use of color and black and white sequences and the penchant for clashing, bright colors" (J. King 184).

More recently, horror movies have become one of Japan's major influences on American cinema and directors such as Nakata Hideo, Kurosawa Kiyoshi and Miike Takashi are believed to continue to influence the Western horror genre for the future (McRoy, "Introduction" 2 and 9). Japanese

---

6  For a discussion of Kurosawa's movies in terms of Orientalism and Occidentalism see Rachael Hutchinson's essay "Orientalism or Occidentalism? Dynamics of Appropriation in Akira Kurosawa."

horror has a century old tradition and is deeply rooted in folklore ghost stories (McRoy, "Introduction" 1). Because Japanese horror movies are profoundly embedded in their culture, they need to be made accessible for a Western audience and Japanese horror movies are regularly remade for the Western market. These remakes however, do not replace the original versions, but are adaptations that can serve as a gateway to the more complex world of Japanese horror cinema for audiences interested in the Japanese versions, thereby acting as "a platform for the cultural text's wider availability" (Hills 164). Hence, American remakes are often perceived by the Western audience, especially by fans of Japanese horror movies, as "juvenile" and "excessively fast-paced" whereas the Japanese originals are regarded as "serious, reflective, and less accessible to (or not meant for) the American teen market" (Hills 169). Yet, Japanese horror movies also borrow from the West, thereby closing the circle of a transnational exchange of visual styles in the horror genre. For example, the Japanese horror movie *Freeze Me* (2000) was influenced by American rape-revenge movies (Lafond 78). The Japanese movie *Ringu*, which was later remade in Hollywood as *The Ring*, opens with an establishing shot of two teenagers who are at home alone before the plot focuses on a female journalist who tries to unveil the mystery behind a videotape. The opening shot, as well as the narrative closely resemble Wes Craven's horror movie *Scream* (1996) (Hand 22).

Japanese animated movies or anime, as they are called in Japan, enjoy great popularity in the United States and they are the greatest contemporary Japanese influence on Hollywood. This is not only evident in Quentin Tarantino's *Kill Bill: Volume One* but also in *The Matrix*. According to Roland Kelts, the Japanese visual style "is beginning to dictate the look, style, and even forming the basis, of major Hollywood movies" (114). The Wachowski brothers, who produced and directed *The Matrix*, are known to be fans of Japanese animation and were consequently influenced by Japanese anime such as *Ghost in the Shell* (1995) or *Metropolis* (2001) which were themselves inspired by Hollywood cinema (Park, *Yellow Future* 175). Furthermore, *The Matrix* inspired Japanese directors of animated movies, who produced *The Animatrix* (2003), an anthology film which consists of different short animated movies, all yarned around the real action movie. This connection between anime and Hollywood cinema is not a new development either. Tezuka Osamu, one of the early and most famous and influential directors of anime, was inspired by the storytelling of Walt Disney[7] (Drazen 5; W. Wong 23) and anime always has borrowed cinema techniques established in the West such as close-ups, flashbacks, and time-lapse (Drazen 5).

The increasing influences of anime in contemporary American movie productions further becomes evident when Disney's 2002 animated movie *Lilo and Stitch* and its sequels and TV mini-series are compared to the Japanese *Pokémon* movie and TV series. Not only does the non-human central character of Disney's animated feature, a genetic alien experiment called Stitch, visually resemble the Japanese "pocket monster" Pikachu in form and usage of bright colors, but Disney started a TV mini-series after the success of the movie and the popularity of the character. The TV series as well as movie sequels enabled the Walt Disney Company to extend the numbers of genetic experiments, which could then be merchandised like the different Japanese pocket monsters. Like in the Japanese Pokémon series, the many different genetic experiments all have an individual persona, special powers, and a cute visual appearance. Also, like the Pokémon series, the narration of single episodes focuses on the task of collecting the different experiments and "taming" or "training" them. Although there are some differences between the two series, an overall influence of the Japanese Pokémon series on Disney's animated feature cannot be denied and it can be argued that the Japanese pocket monsters paved the way for the acceptance of colorful, cute aliens or monster characters in the West.

Finally, cultural exchanges at many levels are a vital part of the movie business. On the production level, it offers directors and actors the possibility to reach an audience beyond their national borders. As Kurosawa Akira stated in 1985,

films are something that carry across to many different kinds of people. In this sense, they have a tremendous power of communication. This has enabled me per-

---

7   The Disney movie *The Lion King* is very contested as well since some comic artists argue that the Disney story closely resembles Tezuka Osamu's *Jungle Emperor* without crediting the movie (see Kuwahara). Later, there was a similar incident which was discussed among animation fans, called the "Nadia versus Atlantis Affair" in which it was suspected that Disney had again used a Japanese original for an animated movie (Patten 185-189).

sonally to speak to people all over the world and to understand them better and form new friendships. People everywhere, seeing a film, share the emotions of the character in the film – the joys, the sorrows, the dramas. (Kurosawa qtd. in Yang 54)

According to Kurosawa cinema involves an interaction of the director, the characters on screen, and the audience. With an internationalization of the movie business, "a film circulates in a sphere which can be described as transnational with none of the specificity so desired by nationalists. It does so because its mode of communication doesn't rely exclusively on the local or the national for success" (Ron Burnett qtd. in O'Regan 262). The cultural background of the movie audience plays a significant role in the reception and since a movie is unlikely to be understood in the same way in different cultural contexts, this of course changes the target group for Hollywood movies as well. However, it has to be kept in mind that movies are still more likely to be financed (and thus influenced) by Western nations.

## *THE LAST SAMURAI*: A MASCULINE EAST

With an ongoing transnational turn in cinema, a shift in the representation of Japan and the Japanese in Hollywood movies can be observed. One example of a movie that supposedly offers a transnational reading of the East is the Hollywood epic *The Last Samurai*, directed by Edward Zwick. Until most recently, the majority of Hollywood movies set in a non-Western culture were shot by American directors, who represented cultures in the way they understood or interpreted them. In doing this, more often than not, films created an exotic image that directed the audience to an Orientalist, sometimes highly inaccurate understanding of the unfamiliar culture. Although *The Last Samurai* is a Hollywood movie, produced and directed by Americans, the movie takes a transnational approach on the production level as well as on the narrative level. A closer analysis, however, reveals that this film still incorporates subtle Orientalist attitudes. At first sight, when looking at the official American theatrical release poster, the *Last Samurai* promises to entertain the audience with an exciting adventure, focusing on a white protagonist (Tom Cruise) in a Japanese setting. Visually, the poster is centered exclusively on the famous Hollywood actor in samurai armor, thus suggesting that this movie will offer both an exotic setting and a familiar action hero.

Yet, unlike earlier Hollywood movies, in which no leading roles were given to Asian actors, Zwick's samurai epic employs several Japanese actors such as Sanada Hirojuki, Watanabe Ken, Nakamura Shichinosuke, and Koyuki, who were not only important for the director in front of the camera, but were asked to share their knowledge about the samurai culture and martial arts as well. Watanabe Ken, who played the Japanese protagonist in the movie, explained that the encounter of East and West not only took place on screen, but continued behind the scenes and interviews in the Japanese movie magazine *Roadshow* reveal that the Japanese actors and crew members of *The Last Samurai* were extremely comfortable with how their indigenous culture was represented in the movie (*Roadshow* 21-23). According to the Japanese actors, the movie offered them the chance to really be seen on the American market and to tell a Western audience more about Japanese culture and history (Yazaki 11) instead of merely serving as decorative backdrops. Yet the fact that *The Last Samurai* was still produced by an American director in Hollywood and mirrors an American perception of the Japanese samurai culture cannot be overlooked, especially since the movie maintains the centrality of the white protagonist. This might have been necessary due to the fact that *The Last Samurai* was the first samurai movie of this epic scale produced in the United States and it therefore constituted the challenge of how to present such an unfamiliar topic of an almost totally unknown culture to a Western audience. Additionally, the casting Tom Cruise certainly helped to draw attention to this project and offered a character with whom a Western audience could easily identify. Furthermore, the plot of the movie follows the classical Hollywood narrative structure, with two plot lines: A mission or quest and a heterosexual romance. Both storylines include a goal, an obstacle, and a climax (see Bordwell).In *The Last Samurai* the audience follows the quest of Nathan Algren (Tom Cruise), a disillusioned Civil War soldier who is hired to fight against the samurai in Japan and who falls in love with a Japanese samurai woman, Taka (Koyuki) and establishes a close friendship to the samurai leader, Katsumoto (Watanabe Ken) he was supposed to fight.

In order to familiarize Western audiences with the culture of the samurai, parallels between Japanese and American history were drawn in both the advertising campaign for the movie and the narrative. In the foreword of the official movie guide for instance, Edward Zwick stated that the "ineluctable march toward a fated end" had not only been a classic theme in the Western genre, but in many samurai movies as well (10). Drawing parallels between radical changes in the Japanese society due to a fast Westernization in nineteenth century Japan, and significant changes in the American society caused by the American Civil War and Indian Wars in the United States, he focused on cross-culturally familiar themes such as loyalty, friendship, and romantic love. Moreover, Zwick not only turned to themes that are familiar on both sides of the Pacific but employed popular and already familiar Japanese visual codes such as falling cherry blossoms (Buehrer xi), a deep rooted image that carries manifold symbolic meaning in Japan (Ohnuki-Tierney, *Kamikaze Diaries* 27-58): One of the meanings attached to the image of falling cherry blossom is their association with the glory of the samurai and their willingness to sacrifice their life for the Emperor (Ohnuki-Tierney, *Kamikaze Diaries* 120-121).

Another characteristic of Japanese movies is their focus on atmosphere. As Donald Richie explains in *Japanese Cinema: Film Style and National Character*, "if the American film is strongest in action, and if the European is strongest in character, then the Japanese film is richest in mood or atmosphere, in presenting characters in their own surroundings" (ix). This focus on atmosphere is created in *The Last Samurai* as well by the repeated use of long camera shots and takes that create tension and, at the same time, slow down the pace of action. Instead of being preoccupied by the action on screen, the audience is invited to pay attention to the surrounding and details on screen as well as the body language and facial expressions of the characters. This is especially important in this movie since in the course of the film, the majority of the conversations between the American soldier Nathan Algren and Katsumoto's sister Taka are non-verbal. The characters seem to communicate on an emotional level that makes verbal communication or explanations obsolete. Instead, the two characters communicate using body language. This emphasis on the non-stated is also typical for the Japanese cinema, in which the cinematic means of implied meaning can be found in a single shot, whereas in Hollywood cinema, everything needs to be explained and verbalized (Richie, *Japanese Cinema* 83 and Hills 169). Finally, the storytelling process is central in Zwick's samurai epos, while Japanese cinema, which is more "'presentational' as opposed to the very 'representational' Hollywood cinema" (Choi xi) gives more attention to the storytelling process of the film. This feature can be traced back to the *benshi*, a storyteller in silent films who explained the story on screen (Choi xi). Zwick's movie revives the tradition of the *benshi*, as it not only opens with a voice-over that introduces the audience to the mythical creation story of Japan, but in fact employs this voice several times in order to add information to the storyline. Thus, it can be concluded that *The Last Samurai* is a Hollywood movie that is influenced by Japanese visual styles as well as cinematic traditions.

On the narrative level, *The Last Samurai* is first and foremost a story about the encounter of two different cultures and a story of redemption. A disillusioned Caucasian protagonist, Nathan Algren, learns the customs of a foreign culture and, in the end, along with new spiritual beliefs, finds his lost sense of self. This storyline of a troubled Western soul which finds renewal in another culture is not unique at all and similar plots can be found in Hollywood movies ranging from Neo-Westerns such as *Dances with Wolves* (1990) to the movie adaptation of *The Last of the Mohicans* (1992), and the most recent eco-critical science-fiction spectacle *Avatar* (2009). Indeed, Native Americans were often used to create binaries in America, where they were regarded as child-like and savage, just as the Japanese were considered immature barbarians. In the U.S. Army *Infantry Journal*, similar analogies were used and Japanese enemies were considered "'as good as Indians ever were' at infiltration" (Dower, *War without Mercy* 152), creating an analogy between the Japanese and Native Americans. Yet, while the idea that Native(s) (Americans) can offer redemptive energy for a white American in distress is not new in movies, such an idea had not existed for Japanese characters in Hollywood at that time. This new perception of Japan, as a new frontier or place of redemption rather than just as an exotic backdrop offers the chance of a new reading of the movie as a transnational encounter of two different cultures. Moreover, the movie's engagement of a Japanese central character, who becomes Algren's spiritual mentor and who helps him to overcome his crisis, Katsumoto, is special and opens a new narrative that does not follow traditional storylines between the East and West.

While it would not be appropriate to completely dismiss the more nuanced and transnational approaches of the movie, one needs to look at the continuation of some of the representational traditions of Japanese in Hollywood movies. The American protagonist, for instance, is shown to not just support Katsumoto's goals to save Japan's traditional culture but to be the central facilitator. This caters to what Deborah Root calls the "salvage paradigm" (100) as he becomes the (white) savior of the vanishing samurai culture and spirituality, thereby clearly echoing ideas of a superior West and inferior East.

## A Tale of Two Cultures: Questioning American Expansionism

While the establishing shot seems to indicate that *The Last Samurai* is yet another movie in which only a Caucasian can solve the problems of an exotic culture, the second shot of the movie already promises a slightly different approach than those of its Orientalist predecessors. The film opens, familiarly enough, with a shot of a beautiful, serene, Japanese landscape. The audience travels with the camera through green, lush fields, where a samurai warrior, Katsumoto, meditates. Japan is represented as a rural, harmonious place which, while it may be mysterious and foreign, does not need to be rescued or civilized. In harsh contrast to this scenery, the second shot introduces the audience to a disorderly America and a disheveled American protagonist: The drunken, shabbily dressed soldier Nathaniel Algren sits in a dark, crammed, dusky room somewhere in San Francisco.

Employing a Western narrative tradition to treat landscapes as morally symbolic terrains, space is geographically and culturally used in this opening frame to set up a binary opposition between Japan and America, contrasting the rural beauty of the East with the industrialized ugliness of the urban West. In this movie, the Japanese landscape allows a Western audience to connote the Japanese setting and character with positive attributes. In contrast, Algren is hardly an elevating figure and does not represent an enlightened man who is to bring civilization to barbarians. On the contrary, the Japanese samurai is portrayed as an enlightened and civilized figure from whom the American soldier will learn. This idea and the positioning of the main characters are underlined by the usage of light: Katsumoto literally appears in an "illuminated" scenery, whereas Algren sits in the dark.

Likewise, this binary set up foreshadows what will happen to Japan if they follow their plans to modernize their country. In this context, Algren functions as a warning example, not as a role model. The movie is set in the late 1860s to 1870s, which were historically the "key years in the crystallization of American perspectives on Japan and Japanese perspectives on America" (Guth, xv). The American protagonist arrives in Japan during the Meji Restoration, an era when Japan ended its self-imposed seclusion and, believing that it needed to become more Western in order to be able to compete with the West, exchanged their Japanese traditions with Western ideas and commodities. These changes led to a clash of Japanese traditionalists with those who were in favor of a modern, Western, Japan.[8]

It is significant that Algren works for an American arms manufacturer at the beginning of the film, advertising rifles in a show. Repeating a scripted text, he declares that "this is the gun that is winning the West" (*The Last Samurai*) thus referring to the long-standing cultural frontier narratives of the Westward movement. However, his seemingly patriotic speech is visually juxtaposed with his memories of the Indian War. Suddenly, Algren starts to tell the audience the truth about using rifles, and hints at the violence of war, telling a young boy that the gun can "blow a hole in your daddy six inches wide" (*The Last Samurai*). Instead of following the original plan, Algren ends his presentation on an ironic note, when he declares "My thanks on behalf of those who died in the name of better mechanical amusements and commercial opportunities" (*The Last Samurai*). These words are interesting, as the American protagonist openly criticizes ongoing globalization processes and the increased focus on consumerism in nineteenth century America. As Christine M.E. Guth explains in her book *Longfellow's Tattoos: Tourism, Collecting, and Japan* on how the United States change after the American Civil War, "the surge of economic growth and industrial progress" as well as "the horrors of the Civil War did much to reconfigure the terms of Americans' encounter with non-European cultures" (50). Thus, many disillusioned Americans ventured out to encounter "cultures they believed to be more innocent and uncorrupted by the modern world" (Guth xv). The character of Algren thus reflects past and contemporary anxieties about globalizing processes and embodies a rather anti-imperialist stance.

The motif of the frontier is introduced to the movie with Algren as he is a soldier who fought in the American Civil War and in the Indian Wars. He has served the powers of imperialism and represents the violent side of the frontier experience as described by Richard Slotkin, who expounds in *Gun-*

---

8   See also chapter two "Here be Monsters."

*fighter Nation: The Myth of the Frontier in Twentieth Century America* that "violence is central to both the historical development of the Frontier and its mythic representation" (11), since most of the legitimate owners of the land, the Native Americans, were not willing to hand their property over to the white man.

Although the idea of the frontier is as well closely connected to white, heterosexual American masculinity, since frontiersmen embodied typical masculine ideals like restlessness, strength, courage, and an inventive mind, Algren feels ashamed after his frontier experience since he questions the killing of Native American civilians. Instead of having been initiated by his frontier experience and having morally grown, he feels traumatized, emasculated and in need of a new or other frontier in order to regain his lost self-respect and masculinity. When Algren is offered the opportunity to go to Japan, however, he is hired by Japanese officials to "help suppress the rebellion of yet another leader" (*The Last Samurai*), that is, to do exactly what he did before. The travel to an unknown country does not promise a way out of this vicious circle and the journey seems to offer just another possibility to earn money by killing. However, Japan and the samurai culture become, in the end, a different frontier for Algren who overcomes his old life and is helped to start over again.

Here and elsewhere the movie does not follow nineteenth century ideas about Japan's role as a new frontier that may be opened after the closing of the American West. By establishing America's frontier spirit as self-destructive, it contradicts both Turner's ideas about the positive value of "The Frontier in American History" and of a "regenerated Orient," where "the long march of westward civilization should complete its circle" (296-297). In *The Last Samurai*, Japan is not seen as an uncivilized frontier, but more as a contact zone, where East and West meet, thereby offering a different reading of Japan as a new frontier. The movie is not about a Westward movement, in which civilized Americans will conquer an uncivilized East but focuses on a guilt-ridden American barbarian who will find his way back to civilized life because he learns from the samurai. Algren gradually turns away from corrupting Western influences by adopting the Japanese code of honor, thereby reversing ideas of the civilized West versus the barbaric East.

Hence, the film replaces the spirit of the "frontier" with the idea of the "border," defined by Amirtijit Singh and Peter Schmidt in *Postcolonial Theory and the United States: Race, Ethnicity and Literature* as means

to connect and divide. Not a frontier, its deadly imagination or a line between the savage and the civilized. Not exodus, with its mirage of a promised-land to end the wandering or diaspora, with its involuntary sense of never-never home. But borders. A part, yet apart, home and not-home, neither 'here' nor 'there'. (7)

The encounter of East and West embodied by Algren and Katsumoto in *The Last Samurai* is set exactly in the range of ambiguity and hybridity that is highlighted in the definition by Singh and Schmidt. The relationship between the two characters in the movie show that borders can serve as both a dividing-line and a point of connection. The mutual friendship between Algren and Katsumoto is no longer tainted with imperialist paradigms but highlights the in-betweenness and possibilities which lie in the liminal experience of border-crossings as reflected in Algren's encounter with the samurai. Their relationship suggests that a harmonious cooperation is possible and that members of both cultures can learn from each other. The movie emphasizes the importance of preserving differences and different cultures and thus criticizes the Westernization of Japan. Cultural conflicts between "traditional" and "modern" Japan generate the main dramatic tension throughout the movie. As one Western expert explains to Algren upon his arrival in Japan "The Emperor is mad for all things Western and the samurai believe it's changing too fast. The ancient and the modern are at war for the soul of Japan" (*The Last Samurai*). This clash is represented by using binaries and constructs the traditional Japanese as the good samurai, while the villainous government officials represent the "new" Japan. While the traditional Japanese samurai are depicted as honorable warriors, the government officials are greedy and corrupt. The modernization of Japan seems to lead to an increased corruption and the loss of all traditional values in favor of supposedly progressive modern ways. This trend is best represented by Omura (Harada Masato), one of the advisors of the Emperor. Omura is the antagonist and archetypal Japanese villain in American movies. According to Ian Buruma, the typical Japanese villain is a "scheming entrepreneur and the conniving politician, both influenced by wicked foreign ways, both, in a way, 'progressives'" (*A Japanese Mirror* 172). Omura is indeed a greedy entrepreneur who is only interested in his economic and political advantage. Completely denying his heritage, and instead emulating the West, he dresses in Western clothes, decorates his office with Western artifacts, and believes in everything that comes from the West. He even prefers to command the Japanese army in English, which estranges his soldiers from him, as they cannot understand him anymore. Omura's viciousness is underlined in the final battle, where the clash of old and new Japan is visually illustrated by the samurai fighting against the modern army of the Emperor. It is obvious that the samurai with their traditional swords will have no chance to win the battle against an army equipped with modern machine guns. When the Japanese army is reluctant to fire at the approaching samurai, Omura relentlessly orders them to open the fire. Visually, "old" and honorable Japan is destroyed on screen by "modern" Japan, leaving the audience wondering what globalizing processes can do to a culture and whether a homogenized, Americanized world is desirable at all, especially since the modern Japanese army is depicted as one, a uniform mass of soldiers, whereas the samurai are individualized as they wear different armors and carry banners bearing their clan symbols.

This binary of a good "old" Japan versus a corrupt modern Japan is problematic as it allows the audience to look exclusively at Japan through the prism of romantic primitivism as only the samurai and their way of life are presented as positive. On the other hand, modern Japan as embodied by Omura is depicted only as cunning, greedy, and dangerous, eradicating all virtuous aspects of its own culture, represented by the samurai. Moreover, according to the narrative, a mutual understanding and respect for another culture can only be expected from representatives of "old" Japan. Whereas Algren and Katsumoto are able to build a deep friendship and learn from each other, Omura and his men do not respect Algren and the American delegates. This becomes clear when the Americans encounter the Japanese delegates for the first time and Algren's supervisor, Colonel Bagley, disparagingly explains that "Japan's got it in mind to become a civilized country and Omura here is willing to spend what it takes to hire white experts to train their army" (*The Last Samurai*). Bagley's explanation clearly reflects imperialist notions and mirrors the idea of Japan being an uncivilized county that needs to be saved by civilized, American experts. Yet, the movie audience learns (via subtitles) that Omura does not perceive the Americans as enlightened and America as a "chosen country." Instead he calls America

"A land of cheap traders" (*The Last Samurai*), hence degrading Americans to people who are willing to do everything for money as they have no honor at all. This first actual encounter of East and West in the movie already sets up a binary that is not overcome at the end of the film and indicates that the ignorance and arrogance between "the Other" is not one-sided. It is only the grace of Katsumoto and Algren who encounter each other open-minded and the Emperor, who gives in to Algren's plea not to sign a treaty that would modernize Japan, which prevents the total failure of the mission of the samurai and their heroic Western helper Algren. The conflict between old "good" Japanese and new "bad" Westernized ways, however, is not resolved in the movie.

## Challenging Ideas of the Feminine East and the Masculine West

Another traditional binary, however, is clearly challenged in *The Last Samurai*. Hollywood productions set in Japan commonly establish a binary of a masculine West against a feminine East. It was crucial to distinguish the barbarian Eastern male from the enlightened Western hero (Kang 75). This binary is challenged and partly revised in *The Last Samurai*. Zwick does not reduce the East to a passive female realm, but with the samurai, he represents the East as very masculine. Like in movies of the Western genre, there is a strong (Japanese) male presence in the movie, which no longer celebrates the Western expansion and violence but follows a more revisionist approach. Especially Katsumoto, the leader of the samurai is presented as a fierce warrior, incorporating virtues such as loyalty and honor which are depicted as increasingly rare in the American society in the movie. Even though Algren first does not care about the samurai and the Japanese culture because he believes that the West is superior to the East, he nevertheless admires the long tradition of warfare in samurai culture from the beginning. Being a professional soldier himself, he is fascinated by the samurai art of fighting. Especially the pride and devotion to their tasks impress Algren and he respects the samurai as worthy enemies, unlike the other American generals who accompany him to Japan and see the samurai as "savages with bows and arrows" (*The Last Samurai*), once more equating them to supposedly uncivilized Native Americans, and thus feeling vindicated concerning their 'frontier-mission.'

Since the audience mainly learns about the samurai culture from Algren's perspective, the male samurai in the movie are never emasculated or depicted as fanatic suicidal persons. In contrast, the audience is exposed to detailed depictions of the art of fighting and the complex Japanese art of warfare. In the past, as Sheridan Prasso has argued, Asian men have seldom been depicted as masculine in Hollywood. Not even martial arts skills were accepted as masculine skills, but on the contrary "martial arts masters were sometimes portrayed as impotent when confronted with Western firepower. No matter how masterful or powerful, the fastest of Eastern hands or most skillful Asian swordplay still can be trumped by the power of a gun" (109). As discussed above, in this movie, however, the audience does not perceive the traditional Japanese warfare with swords as impotent but is rather disgusted by the cowardly usage of guns. Ian Buruma underlines this idea in his study *A Japanese Mirror* as guns were considered in Japan to be weapons "strictly for cowards and foreigners" since "true Japanese heroes fight with their swords" (173). In the movie, the samurai warriors facing their fate and being willing to die for what they believe in seem much more masculine than the Japanese soldiers and American generals behind their modern weapons.

Yet the movie's claim that Algren, a white American soldier, is able to learn and master the skill of the samurai sword as well as the Japanese language and cultural practices within a very short period of time, is less well attuned to the represented culture. Sean M. Tierney argues that the movie conveys an idea of a "supraethnic viability of whiteness" (610) as the American protagonist learns within six months to master the art of the samurai to defeat "with ease six people who have likely spent a lifetime studying the same art" (Tierney 611). This, according to Tierney indicates white supremacy and puts the white character in a position that enables him to establish relationships with the Japanese without losing his superior position. Nevertheless, Algren does not serve as a prime example of white masculinity. On the contrary, he needs to regain his masculinity first and is initiated by the samurai. As a soldier, he killed not only men but also children and women and lost his dignity by being cruel and greedy. As an American soldier, he killed for money and never fought for his ideals. Living in Japan and learning about the way of the samurai, he discovers values and a way of life that he can believe in, he meets people whom he is willing to fight and die for. Thus, the American has to undergo a learning process in the other culture to regain his self-respect. Finally, when he is asked before the last battle why he is going to fight with the samurai against the troops of the West, he replies in Japanese "because they come to kill those who I love" (*The Last Samurai*). This statement shows his change and a transition from an emasculated, imperialist soldier to a noble warrior. Yet, it is not only the American who changes at high speed by the encounter with the East. Katsumoto, similarly greatly improves his language skills within a short period of time and broadens his personal horizon by learning about the American art of war. Although Algren to a certain degree "imitates" the Japanese, it is also true that the Japanese learn from Algren. Reversing a gendered discourse of the masculine West versus a female East, the movie suggests that Japan is no longer only imagined as a docile and passive nation but as well as a nation that becomes aggressive in order to defend its culture.

Furthermore, the depiction of Japanese women in Zwick's movie differs from former movies as well. Taka, Katsumoto's sister and the only female central character does by no means fit Orientalist stereotypes of a Geisha or submissive Madame Butterfly. Instead, she is portrayed as a strong and proud woman, who only houses Algren because she lives according to the samurai codex. Although at first sight an audience not familiar with the behavior of Japanese women could mistake her hospitality and her friendly smiles as signs of interest and affection, the subtitles reveal what Taka really feels. She does not instantly fall in love with Algren but rather despises him for killing her husband and is disgusted by what seems to her a rude, uncivilized behavior. Although in some scenes a notion of eroticism is attached to Taka, especially when the audience sees how she washes herself in a waterfall, the audience and Algren never see her naked. There is no indication of a love scene between the American soldier and the Japanese woman. The only scene of affection takes place when Algren is about to leave with the samurai to fight against the Imperial Army and Taka helps Algren to dress for the upcoming fight. In this scene, she kisses him very lightly before putting her head on his shoulder. Thus, this relationship of an American with a Japanese woman is different from former Japanese-American relationships on screen, where the Japanese woman always was depicted as totally devoted to the Western men, willing to give up her own life and body. Instead, in this movie it is the American soldier who is attracted by her first and who learns her language in order to be able to communicate with her.

Taka is depicted as a strong woman who is able to protect her children on her own when the samurai village is attacked. Obviously she does not need to be taken care of and consequently, it is clear that she will never leave Japan to go back with Algren as a trophy wife or function as his mistress. Instead, she is depicted as an independent, dignified woman with complicated feelings for the American stranger. At the same time, her representation makes clear that the only possibility of the American man and Japanese woman to stay together is that Algren remains in Japan. In the end, the movie suggests that the American might stay in Japan, rather than returning to the United States. The prospect of a long-term relationship is given, which, as Francis Jarman has argued, was denied in previous movies about Japanese-American relationships (164). The suggestion that Algren might stay with Taka in Japan subverts the ending of typical Western movies in which the gunfighter rides away, indicating that he values his freedom more than social structures. Thus, while traditional Westerns celebrate gunfighters as isolationists (Prince 16), *The Last Samurai* offers a new perspective for Nathan Algren as a transnational 'gunfighter' who returns to society, though not to his American society but to the society of the samurai. While the film stages a traditional relationship between a white man and a Japanese woman, the uncommon characterization of Taka in the movie as neither promiscuous nor inferior breaks old stereotypical renditions of gender relations. It further underscores that Japan is no longer merely seen as passive and submissive in the movie, but rather as active and assertive, without constituting a threat.

## Transnational Dialogues

Conversations between the East and the West, represented by Algren and Katsumoto respectively, are central to the narrative of the movie. Katsumoto is interested in learning from and about American culture and, at the same time, he is keen on improving his English. Algren, on the other hand, refuses in the beginning to talk to the samurai leader at all, since he is not attracted by any exchange of ideas and knowledge. However, living with the samurai, he realizes that he does not know anything at all about them and becomes increasingly curious about this unknown culture. The close relationship between the two protagonists from different cultural backgrounds and their reciprocal commitment is based on the conversations they have.

The conversations between Algren and Katsumoto are crucial, as they reveal how people from different cultures might have different perceptions of the same situation. For example, during their first conversation, Algren accuses the samurai of barbarous practices as he witnessed the beheading of a general by Katsumoto. He insists that Americans "don't cut the heads off defeated, kneeling men" (*The Last Samurai*). Yet, he is surprised when Katsumoto explains to him that the beheaded general asked the samurai leader to help end his life as "a samurai cannot stand the shame of defeat" (*The Last Samurai*). Thus, Algren and the audience learn that the act of beheading the general was not a merciless action but rather an act of respect. Katsumoto explains to Algren that "Many of our customs seem strange to you. The same is true for yours" (*The Last Samurai*), thus hinting to the fact that in order to understand another culture, it is important to consider different perceptions before condemning a cultural practice.

The two men start their friendship by discussing American warfare and ideologies, but soon both establish a friendship and begin to debate more personal issues. These conversations and the gentleness as well as the openness of the samurai leader help Algren to reconsider his former life, finally leading him to the conclusion that in order to end his miserable existence and become content with himself, he needs to change his current lifestyle. On the other hand, Katsumoto not only learns about American warfare but the American reassures him in his venture to protect his way of life. When the samurai leader questions the purpose of his mission, concluding that "the way of the samurai is not necessary anymore" (*The Last Samurai*), Algren contradicts Katsumoto and insists that there is nothing more important than the old, traditional ideals which emphasize loyalty, compassion, and total devotion to whatever you do. This American's insight reassures Katsumoto of the importance of his mission and encourages the samurai not to give up their traditional way of life. However, not only Katsumoto, but the Japanese Emperor as well is reminded by Algren, an American that the traditional Japanese culture is valuable and should be preserved by any means. In the movie, both the Japanese and Americans learn from each other, thereby expanding their horizons. The American and the Japanese equally benefit from the cultural encounter and thus no unequal power relation exists in which only one party is enlightened by another. This equal power relation is visually underlined by the frequent use of alternating over the shoulder shots when Algren and Katsumoto have a conversation, thus adding emotional significance to the scene, as the audience is exposed to the perspectives of both characters. The movie suggests that cultural exchanges can be advantageous to both sides if people encounter each other on the same level, without judging the other against one's own, normative ideals. Additionally, the film suggests that there is sometimes the need to be reminded by others of the importance of traditions, thus shedding a positive light on intercultural exchanges.

In this context, it is crucial that neither the American nor the Japanese tries to impose his values on the other, although both are aware of the fact that their cultures are very different. On the contrary, they appreciate their cultural differences and see these differences as an enrichment of their friendship. For example, when Algren is captured by the samurai, one of the warriors treats the American with contempt, since the American does not commit suicide in defeat. As part of the code of honor of the samurai (*bushido*), defeated warriors "slash their stomachs on the battlefield to spite their enemies" (Rankin 9) and to die with honor. However, this practice, called *seppuku* is not part of American warfare and thus unfamiliar to Algren. When a warrior expresses his disgust for the American because of his supposed lack of honor, Katsumoto explains to him that "that's not their custom" (*The Last Samurai*). This short sequence shows how Katsumoto is able to differentiate customs of divergent cultures, not judging the American according to the Japanese code of honor. This scene becomes important once more at the end of the movie, when Katsumoto is wounded and defeated by the Imperial Army. When he asks Algren to help him commit *seppuku* the American warrior respects the wish of his "blood-brother in battle" (Rankin 22) and helps him to end his life honorably. This shows that Algren is indeed able to understand and respect Japanese customs that might have been strange to him before. Yet, the fact that he himself does not commit the ritual suicide after the battle once more underlines that cultural difference is possible: He may have fought with the samurai but has not fully turned into a samurai.

Moreover, language plays an important role in the movie as well. Because Katsumoto is able to speak English, the majority of the conversations between him and Algren are held in English. However, in some scenes, there are Japanese dialogues that are not dubbed in the film, which is unconventional for a Hollywood movie, as Hollywood dialogues in foreign languages are traditionally dubbed. Next to the transnational exchanges in the plot, the movie thus features a surprising innovation in the way in which the language of "the Other" country is rendered more or less accessible for the audience. Many dialogues between Japanese characters are not dubbed but subtitled, thus altering the dominant convention of watching an American movie for a Western audience, since only a few subtitled American productions exist. As Susan Bassnett states on the difference between dubbed and subtitled films "dubbing erases the original voices, and restricts access to other languages. Subtitling, in contrast, makes a comparative perspective possible, as audiences are allowed to access both source and target systems" (136-137) and can hear the Japanese language. The use of subtitles further puts the audience in the position of outsiders who cannot easily understand the language and rely on a translation. This is especially interesting in the subtitled scenes when the Japanese Emperor speaks in *The Last Samurai*. The viewers, just as the American characters in the movie, have to trust the translation of Omura, even though he is not a trustworthy character, leaving the audience with an uncomfortable feeling as one cannot know for sure if the translations are correct. The dialogues between Japanese characters in their native language, which are sometimes not even subtitled at all, can also have a different effect on different audiences. To a Japanese audience, these conversations contribute to a familiar atmosphere in the movie, while for a non-Japanese audience they are markers of difference and lead to irritation and estrangement yet adding to a feeling of authenticity.

Throughout the movie, the American protagonist gradually adapts to the way of the samurai. He does only incorporate Japanese ideals and values, but his outward appearance changes as well. When he lives with the samurai, he is given Japanese clothes, which he first tries on secretly. However, in the course of the film, the Japanese clothes become a part of his new identity. The fact that Algren can assimilate into the Japanese culture and incorporate the code of *bushido*, might suggest that this ancient, traditional, Japanese code can be borrowed and used by anyone, thereby making the ideology available to outsiders. Yet, by mimicry, Algren uses and reenacts the samurai code only to a certain extent.

This becomes evident at the end of the film, when Algren wears samurai armor in order to fight against the Imperial Army and is accepted by the samurai as one of them. Nevertheless, it is important to stress that Algren does not completely turn into a samurai. As Algren reflects, "there is so much here that I will never understand" (*The Last Samurai*). His statement reveals that Algren recognizes the difference between the Japanese and American culture, thereby reflecting a transnational perspective. At first sight, he might look like a samurai but he cannot deny his ethnic roots, he not only looks Caucasian underneath his Samurai helmet, he still is shaped by his American background. There are cultural codes that Algren still does not understand. At the same time, it is obvious that he does not fit into his former American life anymore. Thus, Algren is clearly portrayed as a transnational character, which is neither here nor there but in-between two different cultures. Moreover, it can be argued that in Homi Bhabha's sense, he accomplished to create a Third Space where the Japanese and American culture meet and where a new, transnational identity is created. When the American faces the Imperial Army and the American advisors on the battlefield, a former colleague urges him to make a decision "you ride against us, and you are the same as they are" (*The Last Samurai*). Here, a binary of "us" versus "them" is set up by the American, forcing Algren to decide which side to take – a decision which seems to be impossible for him. Having adapted to the Japanese, samurai way of life, Algren can no longer identify with the American ideology; yet, he does not and cannot deny his American roots either. In the movie, this conflict is visually represented when Algren wear a samurai armor, which reflects his new Japanese identity while his facial features indicate his American identity.

It can be argued that Algren partly takes a transnational position within the narrative since he combines his American heritage with Japanese ideologies. Yet, his transnationality is limited to the battlefield and his unique position is reflected in the sword that is given to him by the samurai. The inscription on the blade reads, "I belong to the warrior in whom the old ways have joined the new" (*The Last Samurai*). The idea of the old ways joining the new ways can be read in different contexts in this film. One such reading could be that Algren joined with his new ideas the samurai, who stand for the old ways. The samurai learned from him to be open towards the modern, American (warfare) culture and new ways of fighting *without* giving up their traditions. A second reading could be that Algren changed his life and his perceptions as well. This idea opens the possibility to a Westerner to identify with Japan and the culture of the samurai, even though he is not, and never will be, Japanese. Although the title of the movie, and the posters advertising the film, could suggest that the character of Tom Cruise was the last samurai, thereby indicating that an American soldier can reinvent himself as a samurai, this is not the outcome of the movie. The American character is by no means supposed to be the last samurai – that is the role ascribed to Katsumoto. This idea is emphasized when Algren takes Katsumoto's sword to the Emperor to remind him of Japan's cultural roots and suggests stopping the rapid modernization processes. When he travels to the capital to see the Emperor, Algren no longer wears the samurai armor, but puts on his Western clothes, thereby visually marking himself as an American. The narrative emphasizes that it is not Algren who convinces the Emperor to stop signing more treaties with the West, but that the Emperor recognizes his mistake in replacing the Japanese culture with modern, Western culture when he receives Katsumoto's sword. In this context it is important to note that the samurai as the most loyal servants dedicated their life protecting the Emperor and Japan. Thus, it is clear to the Emperor and to a Japanese movie audience that Katsumoto sacrificed his life for the traditional culture of Japan. Dressed in Western clothes, Algren neither claims a Japanese identity nor does he try to tell the Emperor about Japanese culture. He has fought in samurai armor with the samurai and has incorporated some of the traditional Japanese values, yet without completely giving up his old ways. Thus, in the end, it is no longer possible to tell where Algren belongs, as he embodies both American as well as Japanese ideals. This notion is taken further by the end of the movie that leaves open whether Algren stays in Japan or returns to the United States.

Despite all these Orientalist aesthetic means, the movie nevertheless received positive reviews in Japan since it allowed the local audience to identify with the Japanese characters and depicted one of the most important decades of social transitions in Japan. The strong female character of Taka, who challenges the sexualization of Japanese women, particularly appealed to the audience. Additionally, it has to be acknowledged that *The Last Samurai* has an international appeal as a story about an individual quest for an identity, an epic battle to protect core values of a culture, and a romantic love story. The dramatic elements of the movie work in the West as well as in the East, and the moral issues such as self-respect and loyalty are shared values throughout all cultures. In the movie, Nathan Algren changes from an arrogant and ignorant American with Orientalist attitudes, believing that he will turn "Orientals into soldiers" (*The Last Samurai*), into a warrior with a more transnational approach. The movie visualizes the complex transaction of modernity and tradition as the conflict centers on Westernizing processes that will probably destroy Japan's cultural uniqueness. Hence, the movie is more about inner conflicts than a conflict between the United States and Japan.

It is tempting to see only transnational traits in *The Last Samurai*, since it focuses exclusively on a Western protagonist who learns specific skills such as sword fighting, but shows how American and Japanese protagonists embrace a foreign ideology and culture. Hence, the movie could be read as an optimistic blueprint of cultural interactions in which two different cultural representatives engage in an open dialogue and are willing to learn from each other. The movie also includes many anti-globalization characteristics which can be also found in transnational discourses, questioning whether modernization and Americanization are worth striving for. In *The Last Samurai* this message is conveyed by erasing "old" Japan which is clearly represented as the ideal state, while "new" Japan seems to be a nation losing its uniqueness. The movie might be understood to suggest that the Western influences corrupt a formerly innocent nation and it might be used to explain Japan's development into a modern, yet inscrutable nation as suggested in more Orientalist movies. In the final scene, after declining to sign new treaties with the West, the Emperor states in English "I have dreamed of a unified Japan ... of a country that is strong and independent and modern ... and now we have railroads, and cannons, and Western clothing. But we cannot forget who we are or where we come from" (*The Last Samurai*). It is striking that the Emperor speaks in English to Algren (and the movie audience), hence making his former translator Omura and the use of subtitles obsolete. The message coming directly from the Emperor does not leave room for interpretation and it emphasizes the importance of cultural roots and heritages – not only for the Japanese but also for Algren and the Americans. This notion is visually underlined by the camera movement in this scene. While the Emperor speaks the words "we cannot forget who we are" he looks at Katsumoto's sword that he is holding in his hand. Then the focus of the camera gradually shifts and a close-up of Algren's face is shown when the Emperor says "or where we come from." Thereby, the movie asserts that it is important not only for the Japanese but also for the Americans to remember their cultural background in an increasingly interconnected world.

However, when one shifts the focus from the characters and their constellation in the movie to the staging of cultural differences between Japan and the United States, it becomes obvious that this movie installs an Orientalist vision by using typical stereotypes. Japan in this movie is the land of noble samurai, women in kimono, and beautiful temples.

According to this vision, Japan is only desirable and worth fighting for in its "original" state. Only traditional Japan, which is not yet completely influenced by the West (and which will later become an imperial power) can serve as a role model. Set in the past, the movie has no direct connection to contemporary economic or political competitions between the two nations and no notion of danger is connected to Japan. Here, the focus is on a pre-industrial nation that does not compete with the United States and that does no longer exist. Thus, traditional, old Japan partly serves escapist purposes by fulfilling a nostalgic longing for the past, based on Orientalist strategies. *The Last Samurai* sends two different messages: on the one hand it offers an anti-imperialist, anti-westernization perspective on Japanese-American relations but at the same time, this movie, which has an international appeal, is nevertheless not completely free from Orientalism.

## TOKYO IRASSHAIMASE!
## TWO AMERICANS LOST IN TRANSLATION

While Nathan Algren, the American protagonist in *The Last Samurai,* is able to integrate into the Japanese culture, Bob, the male American protagonist of Sofia Coppola's 2003 independent movie *Lost in Translation* remains an outsider in contemporary Japan. Although at first sight the movie seems to be again an Orientalist view on contemporary Japan, the film reveals itself as more complicated and offers different readings on closer scrutiny. *Lost in Translation* has to be seen as a movie which works differently with different audiences and plays consciously with Orientalist *and* Occidentalist elements.

*Lost in Translation* is not a typical Hollywood movie. Using only sparse dialogue and including sequences shot with a hand-held, rather unsteady camera and unlikely shots as, for example, framing a longer still-photography shot performed slightly off the focus of the audience, the movie hardly follows formal rules and conventions of Hollywood films. On the level of production, Coppola worked with a mainly Japanese crew when shooting the movie at original locations in Japan, thereby facing the challenge of working with a bilingual team with divergent perceptions and ideas (Coppola DVD *Lost in Translation*). Most of the communication had to be translated into Japanese and back via a bilingual assistant director. This resulted in "an effort similar to that dramatized in the comic sequences in *Lost in Translation* in which Bill Murray's character takes direction through an intermediary during the shooting of his Suntory endorsements" (G. King 12). Furthermore, mistranslations and cultural misunderstandings "slowed down the pace of proceedings" and "in one instance this led to a cross-cultural misunderstanding that resulted in the resignation of the Japanese location manager, deemed to have lost face when the production overran its agreed time limits while shooting in a restaurant location" (G. King 12). Additionally, the director had to cope with different working styles of her Japanese crew members and different restrictions (G. King 11). The management of the hotel, where several sequences of the movie were shot, for instance, only allowed her to use the location at night so as not to disturb the regular guests and the team had no official permission to shoot scenes in the city of Tokyo and the subways.

*Lost in Translation* is a movie set in Tokyo, but it is not a movie *about* Tokyo or Japan. The narration revolves around two American protagonists in temporary exile: Bob Harris (Bill Murray), a middle-aged actor who travels to Tokyo in order to shoot an advertisement for a Japanese company, and Charlotte (Scarlett Johansson), a young Yale graduate who accompanies her photographer husband to Japan. The two characters meet each other in the hotel where they are staying and find out that they have a lot in common: they are not satisfied with their lives and find themselves exposed to a culture that neither of them understands, and they both suffer from insomnia. In order to make their stay as comfortable as possible, Bob and Charlotte start to fraternize and develop a close friendship.

Since the story focuses exclusively on two American characters, central Japanese characters are absent and Tokyo seems to be used merely as an exotic backdrop for the conflict of the two Americans who try to come to terms with their lives. Due to the lack of Japanese protagonists, a cultural connection or interaction between Japanese and American characters does not take place in the movie. Instead, the movie focuses first and foremost on complicated gender relationships and the inability of men and women to communicate properly. According to Coppola, the title refers to the miscommunication between men and women, not only because of the language but because people do not say what they mean (Coppola DVD *Lost in Translation*). Whenever Bob or Charlotte tries to communicate with their spouses, misunderstandings prevail. While Charlotte's husband is always busy and does not even bother to listen to her, Bob's wife in the United States sends him ridiculous fax messages. Therefore, Bob and Charlotte not only feel lost and disconnected because of their unfamiliar surroundings in Japan, but there is also a lack of understanding between them and their partners.

Nevertheless, since the movie's characters are Americans who have to cope with an unknown culture, the title also plays on cultural disconnection and misunderstandings. Interestingly enough, Bob and Charlotte manage to communicate properly and there are only few occasions where they misunderstand each other. Hence, one might conclude that unfamiliar surroundings can lead to improved communication.

## Blinding Lights: Tokyo as a Character

The setting of *Lost in Translation* is, in fact, of crucial importance to the narration. Chris MaGee observes in his introductory chapter to *World Film Locations: Tokyo*, "Cities are cast in films in much the same way casting directors hire actors. Each have their own characters that have been refined in the popular imagination by their repeated appearances in the movies" (5). Even though there is no central human Japanese protagonist in the movie, it can be argued that the city itself acts as a character. To Bob and Charlotte, Tokyo is a glittering, fascinating, yet confusing being, in which modern and traditional Japan exist side by side. The movie audience sees Tokyo as it is seen by the protagonists, starting with Bob's contemplative puzzlement when he rides jet-lagged a taxi from the airport to the hotel. Overwhelmed by the dazzling, flashing neon signs he is unable to decipher and the numerous, modern, high buildings, to Bob the city seems blurred and the rather unfocused camera further creates a feeling of disorientation. Bob's facial expression reveals that he not only already feels lost in the "Empire of

Signs," as Roland Barthes has named Japan, but also overpowered by the city.

Throughout the movie Bob remains an outsider in Japan, because of his ignorant, sometimes even arrogant attitude towards the unknown culture. He is not interested in Japan at all and does not make any effort to try to learn some Japanese words in order to communicate. Bob is never seen with a guide book and prefers to remain in the presumably "safe" transnational space of his hotel instead of exploring the city. The hotel "acts as a cocoon, keeping [him] away from any real contact with the city" (J. King 236). Even if everything from the shower to the other Japanese guests and the English-speaking hotel staff seem to be too small, the hotel is nevertheless a Westernized environment where the rooms feature king size beds, Western bathrooms, and even English television channels. Most of the time, Bob prefers to stay in a space that bears only few markers of Japaneseness. Everything that is not Western makes him feel uncomfortable and therefore he is not interested in exploring his Japanese surroundings. Nonetheless, the hotel is still a Japanese hotel with a mainly Japanese staff and Bob cannot ignore the fact that he is outside America and consequently feels out of place. His sense that he does not fit in his environment is best visualized in the movie when he stands in a crowded elevator in the hotel and literally sticks out of the mass because he is much taller than the Japanese occupants, visually representing an American out of context.

The second protagonist, Charlotte, has a different approach to Japan and the unknown. Standing at a crossroad of her life, she has no idea what to do next. Charlotte hopes to find an answer to the question what to do with her life in Japan which she expects to be a spiritual country. Unlike Bob, she tries to negotiate the urban space as a flâneuse and makes an effort to inspect the city. Deborah Parsons has explained how flânerie "parallels with the idea of the search, and in the abstract wandering in the city this search would seem to be not for place but for self or identity. *Flânerie* can thus be interpreted as an attempt to identify and place the self in the uncertain environment of modernity" (41). By wandering through the streets of Tokyo, Charlotte tries to detect a meaning in her life, yet is only confused by the megapolis. She tries to interact with the unknown culture, yet she does not know how to approach the city and its inhabitants. Visually this is underlined by numerous shots that show Charlotte standing at a window and gazing longingly outside. Even when she walks the city, she carries a transparent umbrella with her. This umbrella functions as a portable window, as it allows her to still see what is happening around her, yet it keeps her physically from fully engaging with the city as it shields her not only from the rain but also creates a spatial distance between her and other people in the city. Hence, Tokyo, represented as a confusing, buzzing city of contradictions, reflects the emotions and inner life of Bob and Charlotte and indicates how both are lost in their lives. The two are not only overwhelmed by the city and the possibilities it offers, but the protagonists are likewise overpowered by the options they have in their lives.

The anxiety of the American protagonists about the city can be interpreted as a reflection of their concerns over their future. Moreover, in her analysis of the role of Tokyo in *Lost in Translation*, Anna Gwendoline Jackson argues that "Tokyo is the City personified, a character that represents the externalization of the alienation, frustration and unfulfilled desires of Bob and Charlotte's inner lives" (158). The two Americans are geographically in the middle of Tokyo, but still, at the same time, they remain "outside" (A. Jackson 154). No matter how often Charlotte strives to understand and connect with the city (and Japan) she never succeeds. When she visits a shrine, hoping to find some spiritual connection and answers to her life, she is disappointed because it does not affect her at all. Instead, back at the hotel, she decorates her room with artificial cherry blossoms to give it an "authentic" feel and listens to an American CD about finding ones purpose in life, which seems much more convenient and tangible for her. The idea of Japan as a place for spiritual re-creation as depicted in *The Last Samurai*, as a personal frontier where the protagonist is changed, is questioned by *Lost in Translation* since it is impossible for the Western characters to find spiritual guidance in Tokyo. Seemingly an invisible border keeps them separated from the city. The idea that there is something ungraspable between the protagonists and the city is visualized in the movie by time and again depicting Tokyo through glass (A. Jackson 158). The characters gaze at the city from the inside of a taxi or through the hotel windows. This spatial separation between Tokyo and the protagonists can be interpreted as an invisible cultural boundary. Since Bob and Charlotte are "outsiders" or *gaijin*[9] they are not able to assimilate to the city. The cultural differences and indifference to the Japanese culture keep the two protagonists at a distance.

However, the self-seclusion of the protagonists enables them to communicate with each other and to share their emotions. In the alien territory, sharing the same sense of alienation, insomnia, and the same language, they become allies who try to cope with this unsettling situation. Although Tokyo is not a place of cultural interconnection and understanding in this movie, it serves as a place where Americans, who may never have become friends with each other and who may have suffered from gender-based miscommunication, learn to take care of each other.

## Make it Suntory Time: Reflecting Orientalism

While many critics hailed Sofia Coppola's movie as a sophisticated, funny motion picture with extremely beautiful pictures of Japan (see Caro; Mitchell; Schwarzbaum), the movie was harshly criticized by the Asian American organization Asia Media Watch. The organization launched a campaign on the Internet, in which they asked members of the movie industry to vote against *Lost in Translation* at all awards. What outraged Asia Media Watch was the "film's heavy reliance on Japanese stereotypes for humor" and they condemned the dehumanization of the Japanese "by portraying them as a collection of shallow stereotypes who are treated with disregard and disdain" (Asia Media Watch). Indeed, the movie does employ several Orientalist, even racist stereotypes, and therefore could be placed among other monolithic depictions of Japan. Homay King explains in *Lost in Translation: Orientalism, Cinema, and the Enigmatic Signifier* that the movie focuses on an American perception, which is problematic as a Western audience tends to "interpret Bob and Charlotte's behavior through a normative Western lens" (162).

Indeed, some Japanese responses to the film were positive. One Japanese moviegoer commented on the Internet that he thought that "the movie captures fairly well how contemporary Japan, in which the modern, busy

---

9   *Gaijin* literally means "outside person". By classifying mainly Caucasians as gaijin a Japanese power relation is established by strictly distinguishing "us" from "them". Today, the term is sometimes considered to be a derogatory term.

parts are mixed with old, serene traditions in a characteristic way, looks to the two Americans who have little knowledge about or interest in the country they are staying in" and he continues that he was "rather amused by the Americans who are confused in a foreign country which they have little knowledge [about]" (Japan Today). This Japanese response touches the important issue of perspective, since the movie does play differently with a Japanese audience. For them, it is a motion picture made by an American director about Americans who stay in Japan. Thus, the movie displays a Western perception of Japan, which is in some parts Orientalist. Nevertheless, from a Japanese perspective, this only reflects the ignorance or rather inability of Westerners to fully comprehend Japan.

Bob for example, who has a strong Orientalist attitude in the movie, completely rejects anything Japanese, thereby representing a hopelessly arrogant American in a foreign country, one who does not care about the "Other" and who cannot find anything exciting in unknown cultures.[10] To the Japanese audience, Bob is the perfect Occidentalist stereotype of a Yankee tourist who believes that everyone has to speak proper English and who never questions himself. For him, the Japanese are just two-dimensional, comical sidekicks whom he does not treat with respect but neglect. Yet, for Japanese viewers it is exactly this ignorant behavior that makes Bob a funny character. It can be further argued that while some Japanese characters are used as a source of humor to a Western audience, especially in the scene with the Japanese prostitute, for a Japanese audience it is the American and his prudish behavior that work as comic relief (H. King 162).

Bob personifies a typical *gaijin*, the selfish and self-concerned foreigner (Creighton 146), an outsider, who will never get access to the Japanese culture. Additionally, the fact that Bob is hired by a Japanese whiskey company to advertise their products alludes to a popular practice in the 1980s and 1990s, when numerous American actors such as Arnold Schwarzenegger, Sylvester Stallone, or Brad Pitt were regularly hired by Japanese companies for advertising purposes. As Millie Creighton argues in her essay "Imagining the Other in Japanese Advertising Campaigns," the use of Western celebrities in Japanese advertisements, who are "often shown overtly breaking

---

10 The cast of Bill Murray is further underlines Bob's character, since Murray is famous for his roles as the "ugly American" in his oeuvre.

the conventional rules of Japanese society" (137) helped to create a binary "Other" to the Japanese. Furthermore, by using Westerners in advertisements, the foreigner becomes reduced and is essentialized into the category of "the Other" (137), thereby turning around the stereotypization which Easterners experience in the West.

In Coppola's movie, Bob is used by the advertising company as an Occidental extra on whom Japanese ideas about Hollywood masculinity are projected. During the commercial shoot, the photographer places Bob, who wears a tuxedo, in an old English-style room and demands him to look "mysterious" like Frank Sinatra or Roger Moore, thereby exoticizing and reducing Bob to an Occidentalist stereotype of a Western gentleman.[11]

One of the most ridiculous characters to appear in the movie is a Japanese show master whom Bob encounters when he is invited to his television show. On closer inspection, however, even this apparently racist representation of a silly, feminized, homosexual Japanese man turns out to be more than just an Orientalist comment on Japanese entertainment shows. As Anna Gwendoline Jackson argues in "Outside in Tokyo: The Gaijin Gaze in Chris Marker's Sans Soleil and Sofia Coppola's Lost in Translation," the Japanese entertainer is based upon a real-life entertainer, who does indeed have a popular TV show in Japan. More accurately, his star persona incorporates an element of *Japanese* racial humor, since "with his blonde wig, dyed eyebrows, whitened eyelashes and wild antics" he is "the Gaijin-superstar stereotype seen clowning on Japanese TV" (A. Jackson 162). A Japanese audience is likely to recognize the show master, who is famous in Japan for *caricaturing* American actors on TV. To them the fact that Bob visits him in his show and messes around with his Japanese host adds to the already bizarre behavior of the American actor, since Bob does not even recognize that he is ridiculed. Such a stereotype of a flamboyant Japanese

---

11 The movie, additionally, employs the stereotype of a young, blonde Hollywood actress, Kelly, who stays in the same hotel as Bob and Charlotte. Kelly embodies the cliché of a shallow, loud, superficial American starlet, who giggles all the time during an interview and reassures everyone that despite her physique she is rather a fast food consumer than an anorexic. On the other hand Kelly represents the "new," transnational generation of Hollywood actors, who - on the surface - seem to get along well everywhere in the world, since she is an American who does not seem lost in Japan.

show master might appear Orientalist to a clueless viewer from the West, from a Japanese perspective however, the host is recognizable as an Occidentalist simulacrum of a Western celebrity. To a Western audience, this allusion is "lost in context" (A. Jackson 162) and instead the scene seems stereotypical.

The movie also plays quite obviously with Western audience expectations as, for example, in the first shot, which shows a close-up of the back of a woman wearing light pink underwear. This shot is held for almost 30 seconds while movie credits fade in and out. This opening is significant since the focus of the first seconds is on the display of a female body, thus objectifying a woman by showing a "close-to-nude status of the lower regions of a body that seems all the more objectified in being removed from its head or its location at this stage in relation to an identifiable character" (G. King 1). Yet, as it turns out, the body is not a Japanese body but the body of the American protagonist of the movie. Instead of reinforcing traditional Madame Butterfly stereotypes, the body of an American woman is objectified and exposed to the gaze of the audience. What is even more, Charlotte is often helpless in the movie and in need of guidance. Yet, when compared to Bob, she seems stronger and more independent. This playing with expectations and turning and twisting of stereotypes can be explained by the fact that Sophia Coppola brings a specific, a consciously female perspective to the movie that does not follow an Orientalist approach. As Reina Lewis has argued in *Gendering Orientalism*, the Orientalist gaze is dominantly a male gaze, and depicts "Orientalist images *of* women rather than representations *by* women" (3). *Lost in Translation*, however, is a female, Western representation of Japan which focalizes gender relations through a female lens and Coppola does not set up a gendered binary between a female, passive East and a male, active West. Instead, she captures the emotions and struggles of two rather naïve Americans far away from home.

### East is East and West is West?

Coppola's movie draws attention to a lack of communication, misperceptions and different forms of exclusion and differentiation, which are the basis for conflicts between Americans and Japanese as well as amongst Americans. In Coppola's movie, there is no real connection between Japan and the Americans. It seems as if the Japanese as well as the Americans prefer to remain among themselves. Relationships between American and Japanese characters are limited to business relationships and passing acquaintances. This lack of real conversations between Japanese and American characters is based on a language barrier. Neither Bob nor Charlotte speak Japanese and the Japanese characters they encounter do not speak English, thereby making any communication impossible. The general lack of communication between the sexes and the inability to express oneself is thus reflected in the intercultural relationship. Metaphorically, the East, Japan or women cannot communicate with the West, America or men since both sides do not speak the same language and no one makes the effort to understand "the o/Other."

On the narrative level of the movie, a Western audience is abandoned in translation since the Japanese lines are not subtitled at all throughout the motion picture, thereby creating a feeling of isolation among the Western audience. Hence, once more the Japanese reception of the movie is different from that of a Western audience, since a Japanese audience is able to understand what the Japanese characters in the movie say and thus does not feel estranged at all. Instead, they can laugh about comments made by the Japanese, which, for a Western audience, remain lost.

Although the movie does not stage an intercultural friendship or a romantic love-affair between the East and the West, *Lost in Translation* is a movie with a transnational approach. The cultural shock and the feeling of isolation experienced by the characters (and partly by the Western audience) are based on the differences between Japan and the United States. They work as metaphors for the alienation and loneliness in the lives of Bob and Charlotte, but they develop their own dynamics in the course of the plot.

According to Ezra and Rowden, many transnational motion picture construct the dynamics of narrative "by a sense of loss" (7). In Sofia Coppola's movie, the protagonists are lost in two different ways: They are lost in their lives at home and they feel disoriented in the unknown environment of Tokyo. Uprooted from their familiar surroundings, they struggle with their emotions and their lives. Although they are not fully aware of it, the encounter with another culture helps them to question their own ways of life. Towards the end of the movie, even Bob, who mainly rejects the Japanese people and culture, mentions to his wife on the phone that he "would like to start eating healthier" and "like to start eating Japanese food" (*Lost in Translation*). It seems as if Bob recognizes that he needs to become active and has to open up in order to change his life and he takes a completely different (food) culture into consideration to start with the change. Neither Bob nor Charlotte are presented as enlightened Westerners who are superior to the East. On the contrary, both are confused and in seeking answers to their lives they get one step ahead in Japan. As the trailer of the movie suggests, "sometimes you have to go halfway around the world to come full circle."

If the "image of the displaced person grounds the transnational, both thematically and in terms of global awareness" (Ezra and Rowden 7), *Lost in Translation* is thoroughly transnational and, at the same time, questions the idea of globalization as homogenization. Japan is clearly a Westernized country, but concurrently, it is clearly *not* the West. It "fluctuates between the phantasmal and real, the foreign and familiar, the strange and everyday life" (Allison "The Japan Fad" 16). This notion is reflected in the movies as well, since the director does not ignore the urban, industrial Japan in favor of an exotic setting. She juxtaposes modern images of the pulsing metropolis with images of traditional Japan such as Mount Fuji, an *Ikebana* class (Japanese flower arrangements), temples, and a traditional Japanese wedding. An opposition within Japan is illuminated and makes it clear that contemporary island nation is both traditional and modern. The country is no longer only rendered a mysterious place but it is also accepted as a modern, maybe even postmodern nation which is technologically extremely developed.[12] Despite globalizing processes, Japan is shown as unique and different from the West.

For temporary visitors from the West, the country remains a fascinating, yet sometimes irritating place as cultural differences are still existent and can lead to confusion and misunderstandings when encountered. Thus, it becomes increasingly important to consider different perspectives when watching a film like Coppola's. To dismiss *Lost in Translation* as an Orientalist film misses the point, as the movie suggests that Bob's ignorant and arrogant and Charlotte's self-centered behavior is unacceptable in a con-

---

12  Indeed the high glass buildings, numerous neon-signs and plasma screed facades remind the audience of science-fiction movies such as *Blade Runner* (1982) or *The Fifth Element* (1997).

temporary world. Moreover, since they can neither cope with their life in Japan nor in the United States, they are denied agency. An Orientalist attitude and the supposedly problematic Orientalist (and Occidentalist) stereotypes that go with it are open to different interpretations by different audiences.

## *LETTERS FROM IWO JIMA*: JAPANESE WRITINGS – AMERICAN PICTURES

While *The Last Samurai* and *Lost in Translation* both move in the direction of a less hostile, less unreservedly Orientalist representation of Japan and towards a more transnational depiction by recognizing and appreciating the differences between American and Japanese culture, actor and director Clint Eastwood goes one step further with his movies *Flags of Our Fathers* and *Letters from Iwo Jima*. The movies are set during the thirty-six days Battle of Iwo Jima in which the Americans lost 6,000 soldiers while 25,000 soldiers were wounded. On the Japanese side, the defense force of 20,000 soldiers was almost completely annihilated (Dower, *War without Mercy* 92). Eastwood decided to set his two movies during a war that was not only territorial but soon turned into a ferocious crusade in which the question of race became central. To Americans especially the Japanese and their warfare seemed incomprehensively cruel and at the Battle of Iwo Jima the different warfare cultures of Japan and the United States clashed. Author James Bradley, described the situation in the biography of his father, *Flags of Our Fathers*, on which the movie was based, as follows:

> This will not be a mere battle. It will be a colossal cultural collision, a grinding together of the tectonic plates that are East and West. The Western "plate" will be the cream of American democracy and mass-production: in voluntary manpower; in technology, training and industrial support. The Eastern "plate" will be the elite minions of a thoroughly militarized society whose high priests have taught that there is no higher virtue than death in battle. The result of this collision will alter the fates of both East and West for the next century to come. (193)

Indeed Americans were shocked and disgusted by the supposedly inhumane enemy, while the Japanese believed in their spiritual purity and superiority and aimed to "smash the 'Anglo-American beasts'" (Buruma, *Inventing Japan* 113). The differences in warfare and national ideologies turned the war in the Pacific into a nightmare that culminated in the dropping of the atomic bombs on Hiroshima and Nagasaki.

Eastwood was less interested in shooting movies about the winning or losing of the battle than telling the stories of those young men who had experienced the war and were affected for the rest of their lives. Therefore, both movies focus not on the historical battle itself but on the individual stories of soldiers and generals from both sides. This makes Eastwood's project extraordinary and different from former World War II movies as the battle is depicted from two oppositional perspectives: *Flags of Our Fathers* depicts the battle from the American point of view, whereas *Letters from Iwo Jima* tells the story from the Japanese troops' perspective.

In academic discussions, historian John Dower has also aimed at a balanced representation of the aims and the course of the war. He observes in his book *War without Mercy* that the Japanese were dehumanized in the United States during World War II. After the attack on Pearl Harbor, sentiments of fear and outrage about such a treacherous act swept across the United States, and there was a need to visualize the enemy as was done in countless propaganda movies. These movies reflected the hostile sentiment of the majority of Americans by depicting the enemy as subhuman, inscrutable, and dangerous. In addition, propaganda posters employed these fears, depicting Japanese people as monsters, thus ascribing them only negative qualities which helped to exploit and use the threat they posed. Although some Americans who had contact to Japanese prisoners of war realized that not all the Japanese were aggressive and fanatic, only few managed to overcome their prejudices (Dower, *War without Mercy* 77). Dower aims at a differentiated perspective on Japanese-American relationships during the Second World War by pointing out also the Japanese perspective on the war and their motivations and by criticizing the monolithic, racist depiction of the enemy, both in the United States and Japan.

In a similar vein the Japanese historian Sadao Asada conducted research on the historical relationship between Japan and the United States. Asada analyzed English and Japanese material, reflecting the viewpoint of Japanese and American contemporary witnesses. His book *Culture Shock and Japanese-American Relations* sheds light on the conflicted course of Japanese-American relations. Recently, Emiko Ohnuki-Tierney published a book in which she endeavors to focus on the human side of *kamikaze* pilots. In *Kamikaze Diaries* she reveals how *kamikaze* pilots, who are dominantly portrayed as cunning and unscrupulous in the West, did not happily sacrifice themselves but instead were frequently forced to "volunteer" for the missions (xvii). She explains the highly complex structure of Japanese warfare in Japan during World War II and reveals that the military ordered young men to die for their country, making suicide a moral obligation rather than a choice. Moreover, she brings to light that those who tried to resist the order were often severely punished (4-8).

With her book Ohnuki-Tierney aspires to deconstruct the dominant image of the *kamikaze* as "synonymous with reckless people, fanatical chauvinists, the inscrutable and untrustworthy 'other,' and even 'suicide bombers'" (xv) and she enables readers all over the world to learn more about the infamous pilots and their lives. Along the same line, in 2007, a Japanese movie entitled *Ore Wa Kimi No Tame ni Koso Shini ni Iku* (*For Those We Love*) was released in Japan. The movie covers the still controversial topic of *kamikaze* pilots during World War II as well and endeavors to depict the humanity of the pilots, who believed that they sacrificed their lives for their families and loved ones. It is also an attempt to replace stereotypical images of old, buck-toothed, dull-looking pilots who relished war and the prospect of killing.

Yet, balanced approaches remain the exception and hardly any movie shows differentiated images of the Japanese in World War II. Instead, the dominant war image of the Japanese enemy as inhuman yellow peril was canonized in mainstream American movies of the last decades, in which the world on screen is clearly divided in good (America) and evil (Japan). This American cinematic version of the Pacific War proved to be extremely powerful in shaping the idea of the Japanese as more severe and cruel than the Americans. It overshadows other versions of the war which remain almost unrecognized in the West. World War II movies from *Flying Tigers* (1942) to *Tora! Tora! Tora!* (1970) to *Pearl Harbor* (2001) have continued to shape and reinforce negative stereotypes of Japanese soldiers. Differently, Eastwood's depiction of the Battle of Iwo Jima from both sides of the Pacific blurs the clear boundary between good and evil and questions whether such a categorization is possible at all. Alternatively, the movies focus on the devastating effects of war on soldiers on both sides and since Eastwood is an *American* who tells the story of war from a Japanese perspective, he can hardly be accused of having produced a movie out of Japanese nationalistic interests. Instead of arguing that *Letters from Iwo Jima* traces an Orientalist approach because an American stages the Japanese perspective, the fact that an American director has an interest in depicting a battle from the perspective of the "Other" demonstrates once more that new, transnational approaches are becoming increasingly important in Hollywood.

*Flags of Our Fathers* was released in the United States in October 2006, four months prior to *Letters from Iwo Jima* which was first released in Japan. *Flags of Our Fathers*, is centered around three American soldiers who accidentally become renowned heroes when a picture is taken of them while they hoist a flag on Mount Suribachi on Iwo Jima. While *Flags of Our Fathers* questions the prize that is paid by soldiers when they fight a war and reveals that often the value of individual lives is underestimated by the government, *Letters from Iwo Jima* shows how the Japanese soldiers were utilized and misused by their government that did not even bother to explain the causes for this battle to the soldiers. These changing perceptions are interesting as both movies were directed by the same American director. *Flags of Our Fathers* seems at first sight to follow typical American World War II movie narratives, yet, at closer scrutiny it focuses on personal experiences and the question of how to deal with trauma. *Letters from Iwo Jima*, also diverges from traditional American combat movies, as it does not follow the jingoistic stance of predecessors such as *Sands of Iwo Jima* (1949). Instead, this movie proves to be a cross-cultural production that incorporates many Japanese styles and indeed offers an interesting, heterogeneous perception of the battle.

### Deconstructing the Image of the Inhumane Japanese

Although the movies were released only a few months apart from each other and portray the same battle, there are no direct connections between them on a narrative level: the protagonists never meet and the stories concentrate on different issues. However, the movies have to be understood as a unit. Like mirror-images, they reflect the two opposing sides of the same battle.

*Flags of Our Fathers* tells the story of the three surviving flag-raisers in the famous Joe Rosenthal photograph.[13] The movie uncovers how a single picture turned three soldiers into national icons, who were used by the American government to sell war bonds in order to raise money for the Pacific War. While the hoisting of the flag is a crucial scene in *Flags of Our Fathers*, it has almost no meaning in *Letters from Iwo Jima* and is only briefly shown as a background action in one scene. The storyline of *Letters from Iwo Jima* was based on actual letters written by General Kuribayashi Tadamichi and other soldiers to their families.[14] Thus, Clint Eastwood did create a fictive Japanese story but based his storyline on actual, Japanese voices. The Japanese perspective concentrates on two protagonists: Saigo, a young Japanese baker, who is part of the troops who are forced to defend the island of Iwo Jima and General Kuribayashi, who is ordered to lead the defense. The former dominant Western perception of all Japanese soldiers as being cruel fanatics, who happily went to battle in order to sacrifice themselves for the Emperor, is already deconstructed when the Japanese protagonists is introduced. Saigo is not a volunteer but was drafted and had to leave his pregnant wife. The audience witnesses in a flashback, how the

---

13 Joe Rosenthal covered the invasion of Iwo Jima for the Associated Press and photographed six Marines who raised the American flag on Mount Suribachi. The picture was published in newspapers all over the United States, immediately became an icon of American victory and was awarded with the Pulitzer Price for Photography. Yet, as James Bradley reveals in his book *Flags of Our Fathers*, the picture only showed the second raising of the flag, after the first flag was removed for The Secretary of the Navy, James Forrestal, who wanted to take it back as a souvenir (Buell). Furthermore, the raising of the flag on Mount Suribachi did not signal the success of the invasion, but the battle went on for thirty-one days before the island was declared secured. As James Bradley writes in his book, "the facts didn't matter. The photo looked heroic, and that was enough" (403). The Marine Corps Memorial in Arlington, which is modeled after the photograph, was unveiled in 1954.

14 The Japanese author Kakehashi Kumiko has written on the same topic in her book *So Sad to Fall in Battle: An Account of War Based on General Tadamichi Kuribayashi's Letters from Iwo Jima*. The book was published in Japan in 2005, one year before the release of the movie and is said to have inspired Watanabe Ken for his role.

young man is informed that he will have the honor to fight for his country. Instead of pride and joy, Saigo's facial expression reveals that he is more shocked than honored and his wife begs the officials to have mercy and not take away her husband. This scene makes overtly clear that this young Japanese soldier is dragged out of his life. Seen from this perspective, Japan is indeed negatively affected by war, since the ongoing invasion by the American troops make it necessary for Saigo to leave. Not being interested in the war, he is punished at the beginning of the movie for his supposedly unpatriotic behavior when lamenting to a friend that he does not see any sense in fighting and dying for an island where "nothing grows" and where "bugs are crawling everywhere" (*Letters from Iwo Jima*). The young reluctant soldier even dares to voice his opinion that "we [the Japanese] should better hand the island to the Americans so that we can go home" (*Letters from Iwo Jima*). Frequently questioning his orders and the purpose of defending the island, he refuses to commit ritual suicide and instead runs away to save his life. Saigo does not fit any previous yellow peril war-time stereotypes of unattractive, merciless Japanese soldiers. Instead, with him the "Other" becomes a handsome young, scared man, who cannot handle weapons and only wants to go home and thus resembles the historical soldiers who were ordered to defend Iwo Jima and were an inexperienced "ill-equipped bunch of randomly cobbled-together units" (Kakehashi 11).

Similarly, not only soldiers like Saigo and his companions are depicted as human beings but General Kuribayashi, a historical figure, as well is introduced to the audience as an intelligent, charismatic, and gentle general. Having studied in California, and being friends with many Americans, he respects and appreciates the American culture. The general embodies the tragedy of the war, since he has to fight a nation that he personally does not consider to be an enemy. Historically Kuribayashi was aware of the military superiority of the United States and strictly opposed a war against America, stating that "America is the last country in the world Japan should fight" (Kakehashi 106). This attitude is reflected in the movie as well and further indicates that not all Japanese people were keen on fighting this war. The general, however, remains loyal to his country and the Japanese code of honor, although he refuses to execute a disobedient serviceman who is unwilling to commit suicide on demand, a common practice in the

Japanese army when facing defeat.[15] Kuribayashi is not willing to sacrifice his soldiers easily, since he believes that a soldier still able to fight is of more use than a dead solider. He is modern enough to break some of the traditional rules and proves that not all Japanese generals were fanatic fools who did not question their orders. His ambivalent position is visualized in the movie as Kuribayashi carries both a Colt 46, which he once received as a gift during a stay in the U.S., and a samurai sword. Saigo and Kuribayashi are depicted neither as cowardly nor cold-blooded characters interested in killing as many Americans as possible; they are presented as husbands, fathers, and friends who care more about their families than about the Emperor and thereby make it easy even for a non-Japanese audience to identify with them.

Yet with his movie, Eastwood introduces the Western audience to aspects of the Japanese war-time mentality which are hard to understand, such as the practice of collective suicide. In several scenes, the actions of the Japanese strike the Western audience as strange and illogical. But since the codes of action are clearly articulated in Eastwood's movie, they never seem inhumane and in turn only underline the desperate and tragic situation of the soldiers. For instance, in *Flags of Our Fathers* some Marines discover the distorted corpses of Japanese soldiers in a cave. They assume that the Japanese soldiers must have committed suicide and, like the audience, they are unable to understand their senseless death. This scene is not resolved and neither the soldiers in the movie nor the audience is given an explanation and thus, to a Western movie audience Japanese warfare appears to be totally illogical, inhumane, and insane. However, although the act of the soldiers seems insane, the movie mise-en-scène presents the Japanese soldiers as victims. The audience cannot help but feel pity when one of the protagonists finds the mutilated bodies, torn apart by grenades of very young Japanese soldiers, some of them in fetal-position. In *Letters from Iwo Jima*, Eastwood focuses as well on an emphatic American perception on World War II, by following James Bradley's notion that the Japanese

---

15 Historicalloy General Kuribayashi also refused to command common "bazai-suicide-attacks" and instead conducted a defensive style of combat. His uncommon tactics were suspicious to other Japanese commanders but Kuribayashi's tactics proved successful to the extent that he withstood the invasion longer than expected (Kakehashi 54).

soldiers were victims of their own nation. Bradley described the desperate situation of the Japanese in his book and assumed that to the Japanese soldiers, the war was "a tragedy brought about by the Japanese military leaders who forced their brutalized young men to be brutal themselves" (104), thus casting light on the fact that most Japanese soldiers were victims of the fanatical warfare of their own country during World War II. The author explains how the Japanese military regime perverted traditional samurai virtues and declared suicide to be "an expression of ultimate sacrifice for one's country" (315). Indeed, in *Letters from Iwo Jima*, the audience is confronted with another group of Japanese soldiers who are supposed to commit the ritual suicide. This time, from the perspective of the Japanese soldiers, the nightmarish situation seems even more hopeless and tragic, as these young soldiers are afraid and do not want to die, but have to follow an order. When watching both movies, *Flags of Our Father* and *Letters from Iwo Jima*, the audience gets a more complete image of this battle during World War II and by mixing an understanding American perception with the Japanese viewpoint of the battle; the movies take a clearly transnational turn and challenge the notion that all Japanese generals and soldiers were imbeciles.

## The Battle of East and West

Although Eastwood avoids depicting the Japanese enemy as subhuman in both movies, he does not completely erase the image of the brutal Japanese soldier. In *Flags of Our Fathers*, the best friend of the American protagonist Doc Bradley (Ryan Philippe) is brutally tortured and slaughtered by Japanese soldiers, leaving the audience shocked and disgusted by such unnecessarily cruel behavior. Here, the image of the Japanese soldier during World War II as being extremely merciless and sadistic seems to be reinforced. Likewise, in *Letters from Iwo Jima* the American enemy is depicted as heartless and cold-blooded, as some American soldiers senselessly kill defenseless Japanese soldiers simply because they are not willing to guard them. Incomparable to the constellation in *Flags of Our Fathers*, one of the murdered soldiers is a close friend of the protagonist and the fact that these murdered Japanese men surrendered because they could no longer stand the brutal treatment by their own commanders makes their death even more tragic. Eastwood underlines in both movies that there are barbaric and vicious soldiers on both sides and that cruelty and inhumanity is not linked to ethnicities but to the individual character and war itself, making it impossible to clearly condemn all Japanese as heinous while hailing all Americans to be heroes and vice versa.

The two movies play with the perspective from which the battle is viewed by the audience. When the young American Marines have to run up the beaches of the island in *Flags of Our Fathers*, they are attacked by Japanese soldiers who are hiding in caves. From this American perspective, the faceless enemy is the devious Other, who lures the Americans into a deadly ambush. Nonetheless, in *Letters from Iwo Jima*, the audience witnesses the same attack from the perspective of the Japanese soldiers inside the caves who are as frightened as the approaching Americans. Besides the large fleet of vessels, they see the endless lines of Americans and they know that they cannot possibly fend off the invasion by such a superior force. The Japanese soldiers fire from caves and holes in the ground at the invading enemy in order to stay alive as long as possible, hoping against hope to survive. What appears to be a shifty attack from the American perspective reveals itself to be a desperate act of self-defense from the Japanese point of view. In *Letters from Iwo Jima*, suddenly the former faceless Japanese enemy becomes individualized and the individual soldiers become victims of a faceless American enemy. This questions the ascription of the roles of aggressor and victim and highlights the importance of the perspective from which a situation is analyzed. Both movies show how Japan and the United States were affected by the war and how soldiers and family members on both sides of the Pacific suffered from the war and the loss of family members and friends.

Since *Letters from Iwo Jima* is a war movie, Americans and Japanese encounter each other first and foremost as enemies on a battlefield. However, unlike former war movies where there was seldom any convergence between the enemies, Eastwood manages to hint at points of contact and similarities between the opposing soldiers despite all separating differences. For example, one scene shows some Japanese soldiers capturing a wounded Marine and dragging him into a cave in order to get some information about the American strategy from him. Their commander, Baron Nishi (Ihara Tsuyoshi) orders his medics to treat him with the scarce medical supplies left. Nishi, a passionate equestrian, traveled to the United States for the Olympic Games in Los Angeles and befriended American celebrities. This experience and his knowledge of the English language make it possible for Nishi and the American soldier to communicate with each other. When the young American dies despite Nishi's efforts, the commander translates and reads out a letter the soldier kept with him. This letter reminds the Japanese soldiers, who treated the American soldier as an enemy that the Americans are human beings too. One Japanese soldier utters in bewilderment that his mother had written almost the same lines to him – only in another language. This scene not only depicts the human side of Japanese soldiers like Baron Nishi, but indicates that "enlisted men from both Japan and the United States were *taught* to think in racist terms" (J. King 31). The soldiers as well as the audience are reminded that "the Other" is not too different from oneself, thus offering a more transnational stance when thinking about World War II.

By staging a movie on the confrontation between Japan and the U.S. in a World War II battle from a Japanese perspective, based on Japanese letters, with Japanese protagonists and, additionally, employing an entirely Japanese cast speaking their mother tongue on screen, American director Clint Eastwood chose a transnational approach to World War II. It can be argued that Eastwood's movie is a transnational product since the film is technically an American movie, though artistically and linguistically it can no longer be identified as such. The fact that this movie is hard to classify is reflected in the different categories in which it was nominated for prizes. *Letters from Iwo Jima* won the Golden Globe in the category "Best Foreign Language Film" and it was nominated for the Academy Awards as "Best Motion Picture of the Year." Thus, while it was nominated for a category in which the majority of movies are not American at the Golden Globe Awards, it was recognized as an American film at the Academy Awards. At the same time, ironically, it received the Japan Academy Prize for Outstanding Foreign Language Film (J. King 33).

This particular position as a hybrid movie can be traced back to the fact that on the one hand the main language used in the movie is Japanese and, on the other hand, the movie includes other typical Japanese elements as well. Voice-over, just as in *The Last Samurai* is employed several times to lead through the narration. *Letters from Iwo Jima* opens with the voice-over of Saigo, who reads a letter that he is writing to his wife. The first line, "Hanako, we are digging the holes in which we will fight and die" (*Letters from Iwo Jima*) already divulges the desperate situation of the soldiers on the island and make clear that the story is not narrated by an extremist Japanese soldier. The audience clearly identifies and emotionally connects with the Japanese characters, regardless of all the cultural and ethnic differences. Ideas of honor and sacrifice, as well as the wish to survive and return home from war, work across national and ethnic borders, these emotions work with audiences in Japan and the United States.

Moreover, *Letters from Iwo Jima*'s cinematic language works in both a U.S. and a Japanese context. As it contains different aesthetic impulses and cinematic traditions, many Japanese moviegoers stated that for them, the movie played like a Japanese film (Schilling). That this impression was intentional is substantiated by an interview with Iris Yamashita, the Japanese-American scriptwriter of the movie, in *The Japan Times Online*. She explained that rather than exoticizing the Japanese for a Western audience, she had intended to write the movie mainly for a Japanese viewership (Schilling). The inclusion of typical elements of Hollywood movies like the figure of the "common man" or scenes of compassion, which may have been estranging in the past, are today unproblematic, as they are now common in Japanese productions as well[16] as the popularity of Hollywood movies in Japan has changed the viewing patterns of the Japanese audience, making it possible for an American movie director to produce a movie which is accepted as a Japanese movie by a Japanese audience.

With *Letters from Iwo Jima*, for the first time, an American director dispelled the traditional depiction of Japanese enemies during World War II as sub-humans, by portraying them instead as people who suffer. Unlike in former war films, like *Pearl Harbor* in which Japanese soldiers were depicted as old and fanatical in order to create a visual contrast to the young and innocent American soldiers, Eastwood's soldiers from both sides are young victims of their nations' war. So far, "first hand Japanese accounts of ground combat against United States forces during World War II are comparatively rare, especially accounts that have been translated into English" (Lofgren 97) and a dominant Western point of view was offered when it came to visual depictions of battles between the United States and Japan.

Eastwood's movies however, do not only hint at the fact that there are indeed two sides of a war (story), but he enables the audience to actually

---

16  Before the occupation of Japan by the United States after World War II, kissing scenes in movies were actually censored in Japan (Buruma, *Inventing* 135-136).

feel with and to get emotionally attached to the characters from *both* sides. His movies no longer ask which side the audience is on, but instead focus on the question from which perspective "the Other" is imagined. *Letters from Iwo Jima* challenges the dominant perception upheld by former Hollywood movies and instead offers a multiple, more differentiated image of the Japanese and the Americans during the war.

## PREVIEW: A TRANSNATIONAL TURN IN HOLLYWOOD

*Letters from Iwo Jima* alongside other contemporary American movies with a Japanese setting or with Japanese central characters reveal how the image of Japan and the Japanese is gradually shifting from an outright Orientalist representation to a more variegated and complex image. Not all approaches were successful, as the movie *Memoirs of a Geisha* demonstrates, in which Japan is reduced to an exotic land of fantasy, where a rags-to-riches story of a young, poor girl who becomes a famous Geisha unfolds.

The movie attempts to explain the traditional institution of the Geisha in Japan, but instead of illuminating the complexities of Geisha culture, it hardens former Orientalist stereotypes by exoticizing the profession of the Geisha for a Western audience. Even worse, the central female Japanese Geisha characters were played by Chinese actresses Michelle Yeoh and Ziyi Zhang. This cast did not only reinforce an Orientalist notion by echoing the idea that "all Asians look the same," but likewise scandalized the Chinese audience. The movie was harshly criticized in the media, especially in Internet blogs, for its cultural insensitivity to atrocities during the Chinese occupation by Japan, when Japanese men captured Chinese women and forced them to work as "comfort women" in so-called "comfort stations" for Japanese soldiers, where these women were constantly raped. As the cast of the movie obviously revived these memories, the movie was banned in China (BBC News "China"). Moreover, since the director of *Memoirs of a Geisha* was not able to find places in Kyoto, where most of the plot is set, that retained the traditional air of pre-war Japan as he imagined it, he decided to build his own filmic fantasy world by borrowing elements from Chinatown, mingling them with different Japanese settings (Napier, *From Impressionism* 121).

In other contemporary Hollywood movies, the differences between Japan and the United States still remain visible, but these differences cease to be only threatening signs of danger. Instead, cultural disjunctions offer the opportunity to rethink one's own position as not only in *Letters from Iwo Jima* but also in *The Last Samurai* or *Lost in Translation*. While in former movies, there was scarcely any sense of friendship between American and Japanese characters, now friendships and negotiations between the former enemies are becoming staged on screen. Nevertheless, Orientalist perceptions have not completely vanished from the screens. Even in a well-meaning representation of Japan like in *The Last Samurai*, it is depicted as an exotic, different culture and serves as a setting for an American adventure and a place of redemption for an American protagonist. It reflects stereotypical American ideas of Japan during the Meiji Period, thereby imagining an artificial Japan for a Western audience. This romanticized and nostalgic Japaneseness is one important selling point of the movie. Although it avoids the classic stereotypes of the Geisha or Madame Butterfly, it nevertheless exoticizes old Japan for a Western audience. This neo-Orientalism is more "open" and does not simply condemn the Japanese as barbaric or uncivilized, but it still recodes them as different and exotic. In *Lost in Translation*, Orientalist stereotypes are employed as cinematic tools in order to challenge and ridicule Orientalist perceptions and stereotypes of Japan. While cultural misunderstandings were not avoided, mainly on account of some viewers' mistaking the genre of comedy as realism, the movie successfully confronted Orientalist delusions about exotic food and uplifting spirituality with the complexity of Tokyo as a real and fast-paced Japanese city. *Letters from Iwo Jima* is the most successful and farthest reaching effort to break with Orientalist images in Hollywood movies to-date. Its American director notwithstanding, it aims at taking a Japanese perspective of the battle and is based on letters of Japanese soldiers. The fact that the movie was made by an American director is particularly interesting in a transnational context, since it supplemented a World War II movie that represented the American perspective and the perspective of the opponents, which significantly shifted the perceptions of "the Other." While the binaries between "us" and "them" could not have been stronger illuminated than by focusing on a battle between the U.S. and Japan in World War II, with this double perspective, the West no longer serves as the normative agency against which the East is judged.

Furthermore, movie characters define themselves in confrontation with cultural alternatives on screen, the movie audience is more and more requested to rethink its position and perception critically. Especially the bilingual nature of *Letters from Iwo Jima* and the choice not to subtitle Japanese dialogues in *The Last Samurai* and *Lost in Translation* emphasizes the culturally different setting of the movies. In contrast to the illusion of familiarity that dubbing creates, subtitles work as markers of differences. They suggest a new reading practice to the audience. It can no longer exclusively rely on translation into "our" language and thereby making "the Other" the same in order to create meaning. Instead, the multilingual nature of these movies, which include subtitled, translated as well as not translated dialogues that cause silences and gaps, offers new heterogeneous movie experiences. Otherness enjoys new visibility, whereas it was before rejected by American audiences (R. Rich 163). The more differentiated representation causes different emotional and intellectual responses in different movie audiences.

The increase in contemporary American movies with a multidimensional Japanese topic, individualized Japanese characters, and settings close to Japanese reality indicates that Western audiences are interested in and capable of imagining Japan differently instead of sticking to practices of phobic Othering. Since representations are never stable but are in a constant flux, many different competing images exist at a time and it remains to be seen how Japan will be depicted in the American mediascape in the future.

# Conclusion

> Cute Power! Asia is in love with Japan's pop culture [...] Everybody loves Japan! Ask anybody in Asia: Western-style cool is out. Everything Japanese is in – and oh, so 'cute'!
> - NEWSWEEK ASIA, NOVEMBER 9, 1999 -

For a long time, Japan was perceived by the West as a rather secluded island nation at the periphery while the United States was perceived as the center of the Western, globalized world. Yet, this notion has increasingly changed with the growing influx and impact of Japanese popular culture – not only in Asia but also the West. Japan's rise as a non-Western center of power hence changed the perception of the island nation in the United States as well, shifting from the notion of a secluded island state, supposedly inhabited by monsters to the idea that Japan is indeed a modern, technological nation. However, changing perceptions of "the Other" do not always eradicate already existing Orientalist or Occidentalist ideas. This tendency can be clearly observed in science-fiction movies, where former Orientalist images of Japan as the land of Geishas, samurai, and *kamikaze* pilots are joined by Techno-Oriental stereotypes, imagining Japan as a land of emotionless, robot-like beings. If once Japan was rendered a backward country which was artistically developed but lacked any knowledge about future technologies, today Japan seems often to be quite the opposite: too mechanized. As the island nation has ascended to one of the technologically most advanced nations it "has become synonymous with the technologies of the future – with screens, networks, cybernetics, robotics, artificial intelligence, simulation" (Morley and Robins 168).

One cinematic example that uses Techno-Oriental stereotypes is Ridley Scott's 1982 movie *Blade Runner*. The movie, based on Phillip K. Dick's science-fiction novel *Do Androids Dream of Electric Sheep?* (1968), was produced and released within the context of a hot phase of economic rivalry between the United States and Japan. In the movie, Japan has economically surpassed the U.S. and the cityscape reflects the domination of Japanese culture with huge, visually overpowering Japanese advertisements, which create an estranging and uncomfortable atmosphere. Set in Los Angeles in 2019, the movie tells the story of the retired police officer Rick Deckard (Harrison Ford), a former "Blade Runner," who has hunted and exterminated bio-engineered replicants. These half-human, half-android creatures can only be distinguished from human beings by a test that measures their empathic response to questions. Hence, empathy or rather the lack of empathy is used in the movie to distinguish humans from non-humans. In this context, the figure of the replicant, or alien "Other" is of interest. Christina Corena argues in "Figurations of the Cyborg in Contemporary Science Fiction Novels in Film" that within the science-fiction genre,

ideas about human subjectivity and identity have most often been established in a comparison between self (human) and Other (non-human) characters. So, in terms of the genre's codes and conventions, it is possible to see how the alien or robot of science fiction may provide an example of Otherness, against which a representation of "proper" human subjectivity is worked through. Images of Otherness in science fiction can be understood as a metaphor for forms of Otherness within society, or between societies, which have traditionally been built upon gendered divides or upon distinctions based on racial differences. (275)

Although, at first sight, *Blade Runner*, like many other science-fiction movies, seems to use the alien as the symbol of the utmost "Other" at closer scrutiny, the movie indeed complicates the issue of clear binaries between "humans" and "replicants" as Otherness is no longer clearly visible. The idea that only humans are capable of having emotions is further questioned, as some replicants in the movie do indeed show concern for one another. Moreover, in one of the key scenes, Roy Batty (Rutger Hauer), a replicant, and Deckard's main antagonist, delivers a very emotional soliloquy before he dies. This short speech was later called by Mark Rowlands "perhaps the most moving death soliloquy in cinematic history" (235). In contrast, Rick

Deckard is presented as a burned-out character, incapable of any emotions, mainly roaming the streets on his own. The audience learns that his ex-wife used to call him "Sushi. Cold fish" (*Blade Runner*). The rather negative association of sushi with coldness makes clear that his former wife perceived Deckard as emotionless and indifferent. Thereby, the American protagonist is clearly rendered as a cold, inhumane person, potentially less alive and human than his replicant antagonist. At the same time, it is sushi that is used to highlight the protagonist's lack of emotions and reinforces stereotypes about Japanese food as disgusting – somehow adverse to humans.

Techno-Orientalist images used in *Blade Runner* are mainly "set up for the West to preserve its identity in its imagination of the future" (Ueno 94) and lead to an "Orientalism of cybersociety" (Ueno 94). As David Morley and Kevin Robinson have argued in *Spaces of Identity*, the West is simultaneously fascinated and scared of a future dominated by Japan. The authors suggest that Orientalist dichotomies between "us" and "them" remain visible in such science-fiction scenarios, for "the barbarians have now become robots" (172). However, in the Techno-Orientalist vision of Japan which heralds a threateningly mechanized Japanized future, the former "Other" is no longer out "there" but among "us" and "here." Thus, it can be argued that *Blade Runner* challenges the audience to rethink ideas of whom or what we consider human and whom or what we consider aliens. Yet, differences remain visible throughout the movie and especially the markers of difference in general and Japaneseness in particular lead to an uncanny feeling within the audience. Furthermore, as the movie is set in Los Angeles, dominated by Japanese corporations, it blames the Japanese technological advances for the fact that biologically engineered replicants exist.

A transnational, (or transgalactical) shift when it comes to the depiction of aliens on screen can be seen in Disney's animated children's science-fiction movie *Lilo and Stitch*. On the narrative level, the message of *Lilo and Stitch* differs from that of most other science-fiction narratives. As Emily Cheng argues in her paper "Family, Race and Citizenship in Disney's *Lilo and Stitch*" order is not restored in this movie by eliminating the alien or sending him home. Instead, the film suggests that an alien can adapt to its new environment, is integrated into the local community, and finally becomes part of human society (123). Cheng clearly reads the alien Stitch as the incorporation of the Asian "Other" (125). Indeed, Stitch does not only resemble the Japanese Pokémon character Pikachu, but his "Asianness" is underlined when he is depicted reenacting a scene from a Godzilla movie, destroying a miniature city that resembles San Francisco. Furthermore, as the movie is set on Hawaii, the alien threat incorporated by Stich echoes American anxieties about Asian labor recruitment and immigration in Hawaii in the early twentieth century (Cheng 123). The outcome of the movie is equally striking, as it suggests that aliens, only partly adapted to the local (human) surrounding, indeed enrich our world. Hence, it can be argued that Disney's *Lilo and Stitch* overcomes stereotypes and prejudices concerning aliens or "the Other" and instead outlines a transnational perspective.

Decentralized and manifold processes of cultural interaction have theoretical and methodological consequences for the analysis of contemporary cultural exchanges, which needs to focus on ambiguity and cultural diversity rather than on unequal power relations and cultural homogenization. As cultural transnationalism highlights the heterogeneous nature of cross-cultural commodities and ambiguity becomes central to contemporary cultural border crossings. Furthermore, these borders cease to be "clear-cut lines between 'us' and 'them'," becoming "zones where 'we' are gradually transformed into 'them', and vice versa" (Batten 7). This is not only evident when investigating the fantasyscape of movies.

A similar shift can be detected within the foodscape, not only with sushi but also with green tea. The American coffee franchise Starbucks for example offers different variations of Japanese *matcha* green tea with beverages such as the "Tazo© Green Tea Latte" or "Tazo© Green Tea Frappuchino." These beverages do not only alter a beverage that is perceived as a significant part of Japanese culture but they completely reimagine the *matcha* green tea for Western consumers by adding milk and cream. On their official website, Starbucks advertises the "Tazo© Green Tea Frappuchino" as follows:

Although matcha tea is best known for its central role in the serene ritual known as the Japanese tea ceremony, tea drinkers all over the world have come to enjoy the gentle, uplifting taste of this finely-powdered green tea in their own way. We particularly like the way it blends with milk and ice in this refreshing Frappuccino® blended beverage. And we think you will too. (Starbucks)

The company hence stresses the Japanese origin of *matcha* tea and its role in the Japanese tea ceremony. At the same time, it is emphasized that the beverage has already proved to be popular with a global green tea drinking audience "in their own way" (Starbucks), indicating that this traditionally Japanese beverage is open for modification. By using the personal pronoun "we" it is further indicated that this adaptation of *matcha* tea is only one way of enjoying this refreshment. However, by adding that "We particularly like the way it blends with milk and ice in this refreshing Frappuccino® blended beverage," Starbucks suggests that their version might be the best way to enjoy *matcha* tea – at least for Western consumers. Blending a traditional, Japanese tea with milk and ice, thus mixing "exotic" ingredients (*matcha* green tea) and familiar ingredients (milk and ice) Starbucks creates a new, transnational beverage that cannot longer be clearly associated with one culture.

The "Tazo© Green Tea Frappuchino" was further adapted and introduced in Japan to a Japanese audience. Here, the refreshment is named "Chocolate Brownie Green Tea Frappuchino©" and ingredients considered "exotic" in Japan (chocolate brownie, milk and ice) are added to the familiar green tea. It can be argued that serving green tea with milk would have met with disapproval in a nation that only accepted milk and dairy products as part of its everyday diet after World War II (Smil and Kobayashi 55). However, in this new "exotic" context, this beverage is perceived as a transnational drink that reimagines the idea of consuming green tea and therefore is not perceived as a substitute for Japanese *matcha* tea.

Within the fantasyscape of entertainment, a reimagination of cultural products can be observed as well. One prime example of how a Japanese commercial image was embraced in the United States is Hello Kitty. Although the cat is nowadays globally recognized as a Japanese cultural product, at closer scrutiny the character of the little white cat with circular black eyes reveals itself as a transnational character. As Ken Belson and Brian Bremner explain in *Hello Kitty: The Remarkable Story of Sanrio and the Billion Dollar Feline Phenomenon*, Kitty was created in 1974 by Sanrio as *English:* Her birthplace is London and she likes to play in the forest and to bake – all attributes closely associated in Japan with an English lifestyle (9). Hence, the character of Hello Kitty is a Japanese imagination of England, or the West and was thus rendered "exotic" and interesting at the Japanese market. Furthermore, with its small size and round features, the little cat fulfills all criteria of being *kawaii* (cute) – an enormously popular concept in Japan.

Despite its rather European background, Hello Kitty is nevertheless perceived as *Japanese* in the United States, where its "exotic," Japanese appeal made the little cat popular in the 1990s and the character was appreciated for its innocence and its supposed Japaneseness (K. Jackson 32). Today, Hello Kitty is mainly perceived in America as a brand, closely associated with celebrities such as Cameron Diaz, Tyra Banks, Christina Aguilera, or Mariah Carey, who all openly confessed that they adored the cat by, for example, carrying around Hello Kitty handbags (Belson and Bremner 106). Singer Lisa Loeb even named one of her albums "Hello Lisa" – a clear homage to Hello Kitty (Belson and Bremner 107), thereby clearly placing the little cat in an American context. Moreover, Hello Kitty is further recontextualized in American popular culture as there are now Hello Kitty dolls dressed as the Statue of Liberty in red, white, and blue (Belson and Bremner 106). Due to effective marketing strategies, and the popularity of the character with American celebrities, today, Hello Kitty has become "synonymous with American upper-class consumerism" (K. Jackson 35). Thus, Hello Kitty can be understood as a transnational phenomenon that attracts Japanese as well as American consumers. Moreover, by traveling from one culture to another, different meanings are attached to the character.

The analyses of flows of commodities in different cultural "scapes" have shed light on the complex issue of Japanese-American cultural exchanges by focusing on different dimensions and facets of cultural flows, in order to detect and understand the pattern of cross-cultural exchanges. Moreover, ideas about a unified national identity are challenged and reconstructed from an American and Japanese point of view: Starbucks' "Tazo© Green Tea Frappuchino" as well as American Sushi are a new, transnational version of a Japanese beverage and dish, imagined by Americans while Tokyo Disney Resort represents a Japanese version of the United States, the Japanese Pavilion in Epcot and the character of Hello Kitty present an American fantasyscape of Japan. The contestation of ideas about a nation and its culture shifts away from antagonistic readings of Japanese-American relations. Although stereotypical ideas of "the Other" existed and continue to exist in different cultural realms, these stereotypes have become increasingly complex and more nuanced. Instead of setting up clear binary oppositions, new cultural practices are developed in order to understand and adapt the unknown culture.

The various scapes have manifested themselves strongly as cultural commodities and practices and "travel" to foreign marketplaces, where they are adapted and modified to fit local consumer tastes. In many cases, these new, localized, often transnational cultural commodities and practices are reimported to the country of origin, where they are no longer identified as part of the culture. Instead, these products are acknowledged as alluring different versions of something familiar and embraced as creative interpretations. It becomes obvious that these cultural practices gain a different meaning when they travel from one cultural context to another. As Timothy J. Craig and Richard King argue in the "Introduction" to their book *Global Goes Local: Popular Culture in Asia*, consumers actively respond beyond mimicry to foreign commodities as they "adopt the icons of alien cultures [and] invest them with meanings that might never have been intended or imagined by their originators"(5). Localizing practices more often than not lead to the creation of new, hybrid products, which question the idea of mutually exclusive categories, as they no longer can be related to only one culture. Especially in a globalized and interconnected world, diverse cultures are connected to each other in what Roland Kelts describes as "the Mobius strip of interrelations" (69) and cultural differences are a vital and important issue in cultural relationships.

Nowadays, various cultures are interconnected due to migrational processes and increasing global communication and information flows. Movies and the Internet, theme parks, and foreign food, each in their own way, grant people access to other cultures without actually traveling to these places, and the inter- and transcultural encounter becomes much more common. In this context, foreign cultural products and practices permeate national borders, not only infiltrating local markets, but, almost at the same token, also influencing the local products and practices. Instead of flattening out all difference, more often than not the results are cross-cultural products and practices which are strongly heterogeneous.

As cultural transfers are never a one-way-street, new theories and approaches are needed in order to analyze the manifold flows of commodities and to understand the multi-layered nature of contemporary cultural exchanges. Former theoretical frameworks such as cultural imperialism or Orientalism do no longer suffice to investigate the cross-cultural exchanges between Japan and the United States. This global interconnectedness calls for the inclusion of multiple perspectives when analyzing these cross-cultural relationships and exchanges, thus adding to a more nuanced understanding of the world. Cultural influences will keep crossing and re-crossing national boundaries, contesting fixed perceptions about other cultures. As these boundaries become increasingly permeable, cross-pollinations between Japan and the United States will continue. How these interactions will increase and what new scapes and dimensions of cultural flows will open in the future, remains to be seen.

# Bibliography

Abarca, Meredith E. "Los Chilaquiles de mi'ama: The Language of Everyday Cooking." *Pilaf, Pozole, and Pad Thai: American Women and Ethnic Food.* Ed. Sherrie A. Iness. Amherst: U of Massachusetts P, 2001. 119-144.

---, "Authentic or Not, It's Original." *Food and Foodways* 12 (2004):1-25.

Abbas, Ackbar and John Nguyet Erni, eds. *Internationalizing Cultural Studies: An Anthology.* Malden: Blackwell Publishing, 2005.

Abrahams, Roger. "Equal Opportunity Eating: A Structural Excursus on Things of the Mouth." *Ethnic and Regional Foodways in the United States: The Performance of Group Identity.* Ed. Linda Keller Brown and Kay Mussell. Knoxville: The U of Tennessee P, 2001. 19-36.

Akam, Helmut Everett. *Transnational America: Cultural Pluralist Thought in the Twentieth Century.* Lanham: Rowman & Littlefield Publishers Inc., 2002.

Allan, Robin. *Walt Disney and Europe.* Bloomington: Indiana UP, 1999.

Allison, Anne. "Japanese Mothers and Obentos: The Lunch-Box as Ideological State Apparatus." *Food and Culture: A Reader.* Eds. Carole Counihan and Penny Esterik. New York: Routledge, 1997. 296-314.

---, Millennial Monsters: Japanese Toys and the Global Imagination. Berkeley: U of California P, 2006.

---, "The Japan Fad in Global Youth Culture and Millennial Capitalism." *Mechademia: Emerging Worlds of Anime and Manga.* Ed. Frenchy Lunning. Minneapolis: U of Minnesota P, 2006. 11-21.

Alvendia, Antonio. *Drifting: Sideways from Japan to America.* St Paul: Motorbooks, 2006.

Anderson, Benedict. *Imagined Communities: Reflections on the Origin and Spread of Nationalism*. Rev. Ed. London: Verso, 1991.
Anderson, Christopher. "Disneyland." *Television: The Critical View*. 6th ed. Ed Horace Newcomb. Oxford: Oxford UP, 2000. 17-33.
Andoh, Elizabeth. *An American Taste of Japan*. New York: William Morrow and Co., 1985.
Appadurai, Arjun. "How to Make a National Cuisine: Cookbooks in Contemporary India." *Comparative Studies in Society and History* 30.1 (1988): 3-24.
---, *Modernity at Large: Cultural Dimensions of Globalization*. Minneapolis: Minnesota UP, 1996.
---, ed. *Globalization*. Durham: Duke UP, 2001.
Ashcroft, Bill, Garth Griffin and Helen Tiffins. *The Empire Writes Back: Theory and Post-Colonial Literature*. 2nd ed. New York: Routledge, 2002.
---, *Post-Colonial Studies: The Key Concepts*. 2000. New York: Routledge, 2007.
Ashkenazi, Michael and Jeanne Jacob. *The Essence of Japanese Cuisine*. Richmond: Curzon Press, 2000.
Ayres, Brenda. "The Wonderful World of Disney: The World That Made the Man and the Man That Made the World." *The Emperor's Old Groove: Decolonizing Disney's Magic Kingdom*. Ed. Brenda Ayres. New York: Peter Lang, 2003. 15-25.

Bacarr, Jina. *The Japanese Art of Sex: How to Tease, Seduce, and Pleasure the Samurai in Your Bedroom*. Berkeley: Stone Bridge Press, 2004.
Baudrillard, Jean. *Simulacra and Simulation*. Trans. Sheila Faria Glaser. Michigan: The U of Michigan P, 2006.
Barthes, Roland. *Empire of Signs*. Trans. Richard Howard. New York: Hill and Wang, 1982.
Bassnett, Susan. "The Translation Turn in Cultural Studies." *Constructing Cultures: Essays on Literary Translations*. Susan Bassnett and André Lefevere. Bristol: Multilingual Matters, 1998. 123-140.
Batten, Bruce L. *To the Ends of Japan: Premodern Frontiers, Boundaries, and Interactions*. Honolulu: U of Hawai'i P, 2003.
Beard, James. *Beard on Food*. New York: Alfred A. Knopf Inc., 1978.

Beasley, W.G. *Japan Encounters the Barbarian: Japanese Travellers in America and Europe*. New Haven: Yale UP, 1995.

Befu, Harumi. "Globalization as Human Dispersal: From the Perspective of Japan." *Globalization and Social Change in Contemporary Japan*. Eds. J.S. Eades, Tom Gill, and Harumi Befu. Melbourne: Trans Pacific Press, 2000.17-40.

---, *Hegemony of Homogeneity: An Anthropological Analysis of Nihonjinron*. Melbourne: Trans Pacific Press, 2001.

Belasco, Warren J. "Ethnic Fast Foods: The Corporate Melting Pot." *Food and Foodways*. 2.1 (1987):1-30.

---, "Food Matters: Perspectives on an Emerging Field. "*Food Nations: Selling Taste in Consumer Society*. Eds. Warren Belasco and Philip Scranton. London: Routledge, 2002. 2-23.

Belleme, John and Jan. *Japanese Foods That Heal: Using Traditional Japanese Ingredients to Promote Health, Longevity, and Well-Being*. North Clarendon: Tuttle, 2007.

Belson, Ken John and Brian Bremner. *Hello Kitty: The Remarkable Story of Sanrio and the Billion Dollar Feline Phenomenon*. Hoboken: John Wiley and Sons, 2004.

Benedict, Ruth. *The Chrysanthemum and the Sword: Patterns of Japanese Culture*. Boston: Houghton Mifflin, 1946.

Benfey, Christopher. *The Great Wave: Gilded Age Misfits, Japanese Eccentrics and the Opening of Old Japan*. New York: Random House, 2003.

Benshoff, Harry M. and Sean Griffin. *America on Film. Representing Race, Class, Gender, and Sexuality at the Movies*. Malden: Blackwell Publishing, 2004.

Bestor, Theodore. *Tsukiji: The Fish Market at the Center of the World*. Berkeley: U of California P, 2004.

---, "How Sushi Went Global." *The Cultural Politics of Food and Eating: A Reader*. Eds. James Watson and Melissa L. Caldwell. Malden: Blackwell Publishing, 2005. 13-20.

Bhabha, Homi K. *The Location of Culture*. London: Routledge, 1994.

Birnbaum, Stephen, ed. *Birnbaum's Walt Disney World: Expert Advice from the Inside Source*. Rev.ed. New York: Disney Editions, 2005.

Black, Jeremy. *Maps and History. Constructing Images of the Past*. New Haven, Yale UP, 1990.

Black, Shameem. "Fertile Cosmofeminism: Ruth L. Ozeki and Transnational Reproduction." *Meridians: Feminism, Race, Transnationalism* 5.1 (2004): 226-256.

Blumberg, Rhoda. *Commodore Perry in the Land of the Shogun.* New York: Lothrop, Lee and Shepard Books, 1985.

Bognar, Botond. "Surface Above All? American Influence on Japanese Urban Space." *Transactions, Transgressions, Transformations: American Culture in Western Europe and Japan.* Eds. Heide Fehrenbach and Uta G. Poiger. New York: Bergham Books, 2000. 45-78.

Booker, Keith. *Disney, Pixar, and the Hidden Messages of Children's Films.* Santa Barbara: Praeger, 2009.

Bordwell, David. "Classical Hollywood Cinema: Narrational Principles and Procedures." *Narrative, Apparatus, Ideology: A Film Theory Reader.* Ed. Philip Rosen. New York: Columbia UP, 1986. 17-34.

Bradley, James. *Flags of Our Fathers.* 2000. New York: Bantam Books, 2006.

Brannen, Mary Yoko. "'Bwana Mickey': Constructing Cultural Consumption at Tokyo Disneyland." *Re-Made in Japan.* Ed. Joseph J. Tobin. New Haven: Yale UP, 1992. 216-234.

Brehm, Margit. "Takashi Murakami: A Lesson in Strategy (Morphed Double-Loop)." *The Japanese Experience Inevitable.* Ed. Margit Brehm. Ostfildern-Ruit: Hatje Cantz Verlag, 2002. 34-83.

Brenner, Leslie. *American Appetite: The Coming of Age of a Cuisine.* New York: Avon Books, 1999.

Brown, Steven T., ed. *Cinema Anime: Critical Engagements With Japanese Animation.* New York: Macmillan, 2006.

Browne, Nick. "The Undoing of the Other Woman: Madame Butterfly in the Discourse of American Orientalism." *The Birth of Whiteness: Race and the Emergence of U.S. Cinema.* Ed. Daniel Bernardi. New Brunswick: Rutgers UP, 1996. 227-256.

Bryman, Alan E. *The Disneyization of Society.* London: Sage Publishers, 2005.

Buehrer, Beverley B. *Japanese Films: A Filmography and Commentary, 1921-1989.* Jefferson: McFarland and Company, 1990.

Buell, Hal. *Uncommon Valor, Common Virtue: Iwo Jima and the Photograph that captured America.* New York: Penguin, 2006.

Buruma, Ian. *A Japanese Mirror: Heroes and Villains of Japanese Culture*. London: Penguin Books, 1985.
---, *Inventing Japan 1853-1964*. New York: The Modern Library, 2004.
Buruma, Ian and Avishai Margalit. *Occidentalism: The West in the Eyes of Its Enemies*. New York: Penguin, 2005.
Byrne, Eleanor and Martin McQuillan. *Deconstructing Disney*. London: Pluto Press, 1999.

Carrier, James G., ed. *Occidentalism: Images of the West*. Oxford: Clarendon Press, 2003.
Chan, Joseph M. "Disneyfying and Globalizing the Chinese Legend Mulan: A Study of Transculturation." *In Search of Boundaries: Communication, Nation-States and Cultural Identities*. Eds. Joseph M. Chan and Bryce T. McIntyre. Westport: Ablex Publishing, 2002. 225-248.
Chan, M. Joseph and Bryce T. McIntyre, eds. "Introduction." *In Search of Boundaries: Communication, Nation-States and Cultural Identities*. Eds. Joseph M. Chan and Bryce T McIntyre. Westport: Ablex Publishing, 2002. xiii-xxvi.
Chen, Constance J.S. "Transnational Orientals: Scholars of Art, Nationalist Discourses, and the Question of Intellectual Authority." *Journal of Asian American Studies* 9.3. (2006): 215-242.
Chen, Xiaomei. *Occidentalism: A Theory of Counter-Discourse in Post-Mao China*. Oxford: Oxford UP, 1995.
Cheng, Emily. "Family, Race and Citizenship in Disney's *Lilo and Stitch*." *Monsters and The Monstrous. Myths and Metaphors of Enduring Evil*. Ed. Niall Scott. New York: Rodopi, 2007. 123-132.
Choi, Jinhee. "Preface." *The Cinema of Japan and Korea*. Ed. John Bowyer. New York: Wallflower Press, 2004.
Chuh, Kandice. *Imagine Otherwise: On Asian Americanist Critique*. Durham: Duke UP, 2003.
Clack, Robert Wood. Rev. of *Jurokuseiki Sekaichizu jo no Nihon (Japan on World Maps of the 16$^{th}$ Century)* by Yoshitomo Okamoto. *Journal of the American Oriental Society*. Vol. 60 No.2 (1940): 275-278.
Clifford, James. "Introduction: Partial Truths." *Writing Culture: The Poetics and Politics of Ethnography*. Eds. James Clifford and George E. Marcus. Berkeley: U of California P, 1986. 1-26.

---, "Traveling Cultures." *Cultural Studies*. Eds. Lawrence Grossberg, Cary Nelson, Paula Treichler. New York: Routledge, 1992. 96-111.

Cohen, Jeffrey Jerome, ed. *Monster Theory: Reading Culture*. Minneapolis: U of Minnesota P., 1996.

Cohen, Robin and Paul Kennedy. *Global Sociology*. Houndmills: Palgrave, 2007.

Cohen, Warren I. *The Asian American Century*. Cambridge: Harvard UP, 2002.

Collier, Marsha. *eBay for Dummies*. Hoboken: Wiley Publishing, 2007.

Conant, Py Kim. *Sex Secrets of an American Geisha: How to Attract, Satisfy, and Keep Your Man*. Alameda: Hunter House, 2007.

Condry, Ian. "Japanese Hip-Hop and the Globalization of Popular Culture." *Urban Life: Readings in the Anthropology of the City*. 4th ed. Eds. George Gmelch and Walter Zenner. Prospect Heights: Wareland Press, 2001. 357-387.

---, *Hip-Hop Japan: Rap and the Paths of Cultural Globalization*. Durham: Duke UP, 2006.

Corena, Christine. "Figurations of the Cyborg in Contemporary Science Fiction Novels and Film." *A Companion to Science Fiction*. Ed. David Seed. Malden: Blackwell Publishing, 2005. 275-288.

Corson, Trevor. *The Zen of Fish: The Story of Sushi From Samurai to Supermarket*. New York: Harper Collins, 2007.

Counihan, Carole and Penny Esterik. "Introduction." *Food and Culture: A Reader*. Eds. Carole Counihan and Penny Esterik. New York: Routledge, 1997. 1-7.

Crafton, Donald. "The Last Night at the Nursery: Walt Disney's Peter Pan." *The Velvet Light Trap*. 24 (1989): 33-52.

Craig, Timothy and Richard King, eds. *Global Goes Local: Popular Culture in Asia*. Vancouver: UBC Press, 2002.

Creef, Elena Tajima. *Imaging Japanese America: The Visual Construction of Citizenship, Nation and the Body*. New York: New York UP, 2004.

Creighton, R. Millie. "Imagining the Other in Japanese Advertising Campaigns." *Occidentalism: Images of the West*. Ed. James G. Carrier. Oxford: Clarendon Press, 2003. 135-160.

Cross, Gary. "Foreword." *Millennial Monsters: Japanese Toys and the Global Imagination*. Allison, Anne. Berkeley: U of California P, 2006. xv-xviii.

Croteau, David and William Hoynes. *The Business of Media: Corporate Media and the Public Interest*. 2<sup>nd</sup> ed. Thousand Oaks: Pine Forge P, 2006.

Cwiertka, Katarzyna. "Introduction." *Asian Food: The Global and the Local*. Eds. Katarzyna Cwiertka and Boudewijn Walraven. Richmond: Curzon, 2002. 1-15.

---, "Eating the Homeland: Japanese Expatriates in the Netherlands. "*Asian Food: The Global and the Local*. Eds. Katarzyna Cwiertka and Boudewijn Walraven. Richmond: Curzon, 2002. 133-152.

Darcy, Jane. "The Disneyfication of the European Fairy Tale." *Issues in Americanization and Culture*. Eds. Neil Campell, Jude Davies, and George McKay. Edinburgh: Edinburgh UP, 2004. 181-196.

De Cordova, Richard. "The Mickey Mouse in Macy's Window: Childhood, Consumerism, and Disney Animation." *Disney Discourse: Producing the Magic Kingdom*. Ed. Eric Smoodin. New York: Routledge, 1994. 203-213.

De Laurentis, Teresa. *Alice Doesn't: Feminism, Semiotics, Cinema*. Bloomington: Indiana UP, 1984.

Decker, Kevin S. and Jason T. Eberl. *Star Wars and Philosophy: More Powerful Than You Can Possibly Imagine*. 2005. Chicago: Open Court, 2011.

Dick, Phillip K. *Do Androids Dream of Electric Sheep?* 1968. New York: De Rey Book, 1996.

Dower, John. *War without Mercy: Race and Power in the Pacific War*. New York: Pantheon, 1993

---, *Embracing Defeat: Japan in the Wake of World War II*. New York: Norton, 2000.

Downer, Lesley. *Japanese Food and Drink*. New York: The Bookwright Press, 1988.

---, *Madame Sadayakko: The Geisha Who Bewitched the West*. New York: Gotham Books, 2003.

Drazen, Patrick. *Anime Explosion! The What? Why? & Wow! Of Japanese Animation*. Berkeley: Stone Bridge Press, 2003.

Dressler, Christopher. "A Dish so Ghastly." *Travellers' Tales of Old Japan*. Eds. Michael Wise. Singapore: Times Books International, 1985. 71-74.

Duke, Benjamin. *The History of Modern Japanese Education: Constructing the National School System 1872-1890*. New Jersey: 2009.

Duus, Peter, ed. *The Japanese Discovery of America: A Brief History with Documents*. Boston: Bedford / St. Martins, 1997.

Eco, Umberto. *Travels in Hyperreality*. 1973. Trans. William Weaver. San Diego: Harvest Book, 1986.

Egoyan, Atom and Balfour, Ian. "Introduction." *Subtitles: On the Foreignness of Film*. Eds. Atom Egoyan and Ian Balfour. Cambridge: The MIT Press, 2004. 21-32.

Ellis, Bret Easton. *American Psycho*. New York: Vintage Contemporaries, 1991.

Emory, Elliott. "Diversity in the United States and Abroad: What Does it Mean When American Studies is Transnational?" *American Quarterly* 59.1 (2007): 1-22.

Engelhardt, Tom. "Ambush At Kamikaze Pass." *American Media and Mass Culture: Left Perspectives*. Ed. Donald Lazere. Berkeley: U of California P, 1987. 480-498.

Esko, Edward and Wendy Esko. *Macrobiotic Cooking for Everyone*. Tokyo: Japan Publications, 1980.

Esko, Wendy. *Introducing Macrobiotic Cooking*. Tokyo: Japan Publications, 1978.

Ezra, Elizabeth and Terry Rowden. "General Introduction: What is Transnational Cinema?" *Transnational Cinema: The Film Reader*. Eds. Elizabeth Ezra and Terry Rowden. London: Routledge, 2006. 1-12.

Feng, X. Peter, ed. *Screening Asian Americans*. New Brunswick: Rutgers UP, 2002.

---, "Introduction." *Screening Asian Americans*. Ed. Peter X. Feng. New Brunswick: Rutgers UP, 2002. 1-18.

---, "False and Double Consciousness: Race, Virtual Reality and the Assimilation of Hong Kong Action Cinema in *The Matrix*." *Aliens R Us: The Other in Science Fiction Cinema*. Eds. Ziauddin Saradar and Sean Cubitt. London: Pluto Press, 2002. 149-163.

Ferrero, Sylvia. "*Comida Sin Par*: Consumption of Mexican Food in Los Angeles: 'Foodscapes' in a Transnational Consumer Society." *Food Nations: Selling Taste in Consumer Societies*. Eds. Warren Belasco and Philip Scranton. New York: Routledge, 2002. 194-219.

Figal, Gerald. *Civilization and Monsters: Spirits of Modernity in Meji Japan.* Durham: Duke UP, 1999.

Fisher Fishkin, Shelly. "Crossroads of Cultures: The Transnational Turn in American Studies: Presidential Address to the American Studies Association." *American Quarterly* 57.1 (2005): 17-57.

Fitts, Robert K. *Remembering Japanese Baseball: An Oral History of the Game.* Carbondale: Southern Illinois UP, 2005.

Francaviglia, Richard. "Walt Disney's Frontierland as an Allegorical Map of the American West." *The Western Historical Quarterly* 30.2 (1999): 155-182.

Frantz, Douglas and Catherine Collins. *Celebration, U.S.A: Living in Disney's Brave New Town.* New York: Henry Holt and Co., 1999.

Frühstück, Sabine. *Uneasy Warriors: Gender, Memory and Popular Culture in the Japanese Army.* Berkeley: U of California P, 2007.

Fuller Slack, Susan. *Japanese Cooking for the American Table.* New York: HP Books, 1996.

Furiya, Linda. *Bento Box in the Heartland: My Japanese Girlhood in Whitebread America.* Emeryville: Seal Press, 2006.

Furuya, Jun "A New Perspective on American History from the Other Side of the Pacific." *The Japanese Journal of American Studies* 18 (2007):59-71.

Fussell, Paul. "Thank God for the Atom Bomb." *Thank God for the Atom Bomb and Other Essays.* Ed. Paul Fussel. New York: Summit Books, 1988. 13-37.

---, "Postscript (1987) on Japanese Skulls." *Thank God for the Atom Bomb and Other Essays.* Ed. Paul Fussel. New York: Summit Books, 1988. 45-52.

Gabaccia, Donna. "What Do We Eat?" *Food in the USA: A Reader.* Ed. Carole M. Counihan. New York: Routledge, 2002. 35-40.

---, *We Are What We Eat.* Cambridge: Harvard UP, 1998.

Gewertz, Deborah and Frederick Errington. "We Think, Therefore They Are? On Occidentalizing the World." *Cultures of United States Imperialism.* Eds. Amy Kaplan and Donald E. Pease. Durham: Duke UP, 1993. 635-655.

Gibney, Frank, ed. *Senso: The Japanese Remember the Pacific War: Letters to the Editor of Asahi Shimbun*. Trans. Beth Cary. Armonk: M.E. Sharpe, 1995.

Giles, Paul. *Virtual Americas: Transnational Fictions and Transatlantic Images*. Durham: Duke UP, 2002.

Gill, Tom. "Transformational Magic. Some Japanese Super-Heroes and Monsters." *The Worlds of Japanese Popular Culture. Gender, Shifting Boundaries and Global Cultures*. Martinez, D.P, ed. Cambridge: Cambridge UP, 1998. 33-55.

Gilmore, David D. *Evil Beings, Mythical Beasts, and All Manner of Imaginary Terrors*. Philadelphia: U of Pennsylvania P, 2003.

Giroux, Henry A. and Grace Pollock. *The Mouse That Roared: Disney and the End of Innocence*. 2001. Lanham: Rowman & Littlefield, 2010.

Gitlin, Todd. "The Unification of the World Under the Sign of Mickey Mouse and Bruce Willis: The Supply and Demand Sides of American Popular Culture." *In Search of Boundaries: Communication, Nation-States and Cultural Identities*. Eds. Joseph M. Chan and Bryce T. McIntyre. Westport: Ablex Publishing, 2002. 21-33.

Gluck, Carol. "Japan and America: A Tale of Two Civilizations." *Asia in Western and World History*. Eds. Ainslee T. Embree and Carol Gluck. London: M.E. Sharpe, 1997. 798-809.

Godoy, Tiffany and Ivan Vartanian. "Introduction." *Style Deficit Disorder: Harajuku Street Fashion Tokyo*. Eds. Tiffany Godoy and Ivan Vartanian. San Francisco: Chronicle Books, 2007. 10-17.

Golden, Arthur. *Memoires of A Geisha*. New York: Vintage Books, 1997.

Goldberg, Wendy. "The Manga Phenomenon in America." *Manga: An Anthology of Global and Cultural Perspectives*." Ed. Toni Johnson-Woods. New York: Continuum, 2010. 281-296.

Greer, John Michael. *Monsters: An Investigator's Guide to Magical Beings*. St.Paul: Llewellym Publications, 2002.

Grewal, Inderpal and Caren Kaplan. "Warrior Marks: Global Womanism's Neo Colonial Discourse in a Multicultural Context." *Multiculturalism, Postcoloniality and Transnational Media*. Eds. Ella Shohat and Robert Stam. New Brunswick: Rutgers UP, 2003. 256-278.

Griffith, Tracy. *Sushi American Style*. New York: Clarkson Potter Publishers, 2004.

Grover, Ron. *Die Disney Story*. Frankfurt: Ullstein Verlag, 1994.

Guth, Christine M.E. *Longfellow's Tattoos: Tourism, Collecting and Japan.* Seattle: University of Washington P., 2004.

Guthrie-Shimizu, Sayuri. *Transpacific Field of Dreams: How Baseball Linked the United States and Japan in Peace and War.* Chapel Hill: The U of North Carolina P., 2012.

Hall, Stuart. "The Spectacle of the 'Other'" *Representation: Cultural Representations and Signifying Practices.* Ed. Stuart Hall. London: Sage, 1997. 223-290.

Halttunen, Karen. "Transnationalism and American Studies in Place." *The Japanese Journal of American Studies* 18 (2007): 5-19.

Hamilton-Oehrl, Angelika. "Leisure Parks in Japan" *The Culture of Japan Through Leisure.* Eds. Sepp Linhart and Sabine Frühstück. Albany: State U of New York, 1998. 237-250.

Hand, J. Richard. "Aesthetics of Cruelty: Traditional Japanese Theatre and the Horror Film." *Japanese Horror Cinema.* Ed. Jay McRoy. Edinburgh: Edinburgh UP, 2006. 18-28.

Hannerz, Ulf. "Scenarios for Peripheral Cultures. "*Culture, Globalization and the World-System.* Ed. Anthony D. King. Minneapolis: The U of Minnesota P, 2000. 107-128.

Harley J.B. *The Nature of Maps: Essays in the History of Cartography.* Ed. Paul Laxton. Baltimore: The John Hopkins UP, 2001.

Harris, Neil. "All the World a Melting Pot? Japan at American Fairs 1876-1904." *Mutual Images: Essays in American-Japanese Relations.* Ed. Akira Iriye. Cambridge: Harvard UP, 1975. 24-54.

Harris, Patricia, David Lyon and Sue McLaughlin. *The Meaning of Food: The Companion to the PBS Television Series Hosted by Marcus Samuelsson.* Guilford: The Globe Pequot Press, 2005.

Hart, Christopher. *Drawing Cutting Edge Fusion: American Comics with a Manga Influence.* New York: Watson-Gunphill Publications, 2005.

Hartwig, Marcel. *Die Traumatisierte Nation? Pearl Harbor und 9/11 als kulturelle Erinnerungen.* Bielefeld: transcript, 2010.

Hebdige, Dick. *Subculture: The Meaning of Style.* 1979. London: Routledge, 2002.

Heldke, Lisa. *Exotic Appetites: Ruminations of a Food Adventurer.* New York: Routledge, 2003.

Hendry, Joy. *The Orient Strikes Back: A Global View of Cultural Display.* Oxford: Berg, 2000.

Heung, Maria. "The Family Romance of Orientalism: From *Madame Butterfly* to *Indochine.* "*Visions of the East: Orientalism in Film.* Eds. Matthew Bernstein and Gaylyn Studlar. London: I.B. Tauris Publishers. 158-183.

Hills, Matt. "Ringing the Changes: Cultural Distinctions and Cultural Differences in US Fan's Readings of Japanese Horror Cinema." *Japanese Horror Cinema.* Ed. Jay McRoy. Edinburgh: Edinburgh UP, 2006. 161-174.

Hirakawa, Takeji. "Harajuku's Start: The Roots of Tokyo's Street Fashion Scene." *Style Deficit Disorder: Harajuku Street Fashion Tokyo.* Eds. Tiffany Godoy and Ivan Vartarian. San Francisco: Chronicle Books, 2007. 22-25.

Hitchcock, Peter. *Imaginary States: Studies in Cultural Transnationalism.* Urbana: U of Illinois P, 2003.

Ho, Jennifer Ann. *Consumption and Identity in Asian American Coming-Off-Age Novels.* New York: Routledge, 2005.

Hogan, Jackie. "The Social Significance of English Usage in Japan." *Japanese Studies* 23.1 (2003): 43-58.

Holland, Clive. *My Japanese Wife: A Japanese Idyll.*1895. New York: R.A. Everett, 1903.

Hooks, Bell. *Black Looks: Race and Representation.* Boston: South End Press, 1992.

Hopkins, Edward Washburn. "The Buddhistic Rule Against Eating Meat." *Journal of American Oriental Society* 27 (1906): 455-469.

Hosking, Richard. *A Dictionary of Japanese Food: Ingredients and Culture.* Tokyo: Tuttle, 1996.

Huang, Yunte. *Charlie Chan. The Untold Story of the Honorable Detective and His Rendezvous with American History.* New York: WW.Norton and Co., 2010.

Hughes, Glenn. *Imaginism and the Imaginists: A Study in Modern Poetry.* New York: Bilblo and Tannen, 1972.

Hunt, Leon. "The Hong Kong/Hollywood Connection: Stardom and Spectacle in Transnational Action Cinema." *Action and Adventure Cinema.* Ed. Yvonne Tasker. London: Routledge, 2004. 269-283.

Hutchinson, Rachael. "Orientalism or Occidentalism? Dynamics of Appropriation in Akira Kurosawa." *Remapping World Cinema: Identity, Culture and Politics in Film.* Eds. Stephanie Dennison and Song Hwee Lim. London: Wallflower Press, 2006. 173-187.

Ikezawa, Yasushi. *Amerika Nihonshoku Wōzu: Sushi, Tofu, Edamame, Nihonshu: Ima Amerika de wa Nihonshoku ga Daibūmu!* (*America Japanese Food Wars*). Tokyo: Asahiya Shōten, 2005.

Imagineers, The. *The Imagineering Field Guide to Epcot at Walt Disney World.* New York: Disney Editions, 2006.

---, *Walt Disney Imagineering: A Behind the Dreams Look at Making the Magic Real.* New York: Disney Editions, 1996.

Iriye, Akira, ed. *Mutual Images: Essays in American-Japanese Relations.* Cambridge: Harvard UP, 1975.

---, "Japan as Competitor 1895-1917." *Mutual Images: Essays in American-Japanese Relations.* Ed. Akira Iriye. Cambridge: Harvard UP, 1975. 73-99.

Issenberg, Sasha. *The Sushi Economy: Globalization and the Making of a Modern Delicacy.* New York: Gotham Books, 2007.

Iwabuchi, Koichi. "Uses of Japanese Popular Culture: Trans/nationalism and Postcolonial Desire for 'Asia'." *Emergences: Journal for the Study of Media and Composite Cultures.* 11.2 (2001): 199-222.

---, *Recentering Globalization: Popular Culture and Japanese Transnationalism.* Durham: Duke UP, 2002.

---. "From Western Gaze to Global Gaze: Japanese Cultural Presence in Asia." *Global Culture: Media, Arts, Policy and Globalization.* Eds. Diane Crane, Nobuko Kawashima and Ken'ichi Kawasaki. New York: Routledge, 2002. 256-273.

Iwahara, Yasuo. "Imagist Shijin to Haiku No Kankei." (*The Relation between Imagist Poets and Haiku*) *Kōgukunin Daigaku Kenkyū Ronsō* 17 (1979): 1-32.

Jackson, Anna Gwendoline. "Outside in Tokyo: The Gaijin Gaze in Chris Marker's Sans Soleil and Sofia Coppola's Lost in Translation." *Cities and Eyes Bronnenboek.* Eds. Nienke Schachtschabel, Sietske Sips, and Layla Tweedie-Cullen. Amsterdam: Amsterdam UP, 2005. 154-163.

Jackson, Kathy Merlock. "Hello Kitty in America." *The Japanification of Children's Popular Culture*. Ed. Mark I. West. Lanham: Scarecrow Press, 2009. 25-40.

Jackson, Kathy Merlock and Roy West. *Disneyland and Culture: Essays on the Parks and Their Influence*. Jefferson: McFarland, 2010.

Jacobson, Matthew Frye. *Roots Too: White Ethnic Revival in Post-Civil Rights America*. Cambridge: Harvard UP, 2008.

James, Wanda. *Driving from Japan: Japanese Cars in America*. Jefferson: McFarland & Company Inc, 2005.

Jameson, Frederic. "Postmodernism, or the Cultural Logic of Late Capitalism." *New Left Review* 146.1 (1984): 53-92.

Jarman, Francis. *The Perception of Asia: Japan and the West*. Hildesheim: Universitätsbibliothek Hildesheim, 1998.

Jehlen, Myra. "Why Did the Europeans Cross the Ocean? A Seventeenth-Century Riddle." *Cultures of United States Imperialism*. Eds. Amy Kaplan and Donald E. Pease. Durham: Duke UP, 1993. 41-58.

Johnson, George A. "The Benjo" *Travellers' Tales of Old Japan*. Ed. Michael Wise. Singapore: Times Books International, 1985. 201-202.

Kakehashi, Kumiko. *So Sad To Fall In Battle: Based on General Tadamichi Kuribayashi's Letters From Iwo Jima*. Trans. Shinchōsha co. Ltd. New York: Presidio Press, 2007.

Kalcik, Susan. "Ethnic Foodways in America: Symbol and the Performance of Identity." *Ethnic and Regional Foodways in the United States: The Performance of Group Identity*. Eds. Linda Keller Brown and Kay Mussell. Knoxville: The U of Tennessee P, 2001. 37-65.

Kamei, Shunske. "The Sacred Lands of Liberty." *Mutual Images: Essays in American-Japanese Relations*. Ed. Akira Iriye. Cambridge: Harvard UP, 1975. 55-72.

Kang, Laura Hyun-Yi. "The Desiring of Asian Female Bodies: Interracial Romance and Cinematic Subjection." *Screening Asian Americans*. Ed. Peter X. Feng. New Brunswick: Rutgers UP, 2002. 71-98.

Kaplan, Amy. "'Left Alone With America.' The Absence of Empire in the Study of American Culture." *Cultures of United States Imperialism*. Eds. Amy Kaplan and Donald E. Pease. Durham: Duke UP, 1993. 3-21.

Kaplan, Caren. *Questions of Travel: Postmodern Discourses of Displacement*. Durham: Duke UP, 1996.

Kato, Hidejoshi. "America as Seen by Japanese Travelers. *"Mutual Images: Essays in American-Japanese Relations.* Ed. Akira Iriye. Cambridge: Harvard UP, 1975. 188-201.

Kato, Hiroko. *Taberu Amerikajin. (Eating Americans).* Tokyo: Taishukan Shōten, 2003.

---. *Sushi Purizu! Amerikajin Sushi o Kūu. (Sushi Please! Americans Devouring Sushi).* Tokyo: Shueisha Shinsō, 2002.

Kawasumi, Ken. *The Encyclopedia of Sushi Rolls.* trans. Laura Diussi. Tokyo: Graph-sha Ltd., 2006.

Keller Brown, Linda and Kay Mussell. "Introduction." *Ethnic and Regional Foodways in the United States: The Performance of Group Identity.* Eds. Linda Keller Brown and Kay Mussell. Knoxville: The U of Tennessee P, 2001. 3-15.

Kellner, Douglas. *Media Culture: Cultural Studies, Identity and Politics between the Modern and Postmodern.* 1995. London: Routledge, 2003.

Kelsky, Karen. *Women on the Verge: Japanese Women, Western Dreams.* Durham: Duke UP, 2001.

Kelts, Roland. *Japanamerica: How Japanese Pop Culture Has Invaded the U.S.* New York: Palgrave, 2006.

Kent, L. Steve. *The Ultimate History of Video Games: From Pong to Pokemon and Beyond.* New York: Three Rivers Press, 2001.

Kerouac, Jack. *Book of Haikus.* Ed. Regina Weinreich. New York: Penguin Books, 2003.

Kim, W. Thomas. "Being Modern: The Circulation of Oriental Objects." *American Quarterly* 58.2 (2006): 379-405.

King, Geoff. *Lost in Translation.* Edinburgh: Edinburgh UP, 2010.

King, Homay. *Lost in Translation: Orientalism, Cinema, and the Enigmatic Signifier.* Durham: Duke UP, 2010. Naficy, Hamid. "Phobic Spaces and Liminal Panics

King, James. *Under Foreign Eye: Western Cinematic Adaptations of Postwar Japan.* Winchester: Zero Books, 2012.

King, Richard C., ed. *Postcolonial America.* Chicago: U of Illinois P, 2000.

Kohler, Chris. *Power Up: How Japanese Video Games Gave the World an Extra Life.* Indianapolis: Bradygames, 2005.

Kondo, Dorinne. "The Aesthetics and Politics of Japanese Identity in the Fashion Industry." *Re-Made in Japan: Everyday Life and Consumer*

*Taste in a Changing Society.* Ed. Joseph J. Tobin. New Haven: Yale UP, 1992. 176-203.

Kumaga, Fumie. *Unmasking Japan Today: The Impact of Traditional Values on Modern Japanese Society.* Westport: Praeger Publishers, 1996.

Kuribayashi, Tadamichi. *Picture Letters from the Commander in Chief.* Trans. Michi Fusayama. Ed. Tsuyuko Yoshida. San Francisco: VIZ Media, 2007.

Kurotani, Sawa. "*Amerika no Omiyage (Souvenirs from America)*: The Question of Selfhood and Alterity in Late Capitalist Japan." *East-West Connections: Review of Asian Studies* 5.1 (2005):27-39.

Kuwahara, Yasue. "Japanese Culture and Popular Consciousness: Disney's *The Lion King* vs. Tezuka's *Jungle Emperor.*" *Journal of Popular Culture* 31.1 (1997): 37-48.

LaFeber, Walter. *The Clash: U.S. Japanese Relations throughout History.* New York: W.W.Norton & Company, 1997.

Lafond, Frank. "Case Study: Ishii Takashi's *Freeze Me* and the Rape-Revenge Film." *Japanese Horror Cinema.* Ed. Jay McRoy. Edinburgh: Edinburgh UP, 2006. 77-85.

Lai, Cherry Sze-Ling and Dixon Heung Wah Wong. "Japanese Comics Coming to Hong Kong." *Globalizing Japan: Ethnography of the Japanese Presence in Asia, Europe, and America.* Eds. Harumi Befu and Sylvie Guichard-Anguis. London: Routledge, 2003. 111-120.

Lambourne, Lionel. *Japonisme: Cultural Crossings Between Japan and the West.* Berlin: Phaidon, 2007.

Laemmerhirt, Iris-Aya. "Riding Blackships to Iwo Jima? Transnational Exchanges and Changing Images of Japan in the United States." *Trans/American, Trans/Oceanic, Trans/Lation. Issues in International American Studies.* Eds. Susana Ataújo, João Ferreira Duarte, and Marta Pacheco Pinto. Newcastle: Cambridge Scholar Publishing, 2010.

---, "Imagining the Taste: Transnational Food Exchanges between Japan and the United States." *The Japanese Journal of American Studies.* 21.2 (2010). 231-250.

Lancaster, Clay. *The Japanese Influence in America.* New York: Abbeville Press, 1983.

Lee, Josephine. *The Japan of Pure Invention: Gilbert and Sullivan's the Mikado*. Minneapolis: U of Minnesota P, 2010.

Lee, Gregory B. and Sunny S.K. Lam. "Wicked Cities: The Other in Hong Kong Science Fiction." *Aliens R Us: The Other in Science Fiction Cinema*. Eds. Ziauddin Sardar and Sean Cubitt. London: Pluto Press, 2003. 111-133.

Lester, Paul Martin and Susan Dente Ross. *Images That Injure: Pictorial Stereotypes in the Media*. Westport: Praeger, 2003.

Lévi-Strauss, Claude. *The Raw and the Cooked. Introduction to a Science of Mythology*. trans. John and Doreen Weightman. New York: Harper and Row, 1969.

---, "The Culinary Triangle." *Food and Culture: A Reader*. Eds. Carole Counihan and Penny Esterik. New York: Routledge, 1997. 28-35.

Lewis, George H. "The Maine Lobsters as Regional Icon: Competing Images over Time and Social Class." *Food and Foodways* 3.4 (1989): 303-316.

Lewis, Reina. *Gendering Orientalism: Race, Femininity and Representation*. London: Routledge, 1996.

Lim, Shirley, Geok-lin. "Identifying Foods, Identifying Selves." *Food Matters: A Special Issue of the Massachusetts Review* 45.3 (2004): 297-305.

Littlewood, Ian. *The Idea of Japan: Western Images, Western Myths*. Chicago: Ivan R. Dee, 1996.

Lockwood, Cara. *Dixieland Sushi*. New York: Down Town Press, 2005.

Lofgren, J. Stephen, ed. "Diary of First Lieutenant Sugihara Kinryu: Iwo Jima, January – February 1945." *The Journal of Military History* 59.1 (1995): 97-133.

Long, Lucy. "Culinary Tourism: A Folkloristic Perspective on Eating and Otherness." *Culinary Tourism*. Ed. Lucy Long. Lexington: The UP of Kentucky, 2004. 20-50.

Looser, Thomas. "Superflat and the Layers of Image and History in 1990s Japan." *Mechademia: Emerging Worlds of Anime and Manga*. Ed. Frenchy Lunning. Minnesota: U of Minneapolis P, 2006. 92-109.

Lowry, Dave. *The Connoisseur's Guide to Sushi*. Boston: The Harvard Common Press, 2005.

Lupton, Deborah. *Food, the Body and the Self*. London: SAGE, 1996.

Lutz, R.C. "Japanese Trade With the United States." *Historical Encyclopedia of American Business*. Ed. Richard L. Wilson. Pasadena: Salem P, 2009. 474-478.

Ma, Karen. *The Modern Madame Butterfly: Fantasy and Reality in Japanese Cross-Cultural Relationships*. Tokyo: Charles E. Tuttle, 1996.

Ma, Sheng-mei. *The Deathly Embrace: Orientalism and Asian American Identity*. Minneapolis: U of Minnesota P, 2000.

---, "Mulan Disney. It's Like Re-Orients: Consuming China and Animating Teen Dreams." *The Emperor's Old Groove: Decolonizing Disney's Magic Kingdom*. Ed. Brenda Ayres. New York: Peter Lang, 2003. 149-164.

MacKenzie, John. *Orientalism, History, Theory and the Arts*. Manchester: Manchester UP, 1995.

Madge, Leila. "Capitalizing On 'Cuteness': The Aesthetics of Social Relations in a New Postwar Japanese Order." *Japanstudien* 9 (1997): 155-176.

MaGee, Chris. "Introduction." *World Film Locations: Tokyo*. Ed. Chris MaGee. Chicago: U of Chicago P., 2011. 5.

Marchetti, Gina. Romance and the "Yellow Peril:" Race, Sex, and Discursive Strategies in Hollywood Fiction. Berkeley: U of California P, 1993.

Marling, Kraral Ann. "Letter from Japan. Kenbei vs. All-American Kawaii at Disneyland." *American Art* 6.2 1992 (1992): 102-111.

Masumoto, Mas D. "Brown Rice Sushi." *Western Folklore* 42.2 (1983): 140-144.

Masuoka, Jitsuichi. "Changing Food Habits of the Japanese in Hawaii." *American Sociological Review* 10.6 (1945): 759-765.

Mathews, Gordon. *Global Culture/Individual Identity: Searching for Home in the Cultural Supermarket*. London: Routledge, 2000.

Matsumoto, Hirotaka. *Osushi, Chikyū o Mawaru*. (*Sushi around the World*). Tokyo: Kobunsha, 2002.

McRoy, Jay, ed. *Japanese Horror Cinema*. Edinburgh: Edinburgh UP, 2006.

---, "Introduction." *Japanese Horror Cinema*. Ed. Jay McRoy. Edinburgh: Edinburgh UP, 2006. 1-11.

---, "Case Study: Cinematic Hybridity in Shimizu Takashi's Ju-On: The Grudge." *Japanese Horror Cinema*. Ed. Jay McRoy. Edinburgh: Edinburgh UP, 2006. 175-184.
Melville, Herman. *Moby Dick.* 1851. London: Penguin, 1994.
Mignolo, D.Walter. "Globalization, Civilization Processes, and the Relocation of Languages and Culture." *The Cultures of Globalization*. Eds. Frederic Jameson and Masao Miyoshi. Durham: Duke UP, 2004. 32-53.
Miller, Toby et al. *Global Hollywood*. London: Bfi Publishing, 2001.
Mintz, Lawrence. "Simulated Tourism at Busch Gardens: The Old Country and Disney's World Showcase, Epcot Center." *Journal of Popular Culture* 32.3 (1998): 47-58.
Mitchell, Tony. "Introduction: Another Root – Hip-Hop outside the USA." *Global Noise: Rap and Hip-Hop Outside the USA*. Ed. Tony Mitchell. Middletown: Wesleyan UP, 2001.
Mitsui, Tōru and Shūhei Hosokawa, eds. *Karaoke Around the World: Global Technology, Local Singing*. London: Routledge, 1998.
Miyao, Daisuke. "Doubleness: American Images of Japanese Men in Silent Spy Films." *The Japanese Journal of American Studies* 9 (1998): 69-95.
Miyoshi, Masao. *Off Center: Power and Cultural Relations between Japan and the United States*. Cambridge: Harvard UP, 1991.
---, "A Borderless World? From Colonialism to Transnationalism and the Decline of the Nation-State." *Critical Inquiry* 19.4 (1993): 726-751.
Mohand, Uday and Leo Maley III. "Orthodoxy and Dissent: The American News Media and the Decision to Use the Atomic Bomb against Japan 1945-1995." *Cultural Difference, Media Memories: Anglo-American Images of Japan*. Ed. Phil Hammond. London: Cassell, 1997. 139-174
Moriyama, Naomi and Doyle, William. *Japanese Women Don't Get Old or Fat*. New York: Delta Trade, 2007.
---, *The Japan Diet*. London: Vermilion, 2007.
Morley, David and Kevin Robins. *Spaces of Identity: Global Media, Electronic Landscapes and Cultural Boundaries*. London: Routledge, 1995.
Murcott, Anne. "Food as an Expression of Identity." *The Analysis of Subjective Culture*. Ed. Harry C. Triandis. New York: John Wiley, 1972. 49-77.

Naficy, Hamid. "Phobic Spaces and Liminal Panics: Independent Transnational Film Genre." *Multiculturalism, Postcoloniality and Transnation-*

*al Media*. Eds. Ella Shohat and Robert Stam. New Brundwick: Rutgers UP, 2003. 203-226.

Nakashima, Tomoko. "Defining 'Japanese Art' in America." *The Japanese Journal of American Studies* 17 (2006): 245-262.

Napier, J. Susan. *Anime From Akira to Howl's Moving Castle: Experiencing Contemporary Japanese Animation*. New York: Palgrave Macmillan, 2005.

---, "The World of Anime Fandom in America." *Mechademia: Emerging Worlds of Anime and Manga*. Ed. Frenchy Lunning. Minneapolis: U of Minnesota P, 2006. 47-63.

---, *From Impressionism to Anime: Japan as Fantasy and Fan Cult in the Mind of the West*. New York: Palgrave Macmillan, 2007.

Nelson, Steve. "Walt Disney's EPCOT and the World's Fair Performance Tradition." *The Drama Review* 30.4 (1986): 106-146.

Neumann, L. William. *America Encounters Japan: From Perry to MacArthur*. Baltimore: The John Hopkins Press, 1969.

Niiya, Brian, ed. *Japanese American History: An A- to Z Reference from 1868 to the Present*. New York: Facts on File Inc., 1993

Noguchi, Paul H. "Savor Slowly: Ekiben: The Fast Food of High Speed Japan." *Ethnology* 33.4 (1994): 317-330.

Noguchi, Yone. *The American Diary of a Japanese Girl*. 1902. Eds. Edward Marx and Laura E. Franey. Philadelphia: Temple UP, 2007.

Notoji, Masako. *Dizuniirando to Iū Seichi*. (*A Sacred Place Called Disneyland*) Tokyo: Iwakami Shoten, 1999.

Nute, Kevin. *Frank Lloyd Wright and Japan: The Role of Traditional Japanese Art and Architecture in the Work of Frank Lloyd Wright*. New York: John Wiley and Sons, 1994.


O'Regan, Tom. "Cultural Exchange" *A Companion to Film Theory*. Eds. Toby Miller and Robert Stam. Malden: Blackwell Publishing, 2004. 262-293.

Ogawa, Masaki. "Japanese Popular Music in Hong Kong: Analysis of Global/Local Relations." *Globalizing Japan: Ethnography of the Japanese Presence in Asia, Europe, and America*. Eds. Harumi Befu and Sylvie Guichard-Anguis. London: Routledge, 2003. 121-130.

Ohnuki-Tierney, Emiko. *Rice as Self: Japanese Identities through Time*. Princeton, Princeton UP, 1993.

---, "McDonald's in Japan: Changing Manners and Etiquette." *Golden Arches East. McDonald's in East Asia.* Ed. James L. Watson. Stanford: Stanford UP, 1997.161-182.

---, "Cherry Blossoms and Their Viewing: A Window onto Japanese Culture." *The Culture of Japan as Seen Through Its Leisure.* Eds. Sepp Linhart and Sabine Frühstück. Albany: State U of New York, 1998. 213-236.

---, "We Eat Each Other's Food to Nourish Our Body: The Global and the Local as Mutually Constituent Forces." *Food in Global History.* Ed. Raymond Grew. Boulder: Westview Press, 1999. 240-272.

---, *Kamikaze Diaries: Reflections of Japanese Student Soldiers.* Chicago: U of Chicago P, 2007.

Otake, Masaru. "The Haiku Touch in Wallace Stevens and Some Imagists." *East West Review* 2 (1965-66):152-65.

Ozeki, L. Ruth. *My Year of Meat.* 1998. London: Picador, 2003.

Park, Jane Chi Hyun. "Stylistic Crossings: Cyberpunk Impulse in Anime." *World Literature Today* (2005): 60-63.

---, *Yellow Future. Oriental Style Hollywood Cinema.* Minneapolis: U of Minnesota P, 2010.

Parson, Deborah L. *Streetwalking the Metropolis: Women, the City, and Modernity.* Oxford: Oxford UP, 2000.

Patten, Fred. *Watching Anime, Reading Manga: 25 Years of Essays and Reviews.* Berkeley: Stone Bridge Press, 2004.

Pells, Richard. *Not Like US: How Europeans Have Loved, Hated and Transformed American Culture Since World War II.* New York: Basic Books, 1997.

Perry, Matthew. *Narrative of the Expedition of an American Squadron to the China Seas and Japan 1852-1854.* 1856. Mineola: Dover, 2000.

Piehler, G. Kurt. *Remembering War the American Way.* Washington: Smithsonian, 1995.

Phillips, Mark. "The Global Disney Audiences Project: Disney Across Cultures." *Dazzled by Disney? The Global Disney Audiences Project.* Eds. Janet Wasko et al. London: Leicester UP, 2001. 31-61.

Pillsburg, Richard. *No Foreign Food: The American Diet in Time and Place.* Boulder: Westview Press, 1998.

Popham, Peter. *Tokyo: The City at The End Of The World*. Tokyo: Kodansha International Ltd, 1998.

Powell, John. *Encyclopedia of North American Immigration*. N.Y.: Facts on File, 2005.

Prager, Brad and Michael Richardson. "A Sort of Homecoming: An Archeology of Disneyland." *Streams of Cultural Capital: Transnational Cultural Studies*. Eds. David Palumbo-Liu and Hans Ulrich Gumbrecht. Stanford: Stanford UP, 1997. 199-219.

Prasso, Sheridan. *The Asian Mystique: Dragon Ladies, Geisha Girls, and Our Fantasies of the Exotic Orient*. New York: Public Affairs, 2006.

Pratt, Mary Louise. *Imperial Eyes: Travel Writing and Transculturation*.1992. New York: Routledge, 2003.

Prince, Stephen. *The Cinema of Akira Kurosawa: The Warrior's Cinema*. Princeton: Princeton UP, 1991

---,"Genre and Violence in the Work of Kurosawa and Peckinpah." *Action and Adventure Cinema*. Ed. Yvonne Tasker. London: Routledge, 2004. 331-344.


Rankin, Andrew. *Seppuku: A History of Samurai Suicide*. Tokyo: Kodansha, 2011.

Raz, Aviad. *Riding the Black Ship: Japan and Tokyo Disneyland*. Cambridge: Harvard UP, 1999.

---, "Domesticating Disney: Onstage Strategies of Adaptation in Tokyo Disneyland." *Journal of Popular Culture* 33.4 (2000): 77-99.

Raz, Jacob and Aviad Raz. "'America' Meets 'Japan': A Journey for Real Between Two Imaginaries." *Theory, Culture and Society* 13.3 (1996): 153-178.

Rich, Ruby. "To Read or Not to Read: Subtitles, Trailers, and Monolingualism." *Subtitles: On the Foreignness of Film*. Eds. Atom Egoyan and Ian Balfour. Cambridge: MIT, 2004. 153-169.

Richie, Donald. *Japanese Cinema: Film Style and National Character*. New York: Anchor Books, 1971.

---, *A Lateral View: Essays On Contemporary Japan*. Tokyo: The Japan Times Ltd., 1987.

---, *Japanese Cinema: An Introduction*. Oxford: Oxford UP, 1990.

---, *A Taste of Japan*. Tokyo: Kodansha, 1992.

---, *The Honorable Visitors*. Tokyo: IEG Muse, 2001.

Richie, Donald and Paul Schrader. *A Hundred Years of Japanese Film: A Concise History, with a Selective Guide to DVDs and Videos.* 2001. Tokyo: Kodansha International, 2005.

Riessland, Andreas. "Sweet Spots: The Use of Cuteness in Japanese Advertising." *Japanstudien* 9. München: Ludicium, 1997. 129-154.

Ritzer, George. *The McDonaldization of Society: An Investigation into the Changing Character of Contemporary Social Life.* Thousand Oaks: Pine Forge Press. 1993.

Roost, Frank. *Die Disneyfizierung der Städte: Grossprojekte der Entertainmentindustrie am Beispiel des New Yorker Time Squares und der Siedlung Celebration in Florida.* Opladen: Leske und Budrich, 2000.

Root, Deborah. *Cannibal Culture. Art, Appropriation, and the Commodification of Difference. Boulder*: Westview, 1996.

Root, Wavery and Richard De Rochemont. *Eating in America.* New Jersey: Ecco Press.1995.

Ross, Bruce. *Haiku Moment: An Anthology of Contemporary North American Haiku. Rutland*: Charles E. Tuttle, 1993.

Rowland, Mark. *The Philosopher at the End of the Universe.*2003. New York: Thomas Dunne Books, 2004.

Rudzinski, Russ. *Japanese Country Cookbook.* San Francisco: Nitty Gritty Productions, 1969.

Said, Edward. *Orientalism.* New York: Vintage, 1979.

---, *Culture and Imperialism.* New York: Vintage, 1994.

Salamone, Virginia A. and Frank A. Salamone. "Images of Main Street: Disney World Adventure." *Journal of American Culture* 2.1 (1999): 85-92.

Samuelson, Dale. *The American Amusement Park.* St. Paul: MBI Publishing, 2001.

Sardar, Ziauddin. "Introduction." *Aliens R Us: The Other in Science Fiction Cinema.* Eds Ziauddin Sardar and Sean Cubitt. London: Pluto Press, 2002. 1-17.

Schilling, Mark. *The Yakuza Movie Book. A Guide to Japanese Gangster Films.* Berkley: Stone Bridge Press, 2008.

Schlesinger, Christopher and John Willoughby. *How to Cook Meat.* New York: Harper Collins, 2002.

Schlosser, Eric. *Fast Food Nation.* London: Penguin, 2002.

Schneider, Birgit. *From Soldiers to Citizens: The Civil Reintegration of Demobilized Soldiers of the German Wehrmacht and the Imperial Japanese Army after Unconditional Surrender in 1945*. Diss. Washington State University, 2010. *ProQuest Dissertations and Theses*. Web. 23.10.2012.

Schodt, L. Frederick. *America and the Four Japans*. Berkeley: Stone Bridge Press, 1994.

Schueller, Malani Johar. *U.S. Orientalisms: Race, Nation, and Gender in Literature, 1790-1890*. Ann Arbor: U of Michigan P, 2004.

Sen, Amit. *Academic Dictionary of Cooking*. Delhi: Isha Books, 2005.

Server, Lee. *Asian Pop Cinema: Bombay to Tokyo*. San Francisco: Chronicle Books, 1999.

Shibusawa, Naoko. *America's Geisha Ally: Reimagining the Japanese Enemy*. Harvard: Harvard UP, 2007.

Shohat, Ella and Robert Stam. "From the Imperial Family to the Transnational Imaginary: Media Spectatorship in the Age of Globalization." *Global/Local: Cultural Production and the Transnational Imaginary*. Eds. Rob Wilson and Wimal Dissanayake. Durham: Duke UP, 1996. 145-170.

---, "Introduction." *Multiculturalism, Postcoloniality and Transnational Media*. Eds. Ella Shohat and Robert Stam. New Brundwick: Rutgers UP, 2003. 1-17.

Silvio, Carl. "Animated Bodies and Cybernetic Selves: *The Animatrix* and the Question of Posthumanity." *Cinema Anime: Critical Engagements with Japanese Animation*. Ed. Steven T. Brown. New York: Macmillan, 2006. 113-137.

Singh, Amirtjit and Peter Schmidt, eds. *Postcolonial Theory and the United States: Race, Ethnicity and Literature*. Jackson: UP of Mississippi, 2000.

Sklar, A. Martin *Walt Disney's Disneyland*. n.p.Walt Disney Productions, 1969.

Slotkin, Richard. *Gunfighter Nation: The Myth of the Frontier in Twentieth Century America*. New York: Harper, 1993.

Smil, Vaclav and Kazuhiko Kobayashi. *Japan's Dietary Transition and Its Impacts*. Cambridge, MA: MIT Press, 2012.

Smoodin, Eric, ed. *Disney Discourse: Producing the Magic Kingdom*. New York: Routledge, 1994.

---, "Introduction: How to Read Walt Disney." *Disney Discourse: Producing the Magic Kingdom.* Ed. Eric Smoodin. New York: Routledge, 1994. 1-20.
Snodgrass, Judith. *Presenting Japanese Buddhism to the West.* Chapel Hill: The U of North Carolina P, 2003.
Spivak, Gayatri. "Teaching for the Times." *Dangerous Liaisons: Gender, Nation, and Postcolonial Perspectives.* Anne McClintock, Aamir Mufti, and Ella Shohat. Minneapolis: U of Minnesota P, 1997. 468-490.
Steele, M. William. *Alternative Narratives in Modern Japanese History.* New York: Routledge, 2003.
Straubhaar, Joseph, Robert Larose, Lucinda Davenport. *Media Now: Understanding Media, Culture, and Technology.* 7th ed. Boston: Wadswoth Publishing, 2012.
Strada, Judi and Minko Takane Moreno. *Sushi for Dummies.* Hoboken: Wiley Publishing, 2004.
Tatsumi, Takayuki. *Full Metal Apache: Transactions Between Cyberpunk Japan and Avant-Pop America.* Durham: Duke UP, 2006.
---, "Waiting For Godzilla: Chaotic Negotiations Between Post-Orientalism and Hyper-Occidentalism." *Transactions, Transgressions, Transformations: American Culture in Western Europe and Japan.* Eds. Heide Fehrenbach and Uta G. Poiger. New York: Bergham Books, 2000. 224-236.
Theado, Matt, ed. *The Beats: A Literary Reference.* Jackson: Da Capo Press, 2002.
Tobin, Joseph J., ed. *Re-Made in Japan: Everyday Life and Consumer Taste in a Changing Society.* New Haven: Yale UP, 1992.
---, "Introduction." *Re-Made in Japan: Everyday Life and Consumer Taste in a Changing Society.* Ed. Joseph J. Tobin. New Haven: Yale UP, 1992. 1-41.
Tomlinson, John. *Cultural Imperialism: A Critical Introduction.* London: Pinter Publ. 1994.
Tsuchiya, Yuka. "Imagined America in Occupied Japan: (Re-) Educational Films Shown by the U.S. Occupation Forces to the Japanese, 1948-1952." *The Japanese Journal of American Studies* 13 (2002): 193-213.
Turner, Frederick Jackson. *The Frontier in American History.* 1920. New York: Dover Publishing, 1996.

Twain, Mark. *The Adventures of Huckleberry Finn*. 1885. London: Penguin, 1994.

Ueda, Atsushi, ed. *The Electric Geisha: Exploring Japan's Popular Culture*. Trans. Miriam Eguchi. Tokyo: Kodansha, 1994.

Ueno, Toshiya. "Japanimation: Techno-Orientalism, Media Tribes and Rave Culture." *Aliens R'Us: The Other in Science-Fiction Cinema*. Eds. Ziauddin Sardar and Sean Cubbitt. London: Pluto Press, 2002. 94-110.

Van der Veen, Marijke. "When is Food a Luxury?" *World Archeology* 34.3 (2003): 405-427.

Van Duzer, Chat. "Hic Sunt Dracones: The Geography and Carthgraphy of Monsters." *The Ashgate Reaearch Companion to Monsters and the Monstrous*. Eds. Asa Aimon Mittman and Peter J. Dendle. Burlington: Ashgate, 2013. 387-436.

Van Maanen, John. "Displacing Disney: Some Notes on the Flow of Culture." *Quantitative Sociology* 15.1 (1992): 5-35.

Vryzidis, Nikolaus. "Tokyo Drifter Critique." *Directory of World Cinema. Japan*. Ed. John Berra. Fishponds: Intellect Publishing, 2010. 282- 283.

Walker, Samuel. "The Decision to Use the Bomb: A Historiographical Update." *Hiroshima in History and Memory*. Ed. Michael J. Hogan. Cambridge: Cambridge UP, 1996. 11-37.

---, "History, Collective Memory, and the Decision to Use the Bomb." *Hiroshima in History and Memory*. Ed. Michael J. Hogan. Cambridge: Cambridge UP, 1996. 187-199.

Ward, Annalee. *Mouse Morality: The Rhetoric of Disney Animated Film*. Austin: U of Texas P., 2002.

Warren, Stacy. "Disneyfication of the Metropolis: Popular Resistance in Seattle." *Journal of Urban Affairs* 16.2 (1994): 89-107.

Wasko, Janet. *Understanding Disney*. Cambridge: Polity Press, 2001.

Wasko, Janet and Eileen R. Meehan. "Dazzled by Disney? Ambiguity in Ubiquity." *Dazzled by Disney? The Global Disney Audiences Project*. Eds. Janet Wasko et al. London: Leicester UP, 2001. 329-343.

Wasser, Frederick. "Is Hollywood America? The Transnationalization of the American Film Industry." *Movies and American Society*. Ed. Steven J. Ross. Oxford: Blackwell Publishers, 2002. 345-357.

Watanabe, Katsumi. "Just Wait Until We Get to the Battlefield." *Senso: The Japanese Remember the Pacific War: Letters to the Editor of Asahi Shimbun.* Ed. Frank Gibney. trans. Beth Cary. Armonk: M.E. Sharpe, 1995. 28.

Watson, L. James, ed. *Golden Arches East: McDonald's in East Asia.* Stanford: Stanford UP, 1997.

---, "Introduction: Transnationalism, Localization, and Fast Foods in East Asia." *Golden Arches East. McDonald's in East Asia.* Ed. James L. Watson. Stanford: Stanford UP, 1997. 1-38.

Watson, James L. and Melissa C. Caldwell, eds. *The Cultural Politics of Food and Eating: A Reader.* Malden: Blackwell Publishing, 2005.

Watters, John G. "The Manners of Mass Murder: Eating Fear." *Feeding Culture: The Pleasures and Perils of Appetite.* Eds. Wojciech Kalaga and Tadeusz Rachwal. Frankfurt: Peter Lang, 2005. 91-100.

Whiting, Robert. *The Chrysanthemum and the Bat: Baseball Samurai Style.* New York: Avon Books, 1977.

---, *You Gotta Have Wa.* New York: Random House, 1989

---, *The Meaning of Ichiro: The New Wave from Japan and the Transformation of Our National Pastime.* New York: Time Warner Book, 2004.

Whitman, Walt. "A Broadway Pagant." *Leaves of Grass.* 1892. New York: Bantam Books, 1983. 196-199.

Wiegand, Wayne. *U.S. History for Dummies.* New York: IDG Books Worldwide, 2001.

Wiley, Peter Booth. *Yankees in the Land of the Gods: Commodore Perry and the Opening of Japan.* New York: Viking, 1990.

Wilkinson, Endymion. *Japan Versus the West: Image and Reality.* London: Penguin, 1991.

Williams, Samuel. "Hot and Cold Saki." *Travellers' Tales of Old Japan.* Ed. Michael Wise. Singapore: Times Books International, 1985. 15-16.

Wilson, Alexander. "The Betrayal of the Future: Walt Disney's Epcot Center." *Disney Discourse: Producing the Magic Kingdom.* Ed. Eric Smoodin. New York: Routledge, 1994. 118-128.

Wise, Michael, ed. *Travellers' Tales of Old Japan.* Singapore: Times Books International, 1985.

Wong, Wendy Siuyi. "Globalizing Manga: From Japan to Hong Kong and Beyond." *Mechademia: Emerging Worlds of Anime and Manga.* Ed. Frenchy Lunning. Minneapolis: U of Minnesota P, 2006. 23-45.

Wright, Terri Martin. "Walt Disney's Adaption of the Grimms' 'Snow White.'" *Journal of Popular Film and Television* 25.3 (1997): 98-108.

Xing, Jun. *Asian America through The Lens: History, Representations and Identity*. Walnut Creek: Altamira Press, 1998.

Yamamoto, Traise. *Masking Selves, Making Subjects: Japanese American Women, Identity, and the Body*. Berkeley: U of California P, 1999.

Yang, Jeff. et al. *Eastern Standard Time: A Guide To Asian Influence on American Culture From Astro Boy to Zen Buddhism*. Boston: Houghton Mifflin Company, 1997.

Yates, Ronald E. *The Kikkoman Chronicles: A Global Company With a Japanese Soul*. New York: McGraw-Hill, 1998.

Yau, Esther C.M. "Introduction. Hong Kong Cinema in a Borderless World." *At Full Speed: Hong Kong Cinema in a Borderless World*. Ed. Esther C.M.Yau. Minneapolis: U of Minnesota P, 2001. 1-28.

Yazaki, Michiko. "Tomu Kuruūsu vs. Nihon no Meijūu Minagiru." ("Tom Cruise vs. Rising Japanese Beasts"). *Roadshow*. 2004 (1):9-23

Yegenoglu, Meyda. *Colonial Fantasies: Towards a Feminist Reading of Orientalism*. Cambridge: Cambridge UP, 1999.

Yoshihara, Mari. *Embracing the East: White Women and American Orientalism*. Oxford: Oxford UP, 2003.

---, "The Flight of the Japanese Butterfly: Orientalism, Nationalism, and Performances of Japanese Womanhood." *American Quarterly* 56.4 (2004): 975-1001.

Yoshimi, Shunya. "Amerikanizēshon to bunka no sēijigaku." ("Americanization and Cultural Studies") *Gendaishakai no Shakaigaku*. Ed. S. Inoue. Tokyo: Iwakami Shoten, 1997. 157-231.

Yoshimoto, Mitsuhiro. "Images of Empire: Tokyo Disneyland and Japanese Cultural Imperialism." *Disney Discourse: Producing the Magic Kingdom*. Ed. Eric Smoodin. New York: Routledge, 1994. 181-199.

Young, Robert J.C. *Colonial Desire: Hybridity in Theory, Culture and Race*. London: Routledge1995.

Yu, Henry. *Thinking Orientals: Migration, Contact, and Exoticism in Modern America*. Oxford: Oxford UP, 2001.

Zia, Helen. *Asian American Dreams: The Emergence of an American People*. New York: Farrar, Straus and Giroux, 2001.

Zwick, Edward. "Foreword." *The Last Samurai Official Movie Guide.* Warner Bros. Pictures et.al. New York: Time Inc. Home Entertainment, 2003. 10-11.

## INTERNET SOURCES

Anderson, Jason. "Eastern Exotica." 07.12.2005. *Canadian Broadcasting Corporation.* 12.01.2006. http://www.cbc.ca/arts/film/geisha.html.

Asian Media Watch. 29.02.2004. *Asian Media Watch.* 27.07.2004. http://www.lost-in-racism.org.

BBC-News "Disney Bets on Asia." 04.09.2001. *BBC.* 15.01.2003. http://news.bbc.co.uk/1/ni/business/1525517.stm.

BBC-News. "China Ban for Memoirs of a Geisha." 02.02.2006. *BBC.* 17.03.2006. http://news.bbc.co.uk/2/hi/entertainment/4672840.stm.

California Sushi Academy. 2006. "About CSA." 20.04.2007. http://www.sushi-academy.com/pages/aboutcsa.html.

Caro, Mark. Rev. of *Lost in Translation*, dir. Sophia Coppola. *Metromix Chicago.* 11.09.2003. 21.05.2004 "http://chicago.metromix.com/movies/review/movie-review-lost-in/.

Cho, Margaret. Blog. 31.10.2005. "Harajuku Girls." 16.06.2007. Homepage. http://www.margaretcho.com/blog/2005/10/31/harajuku-girls.html.

Dower, John. "Black Ships & Samurai." Massachusetts Institute of Technology. 2008.
Visualizing Cultures http://visualizingcultures.mit.edu (15.11.2011)

Faiola, Anthony. "Japan's Empire of Cool: Country's Culture Becomes Its Biggest Export." 27.12. 2003. *Washington Post Foreign Service.* 30.09.2004. http://www.washingtonpost.com/wp-dyn/articles/A33261-2003Dec26.html.

Flags of Our Fathers. 2006. Official Movie Homepage. Warner Bros. Pictures. http://www.flagsofourfathers.com/ 15.01.2007.

Japan Today. 19.04.2004. "Letters to the Editor: Lost in Translation Fine." 27.07.2004. http://www.japantoday.com/e/?content=letter&id=127.

JETRO. "Starbucks' Green Tea Success With Japanese Consumers Leads to Worldwide Popularity." 03.04.2006. *JETRO Newsletter: Spotlight No. 9*. 23.07.2008. http://www.jetro.org/content/354.

Laemmerhirt, Iris-Aya. "'The Tiger's Eyes Are Like My Own': Depictions of Japaneseness in Contemporary American Movies." *COPAS - Current Objectives of Postgraduate Students*. Vol. 8 (2007). http://copas.uni-regensburg.de/article/view/97/121. 23.07.2008.

The Last Samurai. 2003. Warner Brothers. Official Homepage. http://lastsamurai.warnerbros.com

Letters from Iwo Jima. 2006. Warner Brothers. Official Homepage. http://wwws.warnerbros.co.jp/iwojima-movies/ 22.02.2007.

McDonalds. "Asian Chicken Salad." 10.07.2007. Homepage. http://www.mcdonalds.com/usa/eat/features/salads.html 17.07.2007.

McGray, Douglas. "Japan's Gross National Cool." May/June 2003. *Foreign Policy*. 30.09.2004. http://www.foreignpolicy.com/story/cms.php?story_id=178

NBC. Interview. "Sushi Chef Tracy Griffith Makes Sushi American Style." 01.11.2005. *California Sushi Academy*. 16.06.2007. http://www.sushi-academy.com/pages/article/nbctoday.html.

Oriental Land Company Group Homepage. http://www.olc.co.jp/en/company/philosophy/index.html 02.06.2006.

Oriental Land Company Group Homepage. 30.1.2006. "New Attraction to Open in Tokyo Disneyland; Cinderella Castle Mystery Tour to Close." 02.06.2006. http://www.olc.co.jp/en/news_parts/2006013001e.pdf

Oriental Land Company Group Homepage. 2010. "Guest Statistics." 20.01.2012. http://www.olc.co.jp/en/tdr/guest/

Rea, Steven. "Japanese Star Had His Doubts on Eastwood's 'Iwo Jima'." 09.01.2007. *Philadelphia Inquirer*. 12.01.2007. http://www.philly.com/philly/entertainment/movies/6266122.html.

Rainbow Roll Sushi. Homepage. 2008. WDI Corporations.01.06.2007. http://www.wdi.co.jp/ja/re-rainbow.html.

Schilling, Mark. "Scriptwriter talks about Japan hit 'Letters.'" 01.03.2007. *The Japan Times.* 04.03.2007. http://search.japantimes.co.jp/cgi-bin/ff 20070301i1.html.

Schwarzbaum, Lisa. Rev. of *Lost in Translation*, dir. Sophia Coppola. *Entertainment Weekly.* 10.09.2003. 21.05.2004. http://www.ew.com/ ew/article/0,,479937~1~0~lostintranslation,00.html.

Starbucks. "Tazo© Green Tea Latte." 28.04.2013. Homepage. http://www.starbucks.com/menu/drinks/tazo-tea/green-tea-latte.

---, "Tazo© Green Tea Frappuchino." 28.04.2013. Homepage. http://www.starbucks.com/menu/drinks/frappuccino-blended-beverages/green-tea-frappuccino-blended-creme.

---, "Chocolate Brownie Green Tea Frappuchino." 28.04.2013. Homepage. http://store.starbucks.co.jp/beverage/frappuccino/cream/4524785218543/

Stewart, Martha. Martha Stewart Living Omnimedia, Inc. 2008. "Japanese Twist Bridal Shower." 01.06.2007. *Homepage Martha Stewart.* http://www.marthastewart.com/portal/site/mslo/.

Tokyo Disney Resort. 2008. Homepage. 12.07.2008. http://www.tokyodisneyresort.jp/tdr/english/welcome/entire_map.html 3.11.2004.

Tower of Terror. 2006. Homepage. 12.07.2008. http://www.tot1899.com/index.html

Tracy, David. "New Teen Queen Reigns in Japan." 10.12.1996. *The New York Times.* 15.08.2012. http://www.nytimes.com/1996/12/10/news/10 iht-idol.t.html?pagewanted=all.

## MOVIES

*Akira.* Dir. Ohtomo Katsuhiro. Toho, 1988.

*Aladdin.* Dir. Ron Clements and John Musker. Walt Disney Pictures, 1992.

*Avatar.* Dir. James Cameron. Perf. Sam Worthington, Zoe Saldana, Sigourney Weaver. Twentieth Century Fox, 2009.

*Babel.* Dir. Alejandro González Inárritu. Perf. Brad Pitt, Cate Blanchett, Mohamed Akhzam. Paramount Pictures, 2006.

*Batman Begins.* Dir. Christopher Nolan. Perf. Christian Bale, Katie Holmes, Watanabe Ken. Warner Bros., 2005.
*Black Rain.* Dir. Ridley Scott. Perf. Michael Douglas, Andy Garcia, Takakura Ken. Paramount Pictures, 1989.
*Blade Runner.* Dir. Ridley Scott. Perf. Harrison Ford, Rutger Hauer, Sean Young. Warner Bros., 1982.
*Breakfast at Tiffany's.* Dir. Blake Edwards. Perf. Audry Hepburn, George Peppard, Mickey Rooney. Paramount Pictures, 1961.

*Chakushin Ari (One Missed Call).* Dir. Miike Takashi. Perf. Shibasaki Kou, Tsutsumi Shinichi, Fukiishi Kazue. Toho, 2004.
*Cinderella.* Dir. Clyde Geronimi, Wilfred Jackson. Walt Disney Pictures, 1950.
*Come See the Paradise.* Dir. Alan Parker. Perf. Dennis Quaid, Sab Shimono, Tomita Tamlyn. 20$^{th}$ Century Fox, 1990.

*Dances with Wolves.* Dir. Kevin Costner. Perf. Kevin Costner, Mary McDonnell, Graham Greene. Orion Pictures, 1990.
*Dark Water.* Dir. Walter Salles. Perf. Tim Roth; Jennifer Connelly; John C.Reilly. Touchstone Pictures, 2005.

*Flags of Our Fathers.* Dir. Clint Eastwood. Perf. Ryan Philippe, Jesse Bradford, Adam Beach. Paramount Pictures, 2006.
*Freeze Me.* Dir. Ishii Takashi. Perf. Inoue Harumi, Tsurumi Shingo, Kitamura Kazuki. Nikkatsu, 2000.
*From Here to Eternity.* Dir. Fred Zinnemann. Perf. Burt Lancaster, Montgomery Clift, Deborah Kerr. Columbia Pictures, 1953.

*Geisha Girl.* Dir. George P. Breakston, C. Ray Stahl. Perf. Steve Forrest, Martha Hyer, Nakamura Tetsu. Realart Pictures Inc., 1952.
*Godzilla.* Dir. Roland Emmerich. Perf. Matthew Broderick, Jean Reno, Maria Pitillo. Columbia TriStar Film, 1998.
*Gojira.* Dir. Honda, Ishirô. Perf. Takarada, Akira; Kôchi, Momoko; Hrata, Akihiko. Toho, 1954.
*Gung Ho!.* Dir. Ron Howard. Perf. Michael Keaton, Gedde Watanabe, George Wendt. Universal Pictures, 1986.

*Hachi: A Dog's Tale*. Dir. Lasse Hallström. Perf. Richard Gere, Joan Allen, Cary-Hirayuki Tagawa. Stage 6 Films, 2009.
*Hachi-Kō Monogatari (Hachiko)*. Dir. Kōyama, Seijirō. Perf. Nakadai Tatsuya, Yachigusa Kaoru, Ishino Mako. Shochiku-Fuji Company, 1987.
*Honogurai Mizu no Soko Kara (Dark Water)*. Dir. Nakata, Hideo. Perf. Kuroki Hitomi, Kanno Rio, Oguchi Mirei. Toho, 2002.

*Indiana Jones and the Kingdom of the Crystal Skull*. Dir. Steven Spielberg. Perf. Harrison Ford, Cate Blanchett, Karen Allen. Paramount Pictures, 2008.
*Into the Sun*. Dir. Christopher Morrison. Perf. Steven Segal, Matthew Davis, Osawa Takao. Destination Films, 2005.

*Ju-On (The Grudge)*. Dir. Shimizu Takashi. Perf. Okina Megumi, Itô Misaki, Uehara Misa. Xanadeux Company, 2002.

*Karate Kid, Part II*. Dir. John G. Avildsen. Perf. Ralph Macchio, Pat Morita, Okumoto Yuji. Columbia Pictures,1986.
*Kill Bill: Volume One*. Dir. Quentin Tarantino. Perf. Uma Thurman, Lucy Liu, Vivica A. Fox. Miramax Films, 2003.
*Know Your Enemy: Japan*. Dir. Frank Capra and Joris Ivens. U.S. War Department, 1945.
Kôkaku Kidôtai (Ghost in the Shell). Shochiku,1995.

*Letters from Iwo Jima*. Dir. Clint Eastwood. Perf. Watanabe Ken, Ninomiya Kazunari, Ihara Tsuyoshi. Paramount Pictures, 2007.
*Lilo and Stitch*. Dir. Dean De Blois and Chris Sanders. Walt Disney Pictures, 2002.
*Lost in Translation*. Dir. Sofia Coppola. Perf. Bill Murray, Scarlett Johansson, Takeshita Akiko. Focus Features, 2003.

*M. Butterfly*. Dir. David Cronenberg. Perf. Jeremy Irons, John Lone, Barbara Sukowa. Warner Bros., 1993. DVD.
*Memoirs of a Geisha*. Dir. Rob Marchall. Perf. Watanabe Ken, Michelle Yeoh, Ziyi Zhang. Columbia Pictures, 2005.
*Metropolis*. Dir. Fritz Lang. Perf. Alfred Abel, Gustav Fröhlich, Brigitte Helm. UFA, 1927.

*Mononoke Hime* (*Princess Mononoke*). Dir. Miyazaki Hayao. Toho, 1997.
*Monsters Inc.* Dir. Pete Docter. 2001. DVD. Walt Disney Pictures, 2002.
*Mr. Baseball.* Dir. Fred Schepisi. Perf. Tom Selleck, Takakura Ken, Takanashi Aya. Universal Pictures,1992.
*My Japan.* U.S. Treasury Department. 1945. http://archive.org/details/MyJapan1945

*Nora Inu* (*Stray Dog*). Dir. Kurosawa Akira. Perf. Mifune Toshirô, Shimura Takashi, Awaji Keiko. Toho, 1949.

*One Missed Call.* Dir. Eric Vallette. Perf. Shannyn Sossamon, Edward Burns, Ray Wise. Warner Bros., 2008.
*Ore wa, Kimi no Tame Koso Shini ni Iku* (*For Those We Love*). Dir. Shinjo Taku. Perf. Emori Toru, Furuhata Katsutaka, Cleve Gray. Toei Company, 2007.

*Pearl Harbor.* Dir. Michael Bay. Perf. Ben Affleck, Josh Hartnett, Kate Beckinsale. Touchstone Pictures, 2001.
*Per un Pugno di Dollari* (*A Fistful of Dollars*). Dir. Sergio Leone. Perf. Clint Eastwood, Marianne Koch, Gian Maria Volontè. United Artists, 1964.
*Pokémon: The First Movie.* Dir. Michael Haigney and Yuyama Kunihiko. Toho, 1999.

*Ringu.* Dir. Nakata Hideo. Perf. Matsushima Nanako, Nakatani Miki, Sanada Hiroyuki. Toho, 1998.
*Rising Sun.* Dir. Philip Kaufman. Perf. Sean Connery, Wesley Snipes, Harvey Keitel. 20$^{th}$ Century Fox, 1993.

*Sands of Iwo Jima.* Dir. Allan Dwan. Perf. John Wayne, John Agar, Adele Mara. Republic Pictures,1949.
*Sayonara.* Dir. Joshua Logan. Perf. Marlon Brando, Patricia Owens, Taka Miiko. Warner Bros., 1957.
*Scream.* Dir. Wes Craven. Perf. Neve Campbell, David Arquette, Courteney Cox. Dimension Films, 1996.
*Sen to Chihiro no Kamikakushi* (*Spirited Away*). Dir. Miyazaki Hayao. Toho, 2001.

*Shall We Dance*. Dir. Peter Chelsom. Perf. Richard Gere, Jennifer Lopez, Susan Sarandon. Miramax, 2004.
*Shall We Dansu?* Dir. Suo Masayuki. Perf. Yakusho Kôji, Kusakari Tamiyo, Takenaka Naoto. Toho, 1996.
*Shichinin no Samurai (The Seven Samurai)*. Dir. Kurosawa Akira. Perf. Mifune Toshirô, Shimura Takashi, Inaba Yoshio. Toho, 1954.
*Snow White and the Seven Dwarfs*. Dir. David Hand. Walt Disney Pictures, 1937.
*Star Wars Episode I: The Phantom Menace*. Dir. George Lucas. Perf. Ewan McGregor, Liam Neeson, Natalie Portman. 20$^{th}$ Century Fox, 1999.
*Star Wars Episode II: Attack of the Clones*. Dir. George Lucas. Perf. Christopher Lee, Ewan McGregor, Natalie Portman. 20$^{th}$ Century Fox, 2002.
*Star Wars Episode III: Revenge of the Sith*. Dir. George Lucas. Perf. Ewan McGregor, Hayden Christiansen, Natalie Portman. 20$^{th}$ Century Fox, 2005.
*Star Wars Episode IV:* Dir. George Lucas. Perf. Harrison Ford, Carrie Fisher, Mark Hamill. 20$^{th}$ Century Fox, 1977.
*Star War Episode V: The Empire Strikes Back*. Dir. George Lucas. Perf. Harrison Ford, Carrie Fisher, Mark Hamill. 20$^{th}$ Century Fox, 1980.
*Star Wars Episode VI: Return of the Jedi*. Dir. George Lucas. Perf. Harrison Ford, Carrie Fisher, Mark Hamill. 20$^{th}$ Century Fox, 1983.
*Steamboat Willie*. Dir. Walt Disney and Ub Iwerks. 1928. Walt Disney Pictures.
*Suchîmubôi (Steamboy)*. Dir. Ohtomo Katsuhiro. Toho, 2004.

*Tengoku to Jigoku (High and Low)*. Dir. Kurosawa Akira. Perf. Mifune Toshirô, Nakadai Tatsuya, Kagawa Kyôko. Toho, 1963.
*The Animatrix*. Dir. Peter Chung et al. Warner Brothers, 2003.
*The Barbarian and the Geisha*. Dir. John Huston. Perf. John Wayne, Ando Eiko, Sam Jaffe. Twentieth Century Fox, 1958.
*The Black Cauldron*. Dir. Ted Berman and Richard Rich. Walt Disney Pictures, 1985.
*The Bridge on the River Kwai*. Dir. David Lean. Perf. William Holden, Jack Hawkins, Hayakawa Sessue. Columbia Pictures, 1957.
*The Departed*. Dir. Martin Scorsese. Perf. Leonardo DiCaprio, Matt Damon, Martin Sheen, Mark Wahlberg. Warner Bros, 2006.

*The Fast and the Furious: Tokyo Drift.* Dir. Justin Lin. Perf. Lucas Black, Zachery Ty Bryan, Brian Tee. Universal Pictures, 2006.
*The Fifth Element.* Dir. Luc Besson. Perf. Bruce Willis, Gary Oldman, Milla Jovovich. Gaumont Film, 1997.
*The Grudge.* Dir. Shimizu Takashi. Perf. Sarah Michelle Gellar, Jason Behr, Fuji Takako. Columbia Pictures, 2004.
*The Harimaya Bridge.* Dir. Aaron Woolfolk. Perf. Danny Glover, Ben Guillory, Takaoka Saki. T-Joy, 2009.
*The Last of the Mohicans.* Dir. Michael Man. Perf. Daniel Day-Lewis, Madeline Stowe, Russel Means. Twentieth Century Fox, 1992.
*The Last Samurai.* Dir. Edward Zwick. Perf. Tom Cruise, Watanabe Ken, Koyuki. Warner Bros.,2003.
*The Lion King.* Dir. Roger Allers and Rob Minkoff. Walt Disney Pictures, 1994.
*The Little Mermaid.* Dir. Ron Clements and John Musker. Walt Disney Pictures, 1989.
*The Magnificent Seven.* Dir. John Sturges. Perf. Yul Brynner, Eli Wallach, Steve McQueen. United Artists, 1960.
*The Matrix.* Dir. Andy and Larry Wachowski. Perf. Keanu Reeves, Laurence Fishburne, Carrie-Anne Moss. Warner Bros.,1999.
*The Queen.* Dir. Stephen Frears. Perf. Helen Mirren, James Cromwell, Alex Jennings. Miramax Films, 2006.
*The Ring.* Dir. Gore Verbinski. Perf. Naomi Watts, Martin Henderson, David Dorfman. Dream Works, 2002.
*The Teahouse of the August Moon.* Dir. Daniel Mann. Perf. Marlon Brando, Glenn Ford, Kyô Machiko. Metro-Goldwyn-Mayer, 1956.
*The Yakuza.* Dir. Sydney Pollack. Perf. Robert Mitchum, Takakura Ken, Brian Keith. Warner Bros., 1974.
*To End All Wars.* Dir. David L. Cunningham. Perf. Kiefer Sutherland, Robert Carlyle, Mark Strong. 20th Century Fox, 2001.
*Tōkyō Nagaremono (Tokyo Drifters).* Dir. Suzuki Seijun. Perf. Watari Tetsuya, Matsubara Chieko. Nikkatsu, 1966.
*Tora! Tora! Tora!* Dir. Richard Fleischer and Fukasaku Kinji. Perf. Martin Balsam, Yamamura Sô, Joseph Cotten. 20th Century Fox, 1970.

*Yoidore Tenshi (Drunken Angel).* Dir. Kurosawa Akira. Perf. Mifune, Toshirô, Shimura, Rakashi, Yamamoto, Reisaburô. Toho, 1948.

*Yojimbo.* Dir. Kurosawa Akira. Perf. Mifune, Toshirô, Nakdai Tatsuya, Tsukasa Yôko. Toho, 1961.

## MISCELLANEOUS

Coppola, Sofia. Interview. *Lost in Translation.* DVD. Highlight Film, 2004.

*Flags of Our Fathers.* Press Kit. Warner Bros. Pictures Germany, 2006.

*Iwo Jima Kara No Tegami.* (*Letters from Iwo Jima*) Press Kit. Warner Bros. Entertainment, 2006.

*Letters from Iwo Jima.* Press Kit. Warner Bros. Pictures Germany, 2007.

*The Last Samurai.* Press Kit. Warner Bros. Pictures Germany. 2003.
*The Last Samurai.* A Roundtable Press Book. Warner Bros. Entertainment Inc. New York: Time Inc., 2003.
*Tokyo DisneySea.* The Official Guide Map. 2006.
*Tokyo Disneyland.* The Official Guide Map. 2006.

## TV SERIES

*Janguru Taite.* (*Jungle Emperor*).Dir. Yamamoto Eiichi. 1965-1967. Mushi Productions, 1965.

*Kyōryū Sentai Zyuranger.*(*Dinosaur Squadron Zyuranger*). Dir. Toei. Perf. Chiba Reiko, Hashimoto Takumi, Mochizuki Yūta. 1992-1993. TV Asahi.

*Mighty Morphin Power Rangers.* Dir. Jack Olesker. Perf. David Yost, Paul Shrier, Amy Jo Johnson. 1993-1996. MMPR Productions Inc.

*Poketto Monsutâ.* (*Pocket Monster*). Dir. Hidaka Masamitsu and Yuyama Kunihiko. 1997-2002. TV Tokyo.

*Shogun.* Dir. Jerry London. Perf. Richard Chamberlain, Mifune Toshirô, Shimada Yôko. 1980. DVD. Paramount Home Entertainment, 2007.

## Music

Stefani, Gwen. "Harajuku Girls." *Love Angel Music Baby.* Interscope (Universal), 2004.

---, "Rich Girl." *Love Angel Music Baby.* Interscope (Universal), 2004.

# Index

Academy Award · 161, 205
American Psycho · 104, 134, 136
American Sushi · 28, 103, 137, 138, 139, 141, 142, 143, 144, 145, 216
Amusement park · 15, 58, 60, 66, 68
Anderson, Benedict · 25, 28, 33, 58, 61, 107, 145
Anime · 13, 17, 18, 21, 28, 53, 55, 66, 88, 148, 164, 165
Appadurai, Arjun · 24, 26, 30, 129
Asian Chicken Salad · 115, 116, 118
Atomic Bomb · 22, 43, 197

Barbarian · 36, 39, 40, 41, 107, 153, 172, 175
Barthes, Roland · 188
Baseball · 21, 47, 48, 87
Battle of Iwo Jima · 196, 198
Beat · 55
Benihana · 137

Bento Box in the Heartland · 103, 120, 121, 122, 124
Bhabha, Homi · 25, 182
Blade Runner · 159, 195, 212, 213

California Roll · 139
California Sushi Academy · 137, 138, 140, 143
Charlie Chan · 152, 156
Chicago World's Fair · 65
Cohen, Jeffrey Jerome · 18, 48
Colonization · 16, 41, 68, 102, 107, 144, 152
Commodore Perry · 36, 39, 45
Cookbook · 130, 131, 140
Cooking Fusion · 136
Culinary Colonialism · 102, 103, 118, 141, 143
Culinary Culture · 103, 106, 108, 109, 110, 113, 117, 120, 130, 131, 139, 140, 143
Culinary Tourist · 117, 122
Cultural Imperialism · 15, 17, 19, 20, 21, 27, 58, 59, 68, 69, 71, 73, 95, 161, 217

**D**ances with Wolves · 169
Disneyfication · 59, 68, 69
Disneyland · 20, 27, 28, 57, 58, 60, 61, 64, 67, 72, 73, 74, 75, 76, 77, 78, 79, 80, 81, 84, 85, 86, 87, 90, 91, 92, 96, 97, 98, 111
Dixieland Sushi · 103, 118, 120, 124
Dower, John · 36, 37, 44, 154, 157, 169, 196, 197

**E**ast · 12, 15, 16, 21, 26, 39, 45, 52, 53, 63, 93, 95, 96, 97, 108, 110, 111, 115, 124, 127, 147, 151, 152, 153, 159, 160, 166, 167, 169, 170, 172, 173, 175, 177, 178, 183, 193, 194, 195, 196, 203, 208
Eco, Umberto · 67, 73, 129
Empire · 22, 58, 69, 70, 73, 95, 154, 187
Epcot · 61, 64, 65, 66, 67, 73, 80, 91, 97, 101, 102, 216
Exotic · 11, 12, 13, 16, 19, 25, 27, 35, 49, 50, 51, 52, 53, 56, 59, 62, 64, 66, 75, 78, 79, 81, 82, 92, 94, 96, 97, 101, 104, 109, 111, 114, 115, 116, 117, 118, 125, 127, 129, 130, 131, 132, 133, 134, 135, 136, 137, 139, 141, 143, 144, 149, 151, 152, 153, 159, 166, 167, 169, 170, 186, 195, 207, 208, 215, 216

**F**antasyscape · 26, 27, 59, 60, 72, 79, 85, 95, 97, 99, 214, 215, 216
Fisher Fishkin, Shelly · 22
*Flags of Our Fathers* · 196, 197, 199, 200, 202, 203, 204
Foodscape · 26, 27, 101, 107, 116, 122, 129, 137, 139, 144, 214
Frontier · 36, 77, 94, 112, 169, 171, 172, 173, 175, 189
Fusion Cooking · 136

**G**aihin · 190, 192
Gaijin · 190, 191
Geisha · 28, 45, 51, 147, 152, 153, 177, 207, 208
Ginsberg, Allen · 55
Global · 16, 17, 21, 23, 24, 25, 26, 29, 46, 58, 59, 68, 69, 70, 71, 81, 98, 102, 104, 107, 118, 134, 144, 148, 161, 195, 215, 217, 218
Globalization · 15, 17, 19, 24, 25, 29, 30, 35, 49, 65, 68, 96, 102, 103, 134, 137, 144, 160, 171, 184, 195
*Godzilla* · 88, 148, 214
Golden Globe · 205
*Gung Ho!* · 158, 159

**H**aiku · 55
Harajuku Girls · 11, 12, 13, 14, 15, 29, 30
Hello Kitty · 21, 66, 83, 215, 216
Hiroshima · 22, 43, 197

Hitchcock, Peter · 23, 24, 26, 145
Hollywood Movie · 28, 42, 127, 147, 150, 151, 153, 156, 157, 164, 166, 167, 169, 181, 185, 206, 207, 208
Homogenization · 17, 24, 26, 29, 65, 68, 69, 72, 134, 144, 195, 214
Homogenizing · 21, 68, 70, 126
Horror · 66, 119, 149, 161, 163
Hybridity · 25, 173
*Hyperreality* · 67

*Imagineering* · 66
*Imaginist* · 55
Issenberg, Sasha · 103, 104, 113, 114, 132, 133, 134, 142
Iwabuchi Koichi · 17, 21
Iwabuchi, Koichi · 17, 18, 21, 25, 29, 55

Japanese Pavilion · 64, 66, 216
*Japonisme* · 53
Jeffrey Jerome Cohen · 34

Kamikaze · 43, 148, 157, 168, 198, 211
Kerouac, Jack · 55
*Kill Bill* · 149, 156, 163, 164
Kuribayashi, Tadamichi · 200, 201, 202

Language · 11, 20, 55, 71, 101, 122, 129, 150, 168, 176, 178, 180, 187, 190, 194, 205, 206, 209

*Letters from Iwo Jima* · 28, 149, 161, 196, 197, 199, 200, 202, 203, 204, 205, 206, 207, 208, 209
Lévi-Strauss, Claude · 113, 114, 120, 123, 132
*Lilo and Stitch* · 84, 148, 165, 213
*Lost in Translation* · 28, 101, 147, 149, 185, 186, 187, 189, 190, 192, 193, 194, 195, 196, 208, 209
Lowell, Amy · 55

*M. Butterfly* · 155
*Madame Butterfly* · 51, 152, 153, 154, 155, 177, 193, 208
Manga · 18, 21, 55, 148
Masculinity · 38, 126, 154, 155, 156, 160, 172, 176, 192
Mediascape · 26, 28, 148, 160, 209
Meiji · 36, 41, 47, 51, 63, 75, 107, 208
*Memoirs of a Geisha* · 149, 153, 207
*Monster* · 34, 37, 89, 90, 148, 149, 165
Multicultural · 93, 104, 125, 128, 161
*My Year of Meat* · 103, 124, 126

Nagasaki · 22, 35, 43, 197
Napier, Susan · 26, 30, 48, 50, 51, 53, 207

Occidentalism · 39, 40, 163
Occidentalizing · 75, 76, 103
Orient · 12, 36, 39, 40, 50, 52, 53, 63, 92, 115, 130, 135, 152, 153, 159, 172
Oriental Land Company · 72, 74, 76, 82, 85, 87, 89, 90, 94, 96
Orientalism · 12, 13, 39, 40, 50, 53, 63, 69, 103, 118, 130, 145, 147, 148, 149, 150, 152, 159, 163, 185, 190, 193, 208, 213, 217
Orientalizing · 51, 102, 103, 118, 149
Other · 12, 16, 19, 24, 25, 33, 34, 38, 39, 41, 43, 44, 45, 56, 64, 66, 68, 69, 78, 79, 92, 97, 102, 103, 107, 108, 112, 115, 117, 129, 135, 141, 143, 150, 152, 154, 160, 175, 181, 191, 194, 199, 201, 204, 205, 207, 208, 209, 211, 212, 213, 216
Othering · 16, 73, 118, 149, 209

Pacific War · 43, 198, 200
Pearl Harbor · 19, 42, 157, 158, 197, 198, 206
Philadelphia Centennial Exhibition · 63
Pokémon · 66, 88, 114, 148, 165, 213
Popular Culture · 15, 17, 18, 19, 21, 56, 58, 66, 70, 71, 75, 76, 83, 84, 90, 96, 98, 148, 154, 211, 216, 217
Postcolonialism · 161
Pound, Ezra · 55

Propaganda · 42, 44, 150, 157, 197

Raz, Aviad · 19, 20, 27, 59, 76, 81, 85, 87, 89, 96, 98, 148, 151
Remake · 149, 161
*Rising Sun* · 158

Said, Edward · 12, 15, 39, 50, 53, 130, 150
*Salade Orientale* · 115
Samurai · 19, 37, 66, 79, 84, 141, 149, 153, 162, 163, 166, 167, 168, 170, 171, 172, 173, 174, 175, 176, 177, 178, 179, 180, 181, 182, 184, 185, 202, 203, 208, 211
Sandburg, Carl · 55
Starbucks · 19, 71, 214, 215, 216
Stefani, Gwen · 11, 12, 13, 14, 15, 29, 30
Stereotype · 13, 39, 119, 147, 152, 155, 156, 157, 158, 159, 191, 192
Subtitle · 160, 174, 177, 181, 184, 209
Sushi · 21, 27, 28, 82, 101, 102, 103, 104, 108, 111, 113, 114, 119, 120, 124, 131, 132, 133, 134, 135, 136, 137, 138, 139, 140, 141, 142, 143, 144, 145, 148, 159, 213, 214

*The Last Samurai* · 28, 149, 156, 166, 167, 168, 169, 170, 171, 172, 173, 174, 175, 177,

178, 179, 180, 181, 182, 183, 184, 185, 189, 196, 205, 208, 209
The Walt Disney Company · 58, 68, 102
Theme Park · 20, 26, 27, 29, 56, 57, 58, 59, 60, 61, 62, 65, 67, 68, 69, 70, 71, 72, 74, 75, 77, 78, 79, 84, 87, 90, 92, 95, 96, 97, 217
Third Space · 25, 182
Tokyo Disney Resort · 27, 28, 59, 72, 73, 74, 75, 79, 80, 82, 90, 91, 96, 97, 98, 216
Tokyo Disneyland · 20, 57, 58, 59, 62, 72, 73, 74, 75, 76, 77, 78, 79, 80, 81, 82, 83, 84, 85, 86, 87, 89, 90, 91, 95, 96, 97, 98
Tokyo DisneySea · 57, 59, 75, 76, 82, 90, 91, 93, 95
Transnational · 16, 17, 20, 21, 22, 24, 26, 27, 28, 29, 30, 42, 54, 58, 59, 70, 71, 73, 84, 92, 98, 102, 104, 109, 122, 123, 124, 126, 130, 136, 143, 144, 145, 147, 148, 160, 161, 162, 164, 166, 169, 178, 181, 182, 184, 188, 192, 194, 195, 196, 199, 203, 205, 207, 208,213, 215, 216, 217
Transnational Cinema · 160

Transnationalism · 15, 22, 23, 25, 30, 102, 214
Treaty of Kanagawa · 37, 41
Turner, Frederick Jackson · 112, 172

**W**asko, Janet · 60, 61, 70, 98
West · 12, 14, 15, 16, 17, 19, 21, 22, 25, 34, 35, 36, 38, 39, 41, 42, 43, 44, 48, 49, 51, 52, 53, 58, 63, 68, 77, 78, 83, 90, 96, 97, 106, 107, 108, 112, 114, 115, 116, 124, 127, 128, 131, 134, 139, 141, 147, 148, 149, 151, 152, 153, 154, 158, 159, 160, 164, 165, 167, 169, 170, 171, 172, 173, 175, 177, 178, 183, 184, 185, 192, 193, 194, 195, 196, 198, 203, 208, 211, 213, 215
White City · 62, 63
World Disney World · 62, 86
World Exhibition · 50
World Showcase · 61, 65, 80, 101
World War II · 14, 19, 42, 44, 45, 48, 75, 120, 153, 154, 157, 158, 197, 198, 199, 202, 203, 205, 206, 208, 215
Wright, Richard · 50, 51, 69

**Y**ellow Peril · 157
Young, Robert J.C. · 25, 152